MW00624702

ADVANCE PRAISE FOR

Candid Advice for New Faculty Members:
A Guide to Getting Tenure and Advancing Your Academic Career

Drawing on her inspiring story and fueled by a rare coupling of candor, humor, and an abundance of wisdom, Professor Gasman provides tenure-track faculty with a wellspring of promising ideas for surviving and flourishing on their journey to tenure and beyond. I have no doubt that readers will treasure many of her ideas for overcoming the most formidable and often invisible challenges facing many faculty and, no less, her wellspring of lessons for faculty to thrive on their pathway to tenure. I haven't had such fun reading a book in a long time and highly recommend it to faculty, administrators, and students across the landscape of higher education.

Clif Conrad
Villas Distinguished Professor
University of Wisconsin-Madison

Marybeth Gasman has gone beyond creating a window to the almost extraterrestrial world of faculty life in *Candid Advice for New Faculty Members: A Guide to Getting Tenure and Advancing Your Academic Career*. Welcoming us into that world, she has provided veritable bricks for building a durable and rewarding academic career in it. Faculty at every stage of the academic career lifecycle will find Marybeth's transparency—punctuated by daughter Chloë's keen illustrations—illuminating, refreshing, and useful. This book deserves a home in every aspiring, junior, and senior faculty member's personal collection.

Andrew T. Arroyo
Associate Professor, Educational Leadership
Virginia Commonwealth University

Candid Advice for New Faculty Members: A Guide to Getting Tenure and Advancing Your Academic Career is a road map for new faculty on how to navigate the brutal tenure system. It is easy to read and gives essential advice on how to be successful in one's tenure application, how to develop an excellent teaching portfolio, and how to approach research and service, especially for women and faculty of color. Gasman gives simple and clear advice for staying focused on scholarship and teaching, and navigating academic politics.

Abdalla Darwish, Ph.D.
Presidential Professor, Physics & SPIE Fellow
Dillard University

If you have ever met Marybeth, you know first-hand that she cares deeply about academia and shepherding people through the landmines in our field. With her expertise, she weaves that same care and concern through this book. In the academic environment of cloak and dagger duplicity, Marybeth's perspective is refreshingly transparent. She not only demystifies the process, but she also gives sage wisdom that many will not offer. Regardless of institutional type, scholars should consider this a "must read." My only wish is that this text had been available when I engaged the tenure-track.

Leah P. Hollis
Associate Professor, Education
Morgan State University

Starting a tenure-track professorship is a very daunting experience. There are so many unknowns and experiences that must be successfully navigated through to achieve the goal of acquiring tenure. Marybeth Gasman's *Candid Advice for New Faculty Members* offers essential guidance and lessons learned from within the capricious world of academia that will help one attain a flourishing profession. This book is a must-read for those at the beginning and/or mid-portion of their academic career.

Sultan Ali Jenkins
Assistant Professor, Biology
LaGuardia Community College

Marybeth Gasman is one of the most prolific and important voices in higher education today. *Candid Advice for New Faculty Members: A Guide to Getting Tenure and Advancing Your Academic Career* offers access to critical information that every new tenure-track faculty member needs. As a chief diversity officer and director of the Carolina Postdoctoral Program for Faculty Diversity, I highly recommend this book to any graduate student or postdoctoral fellow starting a new tenure-track appointment. Gasman's book is the equivalent of having an academic coach in your back pocket. She has captured the most weighty matters and challenges for early-career faculty—navigating departmental politics, publishing and preparing for the tenure review, securing funding and faculty fellowships while trying to achieve work life balance. An absolute must-read book that you will return to again and again.

Sibby Anderson Thompkins
Special Advisor for Equity & Inclusion and Chief Diversity Officer
Professor of Practice in Public Policy
The University of North Carolina at Chapel Hill

Candid Advice for New Faculty Members: A Guide to Getting Tenure and Advancing Your Academic Career provides an invaluable roadmap for unlocking the mysteries of navigating the academy. Written thoughtfully and authentically, Gasman intertwines her life experiences with lessons from the academy to offer supportive ways new faculty can succeed and not feel alone in their tenure track journey. This is an inspiring and much needed resource!

Dina C. Maramba
Associate Professor of Higher Education
Claremont Graduate University

A must read for anyone considering academia or on tenure-track. As a 3rd year tenure-track faculty with prior industry, non-profit and entrepreneurial experience, I had contemplated leaving academia before reading *Candid Advice for New Faculty Members: A Guide to Getting Tenure and Advancing Your Academic Career*. Gasman shares, in great detail, the value of tenure through a lens I hadn't seen before. Her diverse experience and extensive knowledge allow her to provide the perfect insight in a candid, humorous fashion that is on point and right on time.

Trina Fletcher
Assistant Professor
College of Engineering and Computing
Florida International University

As an African American law professor, Dr. Gasman and I are from different racial and disciplinary backgrounds. But she served as a tremendous guide for me during my early academic career. In short, her advice was indispensable. Now, the advice that took me from Assistant Professor to Full Professor with tenure and Associate Dean in just seven years is in book form. *Candid Advice for New Faculty*

Members: A Guide to Getting Tenure and Advancing Your Academic Career is the path for those who seek to be successful and productive academics.

Gregory S. Parks
Professor of Law
Wake Forest University

Candid Advice for New Faculty Members: A Guide to Getting Tenure and Advancing Your Academic Career is an insightful guide that provides experience-based advice on how to maintain one's focus while navigating tenure, believe in one's own worth, and chart out a fulfilling path—all while following one's passion. In presenting her own experience, Professor Gasman opens a view into her world, with sincerity, humor, and the unabashed intention that others learn from her stories. One is left with a renewed sense of community and inspiration, after her unveiling of the so-called mysteries of the academy that bring into clearer view the importance of what's real-our contributions to making the academy a more collaborative place.

Saúl Jiménez-Sandoval
Interim President, Provost & Professor of Spanish and Portuguese
California State University, Fresno

Colleges and universities that do not have robust faculty development programs could use this book as a roadmap to prepare new faculty with a firm footing to launch a potentially noteworthy career. Marybeth highlights the explicit and, more importantly, implicit nuances to successfully attaining tenure. I will be using many of the points made in this book to develop a best practices document for new faculty in our Physics Program.

B. Kent Wallace
Assistant Professor, Physics
Fisk University

Gasman takes the reader behind the proverbial curtain of the Ivory Tower. Her friendly, conversational tone draws you into the engaging narrative of what she admits to be her unlikely rise in academe. (Of course, anyone who knows Gasman is deeply acquainted with her broad intelligence, sharp insights, and relentless determination to uncover the truth.) But entwined with her individual and absolutely American success story is an essential primer for the aspiring academic. Though an historian of education by training, Gasman delivers advice that transcends the silos of established academic disciplines. She clearly respects and loves the academy, but is not blind to its many and serious shortcomings, particularly with regard to diversity.

With her characteristic generosity, Gasman acknowledges the work of other scholars who have pursued this topic. However, her book pushes into such areas as "work/life balance," what happens (or should happen) after getting the "dream job," and the real challenges that continue to confront women and people of color in academe—subjects that were, frankly, ignored or disparaged when I began my own career as an historian of higher education over thirty years ago.

Simply stated, if Marybeth Gasman's book had existed when I entered graduate school at Princeton University in 1988, I would have avoided many professional missteps and been a more productive and happier citizen of the university, that wondrous place that the late A. Bartlett Giamatti once called "a free and ordered space."

Darryl L. Peterkin
Director, Clara I. Adams Honors College
Morgan State University

Enlightening. Accessible. Replicable. Timely. Direct. Authentic. *Candid Advice for New Faculty Members* should be required reading for both junior faculty navigating the expectations, challenges, and rewards of the academy, and departmental executives guiding new faculty through the tenure process.

Christopher M. Span
Associate Dean for Graduate Programs
University of Illinois at Urbana-Champaign

Marybeth shares insights about faculty life's complexities that many sacrifice years of their careers to learn the hard way. Though her focus is on faculty neophytes, there is valuable information in this tome that anyone interested in junior faculty's success can use immediately. As a scholar and someone who has directly benefitted from Marybeth's care and mentoring, I look forward to sharing this book with my faculty colleagues across the country and my graduate students with faculty career aspirations. This book is a timely reminder that you can meet tenure expectations *and* prioritize your health and family.

Michael Steven Williams
Assistant Professor, Educational Leadership & Policy Analysis
University of Missouri

Gasman's book is an important resource for new faculty members, especially faculty of color, whether at a private elite institution of higher education or at a comprehensive public institution. This book provides straightforward advice to new faculty members on how to work hard, work smart, dream big, and strive to bring balance into your academic and personal life. New faculty members as well as graduate students should read this book.

Timothy P. Fong
Professor, Ethnic Studies
California State University, Sacramento

Candid Advice for New Faculty Members

Candid Advice for New Faculty Members

A Guide to Getting Tenure and Advancing Your Academic Career

BY MARYBETH GASMAN

ILLUSTRATIONS BY
CHLOË SARAH EPSTEIN

Myers
Education
Press

GORHAM, MAINE

Myers Education Press is an academic publisher specializing in books, e-books, and digital content in the field of education. All of our books are subjected to a rigorous peer review process and produced in compliance with the standards of the Council on Library and Information Resources.

Library of Congress Cataloging-in-Publication Data available from Library of Congress.

13-digit ISBN 978-1-9755-0221-8 (paperback)
13-digit ISBN 978-1-9755-0220-1 (hard cover)
13-digit ISBN 978-1-9755-0222-5 (library networkable e-edition)
13-digit ISBN 978-1-9755-0223-2 (consumer e-edition)

Printed in the United States of America.

All first editions printed on acid-free paper that meets the American National Standards Institute Z39-48 standard.

Books published by Myers Education Press may be purchased at special quantity discount rates for groups, workshops, training organizations, and classroom usage. Please call our customer service department at 1-800-232-0223 for details.

Cover and interior design by Teresa Lagrange

Visit us on the web at **www.myersedpress.com** to browse our complete list of titles.

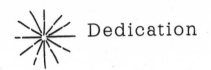 # Dedication

This book is dedicated to my mentors and role models for their honesty and dedication to my success as a scholar:

James D. Anderson
John R. Thelin
Wayne J. Urban
Asa G. Hilliard
Susan H. Fuhrman
Michael T. Nettles
Wanda J. Blanchett

Contents

Acknowledgments   xv

Preface   xvii

Introduction: Reflections on My Journey
to the Professoriate   xix

1. You Got the Offer, Now What?   1

2. How to Plan a Research Agenda and Publish   17

3. How to Teach at Your Best   43

4. How Do I Manage Service?   61

5. Advising for Success   71

6. Do I Have to Apply for Grants?   85

7. Surviving Faculty Politics   95

8. How Do I Achieve Work/Life Balance?   109

9. And the Rest of the Job . . .   119

Concluding Thoughts   131

Epilogue: What if I'm a Woman and/or a Person
of Color? Three Interviews   133

Appendix A: Peer-Reviewed Journal Matrix   189

Appendix B: Books on Writing   191

Appendix C: Establishing a Center or Institute 193

Appendix D: Sample Tenure Essay 199

Appendix E: Tips for Online Teaching 221

Appendix F: Suggested Outline for CV 225

Appendix G: Select Funders for Academic Research 227

Appendix H: Select List of Fellowships 229

Appendix I: Consulting and Public Speaking Log 233

About the Author 235

About the Illustrator 237

Index 239

Acknowledgments

I wrote this book in its entirety during both COVID-19 and the protests of 2020 related to the murders of George Floyd, Tony McDade, Breonna Taylor, and Ahmaud Arbery. I wrote every Monday, Friday, Sunday, and sometimes late at night after spending time with my daughter. It was a strange time to write a guide for achieving professional accomplishments when the world was grappling with its health and the nation was in deep need of racial healing. But I had made a commitment, and one thing that everyone close to me knows is that I always follow through on my commitments.

During my time writing this book, a few people were particularly helpful, not with regard to the book in particular, but as friends and confidants. I want to thank them here. Levon Esters, one of my dearest friends, was a constant source of support, humor, challenge, political information, and overall fun. Alice Ginsberg, also one of my closest friends, provided lots of love, support, and humor. My friend Nelson Bowman caused me to laugh even during the stressful aspects of the pandemic and distracted me from the craziness of having armed National Guard members in front of my home and 4-5 helicopters outside my Philadelphia windows for two weeks as the nation erupted. Andrés Castro Samayoa is really my soulmate in the academy. He was my PhD student for five years, and we had a deep intellectual connection from day one. I appreciate him for his integrity, his kindness, and his intellect. Thai-Huy Nguyen, also my PhD student for five years, makes me laugh so hard my stomach hurts. In 2020, he achieved tenure and decided to leave the academy to work for a policy-related think tank. I supported him 100% in this decision; Thai is an example of someone who chose happiness over the grind of the academy and I am thrilled for him. Camille Charles, my Penn colleague of 16 years and wonderful friend, likes all my Instagram posts (smile) and always makes me feel smarter than I am. I am grateful to all six of these friends for always being supportive, bringing me joy, and having my back 24/7 and 365 days a year. I never, ever have any doubts and I do not think you can ask for anything more than that in friends.

I am also grateful to my mom who came to see me during the middle of the pandemic. She understood that I needed to write nearly every day to finish this book and another one, even though she would constantly ask, "Why are you always writing a book?" My mom is such a sweetheart and provides a beautiful sense of stability in a world that seems insane right now.

Lastly, and as always, I want to express all of my love to my daughter Chloë. She is pure joy and her laugh is the most beautiful sound I have ever heard. She loves in a way I have rarely seen before and accepts everyone, faults and all. Cheers to you, Chloë, for all that you give to me and the world. I had one child, and was blessed with the very best.

Marybeth Gasman
October 2020

 Preface

If you want to achieve tenure, you should know a bit more about what it means, why it exists, and what its benefits are. All too often even faculty do not understand why tenure is important. According to the American Association of University Professors (AAUP) (2020), a tenured faculty position is "an indefinite appointment that can be terminated only for cause or under extraordinary circumstances such as financial exigency and program discontinuation" (n.p.). The way we currently conceptualize tenure stems from the 1940 Statement of Principles on Academic Freedom and Tenure, which has been adopted by university-sponsored faculty handbooks and faculty unions throughout the nation. Tenure is vitally important because it protects academic freedom, which is essential in the areas of teaching and research. If faculty are constantly worried and vulnerable in terms of job security due to what they discuss, explore, and uncover, they cannot fulfill the requirements and responsibilities of their position, which are to produce and share knowledge (AAUP, 2020). Although it may appear that tenure only benefits you as a professor, in actuality, tenure benefits society as a whole. Tenure protects intellectual integrity and provides a marketplace of ideas—popular and unpopular. Many of these ideas will lead to important and life-sustaining changes in medicine, literature, policy, education, art, science, and more.

There are those who object to tenure, claiming it causes laziness and a lack of productivity among faculty. However, research shows that this is not generally the case and in actuality, tenured professors became more productive in their careers (Nikolioudakis et al., 2015). From my faculty-oriented perspective, securing a tenure-track position gives you job security, and although the path can be stressful, the end goal is satisfying.

References

American Association of University Professors (2020). What is academic tenure? https://www.aaup.org/issues/tenure.

Nikolioudakis, N., Tsikliras, A. C., Somarakis, S., & Stergiou, K. I. (2015). Tenure and academic deadwood. *Ethics in Science and Environmental Politics, 15*(1), 87–93.

 Introduction

Reflections on My Journey to the Professoriate

When I became a professor, I had no understanding of what it took to achieve tenure. I learned how to succeed along the way from mentors and colleagues, and by reading handbooks on faculty life. This book is focused on ensuring that new tenure-track faculty achieve tenure. Over the years, I have chronicled in journals and notebooks the knowledge I have gained; this book compiles what I have learned, mistakes I have made, short cuts that work, concrete examples, and motivations that will foster the reader's success towards tenure.

In addition to my own experience, I have also drawn upon research related to faculty. Because I am writing for an academic audience, I am fully aware that I need to provide evidence for my claims; thus, I have included data to support my assertions about everything from writing habits to work/life balance to inequities in academic service. I hope that this book will help, inspire, comfort, and motivate others to succeed on the tenure-track while also enjoying life.

My Journey

As someone who grew up in poverty in an isolated, rural community, with uneducated parents, I had no intention of becoming a professor. Even after deciding to pursue a PhD, I had no understanding of how to become a faculty member. I am not even sure initially why I pursued a PhD, beyond advancing my career as a college/university administrator. I did not have faculty members who served as mentors or role models. I fumbled around, figuring things out as they happened. I asked questions, read everything I could, and begged people to mentor me or share their pathways to success with me. I talked to anyone I could find about their journeys and was intimidated by all of them.

I did not decide to pursue a faculty position until I was three chapters into my dissertation writing. I realize this makes little sense, but I did not understand the process of becoming a faculty member. Most faculty I interacted with did not talk about their careers, and some even told me I did not have what it takes to be a faculty member. One of my professors took me out to lunch and said to me, in what he thought was a helpful and kind way, "You work hard, but you are just not smart enough to be a professor." This is one of the conversations that made me consider being a professor; I have always been someone who is determined to do things when others tell me I do not have what it takes. Any time I have been beaten down, I have picked myself back up.

Once I determined I wanted to be a professor—which was the result of reading James D. Anderson's book *The Education of Blacks in the South* (1988)—I felt invigorated, as if I had found my passion. Anderson's book spoke to me, not only because of what it said about African American history and agency, but because of how it was written. Anderson is a beautiful writer and a gracious story teller, and I wanted to nurture those skills and talents in myself. I did not know if I could ever write like him, but I was determined to find out. I did not know I wanted to be an historian until I read Anderson's book; his technique and voice made sense to me.

Because James Anderson was a faculty member at the University of Illinois and not at my institution, Indiana University (I missed his time at Indiana by just a few years), my next step was to find a professor at Indiana who would mentor me. I found John Thelin, an historian of higher education, a bit of a comedian, and a wonderful human being. He was honest, forthright, attentive, and pushed me to be a curious, dedicated, and a caring scholar. Throughout my career, he has always supported me, offering advice when I asked and having the tough talks that I needed. I remember researching for my dissertation and becoming frustrated that so many archives related to African American history had passages redacted in the archival papers. He told me, "if you cannot get in the front door, try the window, back door, cellar, or chimney." At first, I did not understand, but eventually it made sense: If a letter was redacted by the sender's institution, it might not be redacted by the receiver's institution. If one archive would not allow me to see a set of papers, perhaps another would be more open and have less to hide. According to Thelin, when faced with a problem, there was always another way. I have used this advice many times in my research, professional career, and personal life. I also pass it on to all of my PhD students.

As I moved through the academy, lacking knowledge of how it works and social capital, I encountered people willing to help me. In my first faculty job, I was mentored by two senior faculty members, Wayne Urban and Asa Hilliard, who held endowed professorships at Georgia State University. I was fascinated by each of them and their careers. Although very different, they were both dedicated to their craft and their students. Wayne, an older White man and a historian, mentored and guided me carefully, making sure I was successful. I remember visiting his office once, asking him how he succeeded in his tenure pursuit and secured an endowed professorship, which I did not understand the meaning of at the time. He had one answer: "Don't be a perfectionist." I asked him for clarity and he explained that many new faculty are too focused on being perfect. For example, they will not submit a paper to a peer-reviewed journal outlet until it is perfect—and oftentimes, it will never be perfect. He told me that there is a reason for editors and reviewers—they help us write stronger and better papers—and that I needed to learn to engage their skills. He relayed that too many young scholars have a file full of conference papers that they have not published because the papers are not perfect. If they had published the papers, they probably would have tenure. Wayne's advice stuck with me, and I have never not published a conference paper. I even went back and revised all of my unpublished graduate school papers into peer-reviewed articles. Wayne told me not to waste my words, my research, and my exploration; I have not and will not in the future.

Asa Hilliard, who sadly passed away in 2008, was a beautiful soul who made me smile every time I saw him. He truly believed in all students and never doubted anyone's ability to learn. He was hugely generous. I remember four distinct moments with him that helped shape my career. First, during faculty meetings, while many other faculty spoke to nearly every item on the agenda, I noticed that Asa was typically quiet. I asked him why, and he told me that as a faculty member it is essential to pick your battles. He stressed that his success was the result of focusing on his work instead of focusing on academic politics. I have tried to adhere to this advice as often as possible. I have not always succeeded, but as I have grown older, I am adhering completely. I regret having not always avoided academic politics, because getting involved left me feeling sad, and added unneeded stress to my life. Although I love being a professor—the teaching, the research, and even the service—I have come to know the academy as a place of frequent meanness. I have found that the only way to remain happy is to do what Asa told me in my first year as a faculty member: Stay focused on the work.

The second incident I recall was when Asa came to my office with a stack of his books—each and every one of them. He sat down with me and autographed all of them for me; his beautiful messages showed me that he saw me and that I mattered to him. He knew how to mentor a junior scholar and was always willing to answer my endless list of questions about the academy. He was generous, while all too often people in the academy are not; instead, they hoard opportunity, worry that someone else's gains will be their losses, and complain about having to help others. I have always tried to be generous with others and encouraged my students to be as well. I learned about intellectual generosity from Asa.

The third incident involved Asa's welcoming me to study African American history. When I was a younger scholar, I was far from confident about my role in doing research related to African American history. People of all backgrounds would often ask me why I cared and what drew my interest, and some challenged my right to do so. Early on, I wrote several essays about this topic, exploring my reasons in a semi-public way, often through conversation with trusted African American scholars (Gasman & Payton-Stewart, 2006). Asa never doubted me. He told me that as long as I knew in my heart that my motives were authentic and grounded in an ethic of care, I should research what motivated me, what I cared about, and what I felt passionate about. I believe we should take this approach with scholars and research. If we do not, I fear we are stifling academic freedom and policing who can pursue various topics. I think this kind of behavior is wrong. As a way of showing me his acceptance, Asa once gave me a beautiful outfit from Ghana, where he was an honorary king. I framed it and it hangs in my home. His acceptance of me as a scholar and his willingness to trust me taught me how we all can contribute to knowledge, as long as we do not see ourselves and our work as the only worthy contribution.

Finally, Asa taught me not to take myself too seriously; he encouraged me to laugh, and to laugh at myself. This lesson remains so important because the academy is not a place where laughter is often welcomed. I remember bringing my 18-month old daughter Chloë to my office when I had only enough money to pay for two days of childcare a week. Asa got down on the floor and played with her and made her laugh. I watched this legend of a man, an endowed professor, on the floor with my daughter, laughing and singing. Tears were in my eyes. He loved children and all of their potential, and never forgot why he had become an educational psychologist. He was fierce in his convictions, but humble in his approach—a rarity in the academy where many people at his level are anything but humble.

Both Wayne and Asa taught me much about succeeding in the academy. I listened to them, stopped by their offices frequently, watched them in meetings, and read their work. The most significant academic lesson I learned from them was to watch successful people and the way they lived their academic lives. How did they balance the professional and personal aspects of their lives? How did they manage their time? What did they get involved in and what did they avoid? How did they prepare to do their research and writing? I watched everything and learned as much as I could so that I could succeed as a professor.

Georgia State was a good place for me to start my academic career as I had a lot of time to do my work. I benefited from wonderful mentoring relationships and also learned how to handle academic jealousy. I remember three specific incidents that served as cautionary tales. My department was filled with highly competent people who have gone on to do amazing things—for example, holding provost positions or directing a division of RAND. One of my colleagues was Lisa Delpit, a MacArthur Genius Award winner. She wrote a beautiful book that every person should read called *Other People's Children* (1995), which focuses on teaching with justice in mind. She won the Genius Award right before I arrived and so I did not see her often. However, I heard about her constantly from other faculty, including how she "took too many resources from the department" and "did not pull her weight in the department." When people gossiped about Lisa, I always asked for examples and was given none. I learned about academic jealousy and what happens when a colleague outshines others in the department or school. While colleagues made many assumptions about Lisa, I rarely heard them provide any concrete evidence. As you garner academic success, protect yourself because others are watching and measuring their own self-worth based on your achievements. Make sure you don't fall into this trap.

The second incident happened upon my immediate arrival at the institution. I was an assistant professor for one week when I had a single-authored article published in the top journal in my field—not a sub-field, but the entire field. The acceptance rate for the journal hovered around 3%, although when I applied I had no real understanding of journal rankings or acceptance rates. I naïvely sent in my article, and only began to understand the prestige of the journal when I got a "revise and resubmit" decision and shared it with my advisor. He was astounded and told me he had never been published in that journal. I went on the job market with this article "forthcoming," which helped me to secure 7 on-campus interviews. During my first week at Georgia State, a faculty colleague—a man—put a copy of the article in my faculty mailbox with notes scribbled all over it and a short message on the top that said, "this is a good start, when you are further along in your career, your work will be stronger." What a kick in the gut. Keep in mind that this scholar has never published in this high-ranking journal and at the time had published very little. I learned immediately that if you do well, people will attempt to put you back where they deem you belong.

The final incident was similar to the one I just conveyed. I was asked to give a talk to the school about my work during my first year as a faculty member. I was nervous, honored, and excited, and I prepared extensively. I was giving a talk in front of my colleagues and wanted them to be proud that they hired me. I gave what I thought to be a strong talk; people asked many questions and were engaged by the work. Afterwards, I found a long note in my mailbox from another one of my colleagues—a man with whom I worked closely—that gave a point by point critique of my entire talk. He noted everything I had done wrong and nothing I had done right. I was devastated and felt I had no one to talk with. I could not understand why anyone would feel the need to do this to a young scholar and new assistant professor. Did he consider how this would affect my self-confidence? Maybe he did. After talking with my husband about the experience and calling my PhD advisor, I decided to talk to my department chair. I shared both notes and explained that I was feeling attacked as a woman in the department. I am unsure what he did, but the negative interactions stopped. I learned I have to advocate for myself, because these incidents of sexism and professional jealousy do not just go away. Instead, they will continue if you do not address them. Moreover, future scholars will have to endure them.

After three years at Georgia State University, I moved to the University of Pennsylvania (Penn) and stayed for 16 years, achieving tenure and full professor, and securing an endowed professorship. One of my first mentors at Penn was Susan Fuhrman, my dean. I was intimidated by her—as were many people—but that did not stop me from watching and listening to her. As a woman in the academy, she faced enormous sexism; White men were constantly challenging her leadership. I often heard senior White male faculty refer to her as a "bitch" in faculty meetings and in the hallways. I also watched her endure a great deal of anti-Semitism. Most of the sexism and anti-Semitism was out in the open, and rarely did anyone stand up for her apart from a few faculty and herself.

I carefully watched Susan's leadership and how she used her voice, intellect, and power. Eventually, I summoned the courage to ask her to be my "official" mentor. I remember that she hesitated because she was the dean and worried that it may look like favoritism. However, she agreed to give me feedback on my CV and to provide advice informally. Her advice on my CV really stuck with me. She looked at my document, which I was proud of, and immediately told me that my peer-reviewed articles needed to be upfront and that I should move my professional experience to the back of my CV. She also told me which journals would be valued and which would not, as I sought tenure. It was painful to discover that a few of my articles would not be valued at Penn, but I was glad to know that information rather than to be surprised later. A few years later the faculty codified this information so that journal rankings and value were crowdsourced and transparent. Susan also reminded me to update my CV regularly and often.

Eventually Susan left Penn to be president of Columbia University's Teachers College, but she continued to be my mentor. I received tenure that year. About a year after she left, I had some trouble with three of my more senior peers (all White) who were bullying me; they went to the new dean to tell him I had too much power. I was a newly-tenured associate professor and they were all senior faculty, yet they claimed I had more power. In reality, these faculty were angry that I kept pushing to admit African American women into the PhD program in my field. I was not sure what to do about this situation so I called Susan. She was wonderfully helpful. One of the people who was bullying me was the same person who had called her a bitch and bullied her. He was able to get away with these things because he was well known, vocal about his success, and people regularly acquiesced to his whims and moods. I asked her what to do and her response is something I will never forget—she said, "Walk up to a lion and you get a lamb." At first, I didn't understand, but she expounded, explaining that if you confront a bully, they will back down. She added that if that did not work, I should file a complaint with human resources. I had three lions to confront.

I confronted the man in a meeting after he blurted out something racist (a common occurrence that no one confronted regardless of their race). When I challenged his racist comments, he told me I was naïve and reported me to my dean and department chair. I confronted the other two people in public spaces, one over lunch and another over coffee. The behavior of these three individuals did not change much over the years, but I made it clear that their opinions of me did not matter and that they did not control who I was or what I did in my career. Knowing who you are and what you stand for is essential in the academy. If you do not, academia will devour you.

While at Penn, I was lucky to have two African American women as the chairs of my committees for tenure and promotion to full professor: Margaret Beale Spencer and Vivian Gadsden. They were highly-skilled, savvy, and transparent. I have always been grateful to them for their leadership, advocacy, and honesty. Both of them had encountered copious amounts of racism and sexism within the academy. They protected me and cared for me as I went through the grueling tenure process at Penn, wherein I had to satisfy colleagues in both the education school and the history department, given that I am a historian of education. I needed to author books published by prestigious university presses and publish 12-15 peer-reviewed articles in the top journals in my field.

Although these women were transparent, the process for securing tenure at Penn was like most colleges and universities—unclear, elitist, and lacking feedback along the way. I remember that my third-year review process provided zero feedback. How was I to improve, grow, and learn? One of the reasons I wanted to write this book is to share the knowledge I have learned and received from mentors along the way, to provide clarity to those on the tenure-track. I want to make sure that tenure-track faculty know what questions to ask regardless of the institutions where they work.

Although the academy can be a hard place to work—rife with lack of clarity, jealousy, chaos, and bureaucracy—it is also a place of great joy in terms of students, incredible knowledge, opportunities, and occasional humor at just how bizarre faculty life can be. I once sat in amazement as a group of faculty argued for nearly two hours about whether 'spell check' should remain on student computers during a final exam. Why would we spend two hours arguing about this? And, how many of us regularly use spell check as we write?

Overall, I have loved being a professor most when I have stayed focused on the work and the original reasons I became a professor. When I have been sidetracked by academic politics, life has been stressful. As I write this book, I am in my 20th year of being a professor and my focus is 100% on my work and fostering opportunity for students and new scholars. I have learned to pay no attention to the politics, as they are the underbelly of the academy. As one of my mentors once relayed to me, "academic politics are so vicious precisely because the stakes are so small."[1] This does not mean that what happens in the academy is unimportant—knowledge, learning, students—instead, this statement reveals the ridiculous nature of the infighting in academia, which is usually related to ego. I work hard to live by Asa Hillard's words—focus on the work, not the politics. As faculty, we deserve a happy existence and are more likely to foster positive environments for our students when we have one for ourselves.

Organization of This Book

Chapter 1—*You Got the Offer, Now What?* takes PhD students through the negotiations of a faculty job offer while pushing them to consider all the dimensions of a job and the kind of life they want to have now, and in the future. In Chapter 2— *How to Plan a Research Agenda and Publish*—I discuss how to construct a research agenda, meet one's professional goals, and ensure that the research agenda aligns with one's personal goals and those of the institution in terms of securing tenure. I also discuss how to write consistently and productively. Finally, I discuss the role of research in tenure and how to best prepare for tenure.

Chapter 3—*How to Teach at Your Best*—focuses on designing classes, ensuring that your classes speak to your research, and balancing your course load. I also discuss managing difficult conversations in the classroom, engaging with students around learning, and interpreting and building on teaching evaluations. In Chapter 4—*How Do I Manage Service?*—I talk about the ways for faculty to approach service requirements and how to maximize the work they do to complement their teaching and research. I also discuss when to say "yes" and "no", and how to manage these conversations.

Chapter 5—*Advising for Success*—focuses on advising students, from undergraduates to masters to doctoral students, including how to establish trusting relationships, manage student research collaborations, and motivate students to excel. In Chapter 6—*Do I Have to Apply for Grants?*—I focus on preparing grant proposals and how to make this a part of your research agenda. I also discuss the appropriateness of grants across disciplines and how to match them to one's research.

Chapter 7—*Surviving Faculty Politics*—is about managing politics, including what to get involved with and what to avoid on the tenure-track. I discuss how to manage difficult relationships with colleagues, department chairs, and deans. In Chapter 8—*How Do I Achieve Work/Life Balance?*—I discuss the importance of having a balanced life and how to achieve it. Because achieving work/life balance is very difficult, especially for mothers, I employ some humor in this discussion. And in Chapter 9—*And the Rest of the Job*—I conclude with advice to motivate new faculty to succeed in their positions.

In the Epilogue—*What if I'm a Woman and/or a Person of Color? Three Interviews*—I interview three tenured faculty from three types of institutions: an African American man tenured at a Big Ten, Research 1, American Association of Universities (AAU) institution in the Midwest; a Latina tenured at a Hispanic Serving Institution in the Southwest, which was recently designated as a Research 1 level institution; and an African American women tenured at a Historically Black University in the South, which is a Research 2 level institution.[2]

Before moving into the rest of the book, I want to share a few caveats. First, I wrote this book in a casual tone, with a lot of first-person experiences and examples, and in a practical, sometimes humorous manner. This is not a theoretical book; it is not based on a research study. I write based on my own experiences and those of friends and colleagues across a variety of institutional types, and based on my reading of literature since entering a PhD program in 1994 through the current day. I have always been fascinated by books on faculty life and own most of those currently available. As I came from an uneducated, low-income family—where no one graduated from college—I had no understanding of faculty life and needed to rely on books and mentors to understand everything. My hope is that others can learn from my experiences—the successes and mistakes—and take advantage of the opportunities ahead of them in their career. This book is not THE guide to achieving tenure and a satisfying career as a faculty member, but it is *one* guide, based on my perspective. Make sure to read other available books for a well-rounded view on faculty life. Some of my favorites are *The Black Academic's Guide to Winning Tenure—Without Losing Your Soul* (Rockquemore & Laszloffy, 2008); *The Coach's Guide for Women Professors: Who Want a Successful Career and a Well-Balanced Life* (Seltzer & Rosenbluth, 2015); *The Professor is In: The Essential Guide to Turning Your PhD Into a Job* (Kelsky, 2015); and *The Academic Job Search Handbook* (Vick et al., 2016).

The audience for this book is individuals interested in securing a tenure-track faculty position and achieving tenure. I do not write about adjunct faculty or contingency faculty, non-tenure-track faculty, post-doc positions (beyond their importance in the STEM fields), nor promotion from associate to full professor. If these are areas of interest, I advise you to read books and articles that focus in these areas as there are plenty of scholars writing on these issues.

I hope you enjoy this book and I wish you the very best as you pursue tenure and faculty life. Remember to ask questions along the way, because transparency and information are essential to your success. And, make sure to know who you are and what you stand for, and work hard to avoid straying from your values. The academy is like a glittery ball of gold, but it will burn if you hold it for too long without the occasional release.

Notes

1   This quote, and similar quotes, have been attributed to Henry Kissinger as well as several other scholars and leader (See: https://quoteinvestigator.com/2013/08/18/acad-politics/). For an interesting perspective on faculty in-fighting, which I explore later in this book, see https://www.chronicle.com/article/Why-We-Cant-Just-Get-Along/45742.

2   Higher education likes to classify institutions and there are many ways this is done. Research activity, as well as teaching and community engagement, is classified by the Carnegie Classification. These classifications began in 1970 at the hand of the Carnegie Commission on Higher Education. Over the years, beginning in 1973 and through 2018, the framework for classification has changed as a result of changes in higher education. The next classification will take place in 2021. Colleges and universities are also identified by who they were established to serve or who they currently serve. These institutions include, but are not limited to, Historically Black Colleges and Universities, Tribal Colleges and Universities, Hispanic Serving Institutions, and Asian American and Native American Pacific Islander Serving Institutions (for more information see the Rutgers Center for Minority Serving Institutions at https://cmsi.gse.rutgers.edu). Colleges and universities are also members of various groups, some more prestigious than others. For example, there are eight Ivy League institutions that often hold tremendous prestige. These institutions were formed out of an American collegiate athletic conference in 1953 (see https://ivyleague.com). The Big Ten is the oldest Division I collegiate athletic conference and began in 1805 (see https://bigten.org). Both of these clusters of institutions began as athletic leagues but now have lore round them—with Ivy League equaling prestige in many people's eyes and Big Ten equating to strong athletic and academic standards. Finally, the AAU encompasses a group of 63 highly selective, research-driven universities in the United States and Canada. The AAU is an invitation-only group (see https://www.aau.edu). There are other ways of classifying institutions; these are just a few.

References

Anderson, J. D. (1988). *The education of Blacks in the South, 1860-1935*. The University of North Carolina Press.

Delpit, L. (2006). *Other people's children: Cultural conflict in the classroom*. The New Press.

Gasman, M. & Payton-Stewart, L. (2006). Twice removed: a White scholar studies the history of Black sororities and a Black scholar responds. *International Journal of Research & Method in Education, 29*(2): 129-149.

Kelsky, K. (2015). *The professor is in: The essential guide to turning your Ph.D. into a job*. Three Rivers Press.

Rockquemore, K. A., & Laszloffy, T. (2008). *The Black academic's guide to winning tenure - Without losing your soul*. Lynne Rienner Publishers.

Seltzer, R. & Rosenbluth, F. (2015). *The coach's guide for women professors: Who want a successful career and a well-balanced life*. Stylus Press.

Vick, J., Furlong, J., & Rosanne, L. (2016). *The academic job search handbook*. University of Pennsylvania Press.

1

You Got the Offer, Now What?

Going on the faculty job market is hectic, difficult, daunting, and exhilarating all at the same time regardless of your academic discipline. And given the current academic job market, applying for faculty jobs can be deflating and a bit uncertain (Heemstra, 2020; Olena, 2020; Smith, 2020). I advise you to be positive and believe in yourself and in what you have accomplished thus far. You may not feel prepared, you may stumble throughout the process, and you may feel that people are giving you contradictory advice that takes you in conflicting directions. I suggest that you listen to a variety of people and think about your own needs and wants, then apply what fits and makes you happy. I've organized this chapter in the following way: applying for faculty jobs, negotiating your job offer, and settling into your new faculty role.

Applying for Jobs

There are a few things you need to have in place before applying for faculty jobs. First, you need to have completed or be near completion of a strong and compelling dissertation that demonstrates your intellect, command of literature, and methodological strengths and rigor. Your dissertation, at the point when you are applying for your first faculty position, is the strongest evidence of your knowledge, and faculty search committees will want to hear how you discuss your work, how you connect it to previous work, and how you envision your future research trajectory.

Second, you need to solicit letters of recommendation from three to five individuals. Most institutions will only require three letters, but my advice is to find five people who can readily support you and discuss your work. The relationships that you invest in and develop during your PhD program are incredibly important. During your program, make sure to secure one-on-one time with your advisor, and if possible work with your advisor on research projects to enhance your skills. I also suggest asking your advisor about their career path, including any advice they have based on their successes and failures. However, it is important that you reach out to other professors in your discipline beyond your advisor to gain a diverse array of perspectives and to ensure that several faculty understand your strengths. I suggest setting up regular appointments with faculty with whom you have something in common—these commonalities could be along the lines of research topic or methodology, for example. You may also want to reach out to possible mentors of the same gender, race, or sexuality if you are comfortable doing so. Having a mentor who may have had experiences similar to yours can be powerful in terms of helping you understand how the academy works (Blake-Beard et al., 2006). By the time you finish your PhD, you want to have found three to five individuals who can write the strongest letters possible for you. I advise that you specifically ask them if they can write a strong letter that speaks to your research and where it fits in the field, your teaching strengths and potential to teach a variety of courses in your field, and your preparedness for a tenure-track faculty position. Of note, letters of recommendation need to include examples and specific knowledge about your accomplishments, your ability to conduct research, and your intellect and expertise in your academic area. Search committees will want to know why your research matters and its strength in your discipline.

The career center at UC-Berkeley provides a helpful and expansive overview of what should go in a letter for faculty on the job market.[1] One of their best tips is to make sure that your dissertation chair notes where you are in the dissertation process, as search committees want to know when you will receive your degree. Although I would caution against sending resources on writing letters of recommendation to your references, I would suggest reviewing these resources and ensuring that your reviewers address the most important areas.[2]

Third, depending on your field, you need to have at least one scholarly publication, preferably a peer-reviewed article. Some fields want you to be working on a major book, while other fields want you to have more than a few peer-reviewed articles. In the past few decades, expectations have increased substantially, with some social science disciplines expecting 2-3 peer-reviewed articles or more. When I graduated in 2000, I was not expected to have any peer-reviewed articles—but I did. As mentioned, I had a solo article in a top tier journal. I wrote this article while working on my dissertation because I had severe imposter syndrome—the feeling that you do not belong in the academy—due to my low-income background. I wanted to make sure that I was overprepared for the job market. The norms around publishing as a PhD student vary depending on your academic discipline, so please ask your advisor and mentors to explain the norms in your field.

Fourth, if you are in a STEM field, you will more than likely need to secure one, maybe even two, post-doctoral positions prior to applying for a faculty position. It is beneficial if these positions are at prestigious research institutions and with well-known scholars, especially if you are pursuing a faculty career at a top research university. During your post-doc, you will work in someone else's laboratory, gain the skills to lead your own lab, and enhance your publication track record. I spent about a decade working with and counseling STEM post-docs at the University of Pennsylvania. My own experience confirms the research literature highlighting the difficult experiences many post-docs endure (Hudson et al., 2018). You will be expected to work long hours, often will receive little credit for your work, and will be paid much less than you deserve. Regardless, in order to secure a faculty position in most STEM fields, you may need to work in a post-doctoral role prior to a faculty position. For more information on whether or not to pursue a STEM post-doc, consult "To Postdoc or Not to Postdoc? Tips to Help Determine Whether a Postdoc is Right for You," a helpful and thorough overview of the costs and benefits of pursuing a post-doc in the STEM fields.[3] While post-docs exist in other disciplines, they are not necessary and do not hold the same value in terms of securing a tenure-track faculty position as post-docs in the STEM fields (Hudson et al., 2018).

Fifth, with regard to securing a tenure-track faculty job, your job talk—the formal talk that you will give to faculty, students, and staff during your campus interview—is incredibly important. It gives search committee members, future colleagues, and others in the university community an opportunity to see how you grapple with ideas, methodologies, and theories, and provides a sense of how you teach others about ideas and topics. I practiced my own job talk nearly a hundred times, to both memorize it and become deeply familiar with the content. I know that this approach will not work for everyone, but as a historian I wanted my work to have an impact on the audience, and sought to convey the deep knowledge I had gained from my seven years as a PhD student. Although all disciplines are different (this will become a common refrain), making sure you are prepared is essential to all of them. The best talks I have seen are TED talks, and having given one myself (Gasman, 2014), I know that it takes a hundred practice rounds to be able to give the talk without notes (Anderson, 2017; Donovan, 2013; Gallo, 2015). I recommend seeing your faculty job talk as a TED talk.

Your job talk, which I would recommend outlining as you are applying for positions, should convey three main ideas: 1) How you came to your research topic; 2) Your intellect, methodological skills, and analytical expertise; and 3) Your plans for future research. I suggest, based on listening to hundreds of job talks, that an ideal talk is 35 minutes, and should not exceed 45 minutes. You should divide your talk into three parts: 1) an introduction of you and your work (5 minutes); 2) a spotlight on your dissertation research focusing on your methods, analysis, and findings (25-30 minutes); and 3) a section that highlights your next research project or your future research trajectory (5 minutes). Colleges and universities are making an investment in you and want to know your current capabilities and your future research plans. I believe that job talks should be brief and clear; more than likely, you will not be talking to experts on your topic and most people in your audiences will span various sub-areas of your discipline. You want to be able to speak to all of them and have them understand you. If you are using PowerPoint, make sure the slides are clear and do not include a lot of words; and please do not read the slides. It is also important to use high quality images so your slides do not appear grainy and distorted. Are these suggestions extremely particular? Yes, but people are judging you and if they are looking for reasons to dismiss you as a candidate, they will look at everything. Finally, make sure that you do not have more than 12-15 slides, and ideally no more than 10. You do not have to share your entire dissertation with the audience, only the highlights.

You can prepare the most thorough job talk and have the most rigorous research, yet faculty might still challenge you. I have two pieces of advice in this situation: First, do not argue with faculty in the audience. Thank them for the question, answer it the best you can, and if you cannot, tell them that you are excited to consider their question as you move forward. Remember that people are watching to see what kind of colleague you will be, and tone of voice can be misinterpreted or used against you. Although most questions will be asked in supportive ways, job candidates will usually be challenged by one or two aggressive faculty in the audience. Let me tell you a secret: The faculty who aggressively challenge you in a job talk are the same ones who challenge everyone, and most of their colleagues are used to and embarrassed by the

way they act. These faculty challengers are insecure and are more interested in peacocking for their colleagues than they are in your research. Just let them go on with flaunting their feathers and sit secure in your knowledge and intellect.

My second piece of advice if you are challenged is: Do not guess at answers if you do not have adequate information. Learn to say, "I don't know but I'd be happy to get back to you." There is nothing wrong with not knowing everything and we need to normalize this fact in the academy. None of us can remember everything. It is much better to get back to someone asking a question than it is to give them a wrong or uncertain answer. When I am asked a question that I cannot answer while giving a public talk, I tell the person that I would be happy to follow up in email after the talk and engage in a conversation. If you promise to follow up, you need to do so. If you do not, when it comes time to discuss your candidacy in the search committee meeting, someone will say, "She said she would follow up with me on this matter and did not." Do not be that person.

Negotiating the Job Offer

Most people find negotiating job offers and discussing money to be uncomfortable. I feel the same way, but I have learned that I have to stand up for myself and that I deserve to be paid what I am worth as a scholar. Once you learn how to negotiate, it will get easier. I would advise, however, to be gracious when navigating these processes, as a cocky attitude will give people a lasting negative impression of you.

More than likely your offer will come from either a department chair or a dean and not the search committee chair. In this case, the dean or department chair holds the majority of the power, especially because you are a new professor with little to use as negotiating power. If you have some publications in prominent outlets, another job offer, or meet a specific need that is hard to fill, your negotiating power improves. Regardless, I advise negotiating the following as standard for any first tenure-track faculty offer. First, I suggest asking for a minimum of $10,000 more than you are offered. I advise all of my PhD students to do this and almost all have been met at least half way. It is essential that you negotiate the highest base salary you can, because subsequent raises, retirement contributions, and summer salaries secured through grants are all based on this amount (Aguilar, 2019). You should also do some research on average salaries for assistant professor positions in your academic discipline. You can look up average salaries in *The Chronicle of Higher Education* or the American Association of University Professors' annual reports on faculty salaries. Make sure you account for unrealistic and inflated averages if the institution has a business or medical school; those faculty will always be paid more than faculty in the humanities or social sciences, due to competition from industry employers. In addition, if your offer is from a public college or university, most have salary data online or in the public library.

Second, it is important that you ask for summer salary support for your first two or three years. Remember that faculty are usually on a nine- or ten-month contract and as such, are not paid for summer work unless they secure funding. You may not be offered summer support, but you should ask for it. At a minimum ask for one month of summer funding for the first three years, as this extra money will be helpful as you progress in your career. We will talk about how to secure other summer money in Chapter 6 when we discuss grant writing. In addition, I suggest not teaching during summers unless you absolutely need the money. When I was a new assistant professor in the year 2000, my husband and I had very little money. We were living with our child in Atlanta, GA—an expensive city— on $43,000 a year. We needed more money, as we paid $1300 to rent a two-bedroom apartment and $1000 a month for daycare. We had very little wiggle room. However, I knew that in order to secure tenure, I could not afford to teach in the summer. The pay for summer classes is very low, even at more elite institutions (ranging from $1500 - $5000/course in 2020). You have to ask yourself if the money is worth it (especially after taxes are withheld) or if you can cut back on spending during the year and use the summer to work toward tenure. Cutting back for us meant no vacations, no eating at restaurants, and no new clothes beyond basics—basically, we used what we had and lived in a very minimal way. By doing this, during the summers, I was able to write extensively and my husband was able to paint (as he was an artist).

Third, it is essential to ask for a research assistant to support your research agenda and to strengthen your advising and mentoring skills. I suggest asking to work with a PhD student but if this is not possible, a master's or work study student can help you with various research related tasks. If you are going to work with a student, you will need to train them, mentor them, and offer them critical feedback. Over the years, I have spent a lot of time with students, teaching them how to develop strong writing skills, code data, engage in grant writing, analyze data, and search for appropriate literature for research projects. The time invested was worth it as I have worked with incredible student teams on large projects, and most of these students have gone on to pursue PhDs or become faculty. Students can provide support to you and you can develop their skills at the same time.

Fourth, it is important to ask for travel funds to present your work at academic conferences. Presenting at the premier conferences in your field is an expectation across all academic disciplines; however, many institutions offer little funding for faculty to attend conferences. At some institutions, travel funds are dispersed by departments and at others, they come centrally from your school or college. Travel funds can range from $500 - $2500 a year for new faculty, and average about $1000. In the current COVID-19 pandemic, as institutions work to eliminate spending, many universities have greatly reduced or cut travel funds completely. As $1000 will not even pay for one academic conference, you may be able to negotiate extra travel funds in your start up package. However, if the choice comes down to extra travel funds or salary, always take salary because it is permanent whereas travel funds are not. Also, remember that travel expenses as a faculty member can be deducted from your taxes if they are not reimbursed by your institution, so keep every receipt—even a pack of mints can be deducted if you digest the mints while traveling.

Fifth, depending on your discipline, you will have more or less negotiating power around a start-up package. In non-science fields, start-up packages range from nothing to $25,000 for an assistant professor; of course there are aberrations but anything in this range is the norm, and the amount you receive depends on your institution. In the science fields, especially those requiring a lab, start-up packages are much, much larger and are determined by the nature of what the scientist needs in order to set up their lab and prepare to apply for external funds. Scientists offering advice on negotiating start-up packages suggest putting together an itemized list of what you need to successfully set up your lab, remembering to include less expensive items such as chemicals and glassware and more expensive items such as equipment, post-docs, undergraduate research support, and lab space. It is also important to ask for an unlimited amount of time to spend your start-up funds, as taking more time to spend the funds will be necessary if you do not bring in grant funding right away. For those of you in the sciences, I recommend the article "Top 10 Tips on Negotiating Start-up Packages," in *Nature*. This comprehensive guide also provides the important advice that it is essential to check your ego as you negotiate with an institution (Leeming, 2015).

Sixth, you may want to negotiate a reduced course load during your first year. I suggest reducing your load by one course per semester, if possible. It is important to teach at least one or two courses your first year to hone and demonstrate your teaching skills and show that you are meeting and developing relationships with students. Teaching and mentoring students matter in your annual reviews, third year review, and tenure and promotion reviews. Teaching during your first year is also a good way to learn how to balance the many roles of being a faculty member, which is essential to your success.

Seventh, most institutions will allow you a one semester *sabbatical* during or after your third year on the tenure-track.

Make sure to ask about and take advantage of this release, as it will give you an opportunity to write and focus on your research. It is essential that you do as much research as possible before year four on the tenure-track, as books and articles take a significant amount of time to be published. For example, most top tier journals take a minimum of six months to review a paper, and then you may have one or more requests to revise and resubmit your work. If your paper is accepted, it goes through a production process, which can take anywhere from another six months to over a year, depending on the journal's backlog. Similarly, book publishers often require peer review for both your book proposal and the final manuscript. This process can take several months and once it is complete, your book must go through the production process (copyediting, page proofs, indexing, marketing), which can take six months to a year.

Finally, some candidates on the job market are searching with a partner—someone who is already a faculty member, someone who is finishing a PhD at the same time, or a partner in a non-academic job. When negotiating for your first job, you do not have a lot of negotiating power unless you are highly productive or have a unique skill that the institution needs. When I went on the job market, I was married to a man who was a tenure-track faculty member; he had secured a position three years before I finished my degree. Since I moved with him for his first faculty position, he moved with me for mine. It is important to discuss what you both need, what you value, and what you are willing to sacrifice or give up. As he was an artist, the one thing he would not give up was being in a city. As a result, I only applied for jobs in cities. When I was negotiating for my first faculty position, I asked the search committee chair, who would also be my department chair, if he could assist me in securing a position for my husband. I had little to negotiate with, but the institution was kind. They made introductions to local universities and artists. After roughly six months, my husband found a lecturer position. It would take another year for him to find a full-time faculty position, and it was at a private school rather than a college or university. As you move along in your career and become more productive and well known, it is easier to negotiate a position for your partner, especially if they are an academic or higher education administrator (Blake, 2020). For example, when I was negotiating with the University of Pennsylvania as an assistant professor, I was able to secure adjunct teaching for my husband and a large studio space on Penn's campus. He was willing to move to Philadelphia without a tenure-track position because he wanted to get back to the East Coast art scene, and having a large studio space was a luxury, even if it was a bit run down—plus, he had initially shown me the position advertisement for the job at Penn. I cannot stress enough the importance of discussing your negotiation strategy with your partner if you have one—being a tenure-track professor is highly stressful and it is imperative to have their full support throughout the process.

As you are negotiating with your future institutional home, do not rush; ask for the time you need. Asking for two weeks to make your decision is appropriate and reasonable, as you may have multiple offers. Choosing your first job is important and you do not want to rush. It is also important to realize that you probably will not stay in your first or even your second job forever. I stayed at Georgia State University for three years and at Penn for 16 years. One never knows what the future holds. I often tell the PhD students I work with that it is fine to take a job in a small town—even though you love cities—for a few years. You can always move in the future. It is important, however, to make sure that a small town or rural community can accommodate your needs and is a safe space regarding race, ethnicity, sexuality, religion, etc. There are many considerations in the job search and you must think seriously about your future. One lesson I have learned in my 20-plus years of being a professor is to go where you will have kind colleagues and feel empowered and valued. Your quality of life is more important than the reputation of the college or university where you work or the "name brand" of your faculty colleagues. And one last bit of advice, get everything you have negotiated in writing; if it is not in writing, you are likely not to see it come to fruition.

Settling into Your Role and Establishing Patterns

When you arrive in your new faculty role, you want to make a good impression and be in the best place to do your research and teaching. I recommend spending the summer before you begin your faculty position focused on preparing your upcoming classes, laying out your research agenda (see Chapter 2), and thinking about your weekly schedule. Having these items in place will ensure that you are not behind when you arrive. I called my department chair to find out what I would be teaching, asked for sample syllabi to get a feel for departmental norms, and prepared my syllabi ahead of time. Understanding norms around course requirements and language on syllabi is important. When I arrived at Penn, I was faced with a challenge from students (and a departmental administrator) that my history course syllabus was too hard. I found this odd given that I used the same syllabus at Georgia State University, an institution that I knew my Penn colleagues, and more than likely my students who had complained, believed was less rigorous than Penn. The Georgia State students never complained. I stood up for myself and maintained the level of work on my syllabus, but it was rough for a few years. The rigor of my class and the fact that this was my first time teaching to a class of only White students created difficulty for me initially. Eventually, I realized that the masters students I was teaching at Penn were much more practitioner-focused than my research-oriented students at Georgia State. I made some changes to my syllabus to make it more practical and less focused on "doing" the work of an historian and any and all complaints disappeared. Interestingly, my syllabus at Rutgers University is once again more research-focused.

In addition to preparing my syllabus, I reviewed my dissertation to see how I could create articles from it, and also began thinking about how turn it into a book. I reviewed each chapter, reconceptualized them as articles, and located various journals where I could submit those articles. Potential articles were based on my findings and also my methodological approaches. I also began investigating presses that might be interested in a book that I would develop out of my dissertation.

One of the most important things that I did was figure out my schedule. I knew when I would be teaching, and planned my writing time around my teaching days (see Chapter 2 for an extensive discussion of writing strategies). If you can set

up regular patterns and habits around your role as a professor, you will benefit immensely. Why? Because work expands and the more time you give yourself to do something, the longer it will take. This is not my idea—it was first expressed in a 1955 article in *The Economist* by British historian Cyril Parkinson and is now referred to as Parkinson's Law. He said, "It is a commonplace observation that work expands so as to fill the time available for its completion" (Klimek et al., 2008). This notion is one of the most important lessons I have learned.

Early on, I determined how much time a week I would devote to teaching preparation (See Chapter 3), research and writing, service (See Chapter 4), and advising (See Chapter 5). I also have a family so I need to factor in family time and also work/life balance (See Chapter 8). Although I will discuss all of these items in depth in the subsequent chapters, it is important to think about them early as you are settling into your role as a faculty member. The more upfront preparation you can do, the more successful you will be.

The last thing I want to say in this chapter is that it is essential not to take yourself too seriously in your new role. A faculty career is a good one—it is a privilege to spend your career learning, exploring, and teaching. Do not take it for granted and do not get too wrapped up in it. Far too often, faculty only have that one identity and fail to have a well-rounded life. It is too easy to let your work engulf you and the other aspects of your life. This happened to me for a few years before I received tenure. I deeply regret letting my work consume me and although I continue to work hard, I make time for all the other parts of my life. I hope you do too.

Notes

1   See Academic Job Search: Letters of Recommendation: https://career.berkeley.edu/PhDs/PhDletters

2   I suggest that you ask writers of reference letters to send letters directly to institutions to which you are applying.

3   See https://orise.orau.gov/resources/stem/professional-development/becoming-a-postdoc/to-postdoc-or-not-to-post-doc.html.

References

Aguilar, S. (2019). Yes, you should negotiate. *Inside Higher Education*, https://www.insidehighered.com/advice/2019/03/13/how-and-why-negotiate-starting-salary-opinion

Anderson, C. (2017). *TED talks: The official TED guide to public speaking.* Mariner Books.

Blake, D. (2020). *Dual-Career hiring for faculty diversity: Insights from diverse academic couples.* New Brunswick, NJ: Proctor Institute for Leadership, Equity & Justice.

Blake-Beard, S., Murrell, A. J., & Thomas, D. A. (2006). *Unfinished business: The impact of race on understanding mentoring relationships.* Division of Research, Harvard Business School.

Donovan, J. (2013). *How to deliver a TED talk: Secrets of the world's most inspiring presentations.* McGraw Hill.

Gallo, C. (2015). *Talk like TED: The 9 public-speaking secrets of the world's top minds.* St. Martin Griffin.

Gasman, M. (2014). *Talking justice: Using words and voice to make change.* TEDxBloomington, https://www.youtube.com/watch?v=DHUZFcsTpYE

Heemstra, J. (2020). *The job market is tough. It's wise to explore different career options.* Chemical & Engineering News. https://cen.acs.org/articles/98/i39/job-market-tough-s-wise.html

Hudson, T. D., Haley, K. J., Jaeger, A. J., Mitchal, A., Dinin, A. & Dunstan, S. (2018). Becoming a legitimate scientist: Science identity of postdocs in STEM fields. *Review of Higher Education, 41*(4), 607–639.

Klimek, Peter; Hanel, Rudolf; Thurner, Stefan (14 April 2008), "To how many politicians should government be left?", Physica A, 388 (18): 3939–3947

Leeming, J. (2015). *Top 10 tips on negotiating start-up packages.* Nature. http://blogs.nature.com/naturejobs/2015/11/16/the-faculty-series-top-10-tips-on-negotiating-start-up-packages/

Olena, A. (2020). *The pandemic continues to put a damper on faculty hiring.* The Scientist. https://www.the-scientist.com/news-opinion/the-pandemic-continues-to-put-a-damper-on-faculty-hiring-68020

Parkinson, C.N. (1955). *Parkinson's law.* The Economist. https://www.economist.com/news/1955/11/19/parkinsons-law.

Smith, C. (2020). *The importance of informational interviews.* Inside Higher Education. https://www.insidehighered.com/advice/2020/06/01/given-uncertainty-about-faculty-hiring-fall-job-seekers-should-actively-seek

2

How to Plan a Research Agenda and Publish

In this chapter, I will discuss how to construct a research agenda, meet your publishing goals, and ensure that your research agenda aligns with your personal goals and those of the institution in terms of securing tenure. I will also discuss how to write consistently and productively. Finally, I will discuss the role of research in, and how to best prepare for, tenure.

When crafting a research agenda, you want to think about the expectations for research at your institution. What are the expectations for tenure-track faculty each year at your college or university? Next, ask yourself if you want to stay at this institution or eventually move to one that is more research-focused. Perhaps you want to move to a more teaching-oriented institution in the future. You will need to think through all of these issues when crafting a research agenda.

My first faculty job was at Georgia State University in Atlanta, GA in 2000. Although Georgia State has gained a lot of publicity recently for its service of students of color and low-income students—specifically its ability to graduate African American students at a higher rate than White students—it was fairly unknown when I was there. Georgia State is a public, regional institution. When I arrived, I asked my department chair about the expectations for tenure, and he was clear that I would need roughly 8-10 peer-reviewed articles when I applied for tenure. This goal meant that I needed to produce roughly two peer-reviewed articles a year. I set that goal as my minimum because I knew that I wanted to be flexible in my journey in the professoriate; I have always been a bit of an overachiever given my background, and I knew that I might want to secure a position at a more research-focused institution in the future. This is a decision that you need to make for yourself. Because I believe institutions are never loyal to people no matter how much you give of yourself, I always want to make choices that allow me to have the most flexibility in my career. As a result of this outlook, I aimed for three peer-reviewed articles a year while I also worked on a book and an occasional book chapter if it was invited for an important book. As a new professor, I was teaching classes that were a bit out of my comfort zone and had a teaching load of two courses a semester, which is the norm at most research-focused universities. If you are at a comprehensive institution or teaching-focused college, your teaching load will be heavier; however, your research expectations will be lighter. During this time, I had a fourteen-month old daughter so my research and writing time was limited. Throughout this chapter, I will share more about how I managed my time and was able to focus on research to meet my goals.

I eventually moved from Georgia State to the University of Pennsylvania (Penn), which had much more stringent tenure expectations. Again, I went to the dean (Penn had a much smaller faculty than Georgia State and department chairs had little power or influence in the lives of departmental faculty) and asked about tenure expectations. I was told that I needed roughly 15 peer-reviewed articles, mainly in top-tier journals. I was given a matrix that detailed which journals were valued by my colleagues in the school and told which ones I was expected to publish in.[1] Because I am trained as an historian and solely did historical research up until getting tenure, I was also told that I needed to publish a book not based on my dissertation project, with a highly-respected university press. When I was at Penn, 38% of faculty who made it to their tenure year were awarded tenure. The standards were very high and in order to achieve tenure, I had to be focused, dedicated, and use my writing time wisely. Because Penn has a disciplinary focus in its professional schools, I was expected to satisfy the expectations for tenure in both the history department and the education school, which seems outlandish in retrospect.

It is deeply important that you ask questions about the specific expectations for research and publications at your institution. Ask your dean, your department chair, and your colleagues. Also, explore the CVs of those who were recently awarded tenure. Examine the articles they published, including author order, quality and ranking of publication outlet, number of publications, service, leadership, presentations, etc.—and move yourself in the same direction. Keep in mind that the process of awarding tenure is not a science; it is messy and rife with issues of privilege, racism, gender discrimination, and homophobia. The people making tenure decisions are human and hold biases and grudges, dislike people, and often excuse their faculty friends for not being productive. The more you can prepare yourself for the norms and expectations the better. And if you are a person of color, someone from a low-income background, or part of the LGBTQ+ community, it is essential that your tenure materials are meticulously prepared. Remember that if people do not want you at an institution, they will find every reason—large and small—to find fault with you and your record.

Mining Your Dissertation

One of the first things I tell new faculty is to mine their dissertation for potential articles. Your dissertation is, in most cases, your first large body of work. Sometimes new faculty are tired of reading their dissertation and want to move on to something new—I understand and felt the same way. However, one of the best things that you can do for yourself is to sit down with your dissertation, separate each chapter, and envision articles. It is likely that you can pull three distinct articles related to your findings from the document. You may also be able to craft an article based on your methodological approach if it is unique and rigorous. You might also publish your literature review as an article. You have organized and analyzed a large body of literature, and some journals publish well-crafted and uniquely framed freestanding literature reviews. I suggest that you consider your literature review with this idea in mind. For those of you in a discipline such as history or anthropology that is more focused on books, it is essential to use your dissertation as the foundation for your first book. This goal will require considerable rewriting and refining of your work, but it is much easier to edit and refine than to start a new research project. I turned my dissertation into a book and was also able to draw upon the same data for a few articles. These articles will be different from the chapters in your book but they can draw upon similar themes.

I want to reiterate the importance of using your dissertation to jumpstart your research agenda. I often hear new assistant professors talking about new projects and how they have moved on from their dissertations. What they do not realize is that third year review and tenure committees ask questions such as, "What did this candidate do with their dissertation research?" You want these committee members to see how you built upon your dissertation. It is fine and important to craft a new project, but do not abandon your dissertation to do so.

Setting Research Goals for Each Year

After reviewing your dissertation for ideas, it is essential that you set yearly goals for your research. These goals should align with your career goals. Because I was interested in moving beyond the academic institution where I began my career, my yearly goals were to produce at a level that would allow me to do so. One of the secrets to having a successful research agenda is to stay focused and to go deep rather than wide. I have used an executive coach—someone who is a sounding board and fully understands academic decision-making—for the last 5-6 years and she gave me the same advice: The most successful people have deep knowledge rather than broad knowledge. Having deep knowledge allows you to write and think more freely about your topic. For example, if I am writing about Historically Black Colleges and Universities (HBCUs), I know the research like the back of my hand. I have read everything on HBCUs and I make sure to read everything new that comes out in a timely manner; I keep an updated bibliography that I started in 1994 on my computer. Because I am familiar with the research, I can name from memory all of the prominent authors writing about HBCUs and describe their research. When writing, I do not need the classic texts in front of me because I have read them many times and know their major themes and arguments. Having deep knowledge of a subject allows you to write more easily. I am not suggesting that you ignore various worldly and societal topics—it is important to read widely across such topics—but you do not need deep expertise in these larger areas.

When setting your research goals, make sure they are realistic and doable, and that you have people who are willing to hold you accountable. Share your research goals with peers and mentors to ensure that you follow through. Set deadlines and put reminders on your calendar to encourage you to work on and finish projects. I did that every day while I was writing this book, and I will do it again for the next book I write. You might have to retool and reorganize your goals from time to time, and that is ok, but try to stay as focused as you can.

Your Next Project

Although mining your dissertation is essential, your research goals for your first year should also include ideas about your next research project. I suggest building on your dissertation knowledge base for your next project. For example, my dissertation was an intellectual biography of sociologist and Fisk University president Charles Spurgeon Johnson. I was interested in him as a leader, a scholar, and as an African American man who navigated the world of philanthropy within the context of HBCUs. Doing research related to Johnson led me to understand a variety of research areas, including the Harlem Renaissance, African American leadership, Black colleges, White philanthropy, Black intellectuals, and the history of race and sociology. I also had to learn more about historical methods, oral history, and archival research in order to conduct my research. Deep knowledge about your topic will help you to move to the next level.

My next major project was a history of the United Negro College Fund (UNCF), the major fundraising organization for private Black colleges. This topic emerged from my dissertation defense, when my advisor asked me whether I could have looked at the UNCF papers to gather information that was unavailable at individual Black colleges. I wrote this suggestion down and eventually went back to the idea of looking at the UNCF archival papers. I spent time scouring books and archives and came across an oral history collection at Columbia University that was a godsend. To my surprise, the original papers of the UNCF were at the Atlanta University Center in Atlanta, less than a mile from my faculty office at Georgia State University! Once I determined that no one else had written a history of the UNCF, I dug in. This project took me a total of five years to complete, including research and writing, and resulted in a single-authored book, published by Johns Hopkins University Press. I was also able to secure a grant from the Spencer Foundation to support the research. I used this book in my tenure packet at the University of Pennsylvania. Much like my first large research project, this one drew from literature on Black colleges, Black leadership, and philanthropy, and African American history more generally. I gained a deeper knowledge of my research area. And also, much like my dissertation work, this project sharpened my skills in archival research, oral history, and historical research. Having deeper research knowledge made me more confident.

Reading Regularly and Widely

People often ask me how I can be so productive; my answer is that I read regularly and widely. In a given year, I read between 35-45 scholarly and general books. These include books for research, books for pleasure, and books to give me a broader knowledge base about general issues in the world. I use a combination of print and audiobooks to accomplish this kind of reading agenda. I also read newspapers, blogs, peer-reviewed articles, and other types of essays. How does this help? It makes me more informed, more widely read, and a much better writer. Reading will enhance your vocabulary and provide examples of how to structure introductions, how to creatively share data, and how to communicate ideas. I keep a notebook of writing ideas—including how to write in creative ways and sample phrases of beautiful writing.

Improving Your Writing

I think most faculty are poor writers. The issue is that faculty are taught to do research but are not taught to write. If anything, they are taught to write in horrific ways that embrace passive voice and haughty language, and they forget that someone other than their former dissertation chair is reading what they write. Recently, a faculty colleague shared a report she had written, asking for my advice. I was delicate in my commentary but honest in my critique. I explained to her that when writing you have to consider your audience. With a report, you are often speaking to a more general or policy audience, and your language needs to keep this in mind. When writing for general audiences, scholars often use language more appropriate for scholarly audiences, and they lose their readers. I share the book *Stylish Academic Writing* by Helen Sword (2012) with everyone I know.[2] Sword gives myriad examples of how to make your writing come alive and demonstrates how to tell stories with your data, something we all need to learn, to engage readers.

Another strategy for being a better writer is to write often. To do this, you have to set aside time to write. Let me share the things that suck away writing time: television, gossip, perfectionism, social media, friends, service requirements, overpreparing for teaching, and lack of organization. I believe you can enjoy most things in moderation and be fine, but you cannot indulge, full force, in everything. Yes, I watch television, but I do not watch a lot of it. Yes, I get together with friends, but I do not drop my writing for the day if I have committed to it. I make plans for another day. Yes, I prepare to teach my classes, which we will talk more about, but I do it months in advance, and I do not overprepare. Yes, I do service—in fact, a lot of it—but I do not let it interfere with my writing time, which is blocked off on my calendar. And, yes, I am very organized; this skill is essential. Finally, I have learned that faculty gossip is the worst time suck and it does nobody any good. "Let go and let God" on that gossip—eventually you will be the subject of it anyway. I firmly believe that if people are gossiping to you, they are gossiping about you.

My strategy for getting a lot of writing accomplished each week is to block off time on my calendar. Depending on your teaching load, you can block off more or less time. I am writing this section with the assumption that you are teaching two courses per semester. If you are teaching more, then you should block off less time; and if you are teaching less, you should block off more time. My approach is to block off two days during the work week for writing. I usually choose Monday and Friday, but occasionally I will switch to a different day depending on my schedule. However, I always have a minimum of two writing days during the work week. I also write on Sundays from noon until about 7 p.m. I may write on Saturday instead of Sunday if I have other plans, but my normal writing routine is Monday, Friday, and Sunday. How do I maintain this schedule? I make appointments with myself and keep them. I also tell everyone that these are my writing days. If you ask my students when my writing days are, they can tell you immediately. If you ask my staff, they also can tell you. I do not apologize for reserving these days for writing, I just state in a matter-of-fact manner that these are my writing days. I also explained to my students while I was on the tenure track that I needed to write two days a week in order to achieve tenure, and that achieving tenure was important to my ability to support them throughout their careers. They understood. On Tuesday, Wednesday, and Thursday, from 8 a.m. to 6 p.m., I teach, attend faculty meetings, do service, and meet with students. Because I run a national center (See Appendix C) and institute, my days are filled with meetings that go beyond the schedule of an average faculty member—however, I established the center after becoming a full professor in 2014, and the institute in 2019. My schedule as an assistant and associate professor was more in line with a traditional faculty role.

It is important to understand that everyone will try to impose on your writing time. You will have to work hard to protect it. I love helping people, and am willing to help almost anyone, but I help people on my non-writing days (unless it is an emergency). Teach yourself to say "no" firmly and kindly, otherwise you will not be able to meet your writing goals. Also keep in mind that friends, family, and faculty colleagues will attempt to make you feel guilty for writing—some because they love you and some because they do not want you to accomplish something they are not. I work to have balance in my life and as such, I relax and spend a lot of time with my daughter. I am not suggesting that you say no to everything other than writing, but stating that far too many faculty get distracted, procrastinate, and let others infringe upon their writing time.

My writing days include writing, editing, reading for writing projects, analyzing data, and organizing writing projects. Some days writing is frustrating, or I may not be feeling at my best, so I use those days to edit and add to my drafts rather than to begin new writing projects. I usually have two or three projects to work on per day, and I block off the time on my calendar. For example, today, I began the day by finishing some edits on another book that is in production, I added a few paragraphs and edited a book chapter for someone else's book that I am writing with two of my students, and after a couple hours, I shifted to this book project and wrote about 15 pages. If you like to write in large blocks, it is important to take breaks. I take breaks for lunch and working out. I normally eat lunch at noon or 1 p.m., work out at 4 p.m. or 5 p.m., and finish up at 6:30 p.m. It is a long day but I am able to accomplish a lot—typically 20-40 pages—and that is important to me for meeting my goals (See Figure 2.1 for a sample writing day schedule). Please note that these 20-40 pages are not perfect—remember that I avoid perfectionism—instead, they are in draft form that I edit later. The number of pages is tied to how I feel and how able I am to push out distractions from my personal and professional life.

Writing Day Schedule			To Do
Time ▼	**Appointment** ▼		
7:00 AM			Write on book in the morning
7:30 AM	Wake up & Shower		Work on article revisions in the afternoon
8:00 AM	Eat breakfast		revisit reviewer comments
8:30 AM			prepare letter to the editor with response to comments
9:00 AM	Begin writing		reread article one more time before submission
9:30 AM			
10:00 AM			
10:30 AM			
11:00 AM			
11:30 AM	Check email/messages		
12:00 PM	Eat Lunch		
12:30 PM			
1:00 PM	Begin writing again		
1:30 PM			
2:00 PM			
2:30 PM	Take a break - walk 30 minutes		
3:00 PM	Begin writing again		
3:30 PM			
4:00 PM			
4:30 PM	Take a break - walk 30 minutes		
5:00 PM			
5:30 PM			
6:00 PM	Eat Dinner		
6:30 PM			

Figure 2.1 – Writing Day Schedule

People often ask me where I write. When I was a tenure-track faculty member, I wrote in my office with the door closed on my writing days. I did not answer knocks on the door. On non-writing days, I left my door open. On writing days, I came in at 8 a.m. and stayed in my office all day, with the exception of lunch and bathroom breaks, until 6 p.m. (and sometimes I brought my lunch so I did not even leave for lunch). I was able to write an enormous amount using this approach. Once I became more well known, I started writing at home on my writing days because there were far too many interruptions around my office. I now write exclusively at home. I cannot write with any depth in my faculty office, coffee shops, hotels, or on airplanes. I can edit in those places, but my substantial writing takes place at home. Although I have a home office, I only use it occasionally for writing and I certainly do not use the desk—I am not even sure why I have a desk at home. I do occasionally use the small loveseat and ottoman in my office. However, my favorite place to write is at my dining room table. The hard chair keeps me awake and focused, and I have a view of Philadelphia that inspires me. Sometimes I will also curl up in a big chair in my living room and write or edit. The point here is that you need to figure out what works best for you and where you will be the least distracted. This

may sound odd, but the very best writing I have ever done and the least distracted I have ever been is writing with my daughter across from me—I am writing and she is writing or drawing (she illustrates and writes graphic novels and comic books). She calms me, inspires me, and tells me to focus when I am not doing so. Find what works for you and your writing will flow much more easily.

If you write better in shorter spurts or have to teach every day, you will need to block off time on your calendar through-out the week. It is more likely that you will be interrupted, so be prepared to be tough. I suggest blocking off time in the morning because you will be too exhausted by the end of the day to write. You will probably need to block off time on the weekend, too, if your teaching load is heavier. A heavier teaching load typically means that you will have lower pub-lishing expectations and need fewer peer-reviewed articles; often book chapters, reports, and other scholarly essays will also count toward tenure.

Presenting Your Work at Conferences

Another part of your research agenda involves presenting at academic conferences. Depending on your field, there may be one or more major conferences. Because you will not have unlimited travel funds nor a large salary as an assistant pro-fessor, you will need to decide which conferences are most important. Again, I would look at the CVs of those in your department who have secured tenure and see where they are presenting. You might be saying to yourself, "I am going to pres-ent where I want to present." That is a fine perspective for a tenured faculty member (although you may want to wait until you are a full professor), but for someone on the tenure-track, it is important to present at the major, peer-reviewed, aca-demic conferences in your field. I would suggest choosing one or two conferences and sticking with them. You do not need to present at every conference—it is time consuming and expensive.

I used peer-reviewed academic conferences to motivate myself to complete work when I was on the tenure track. I no longer do this, because I no longer need anything to motivate me (smile). I would make a time line that involved preparing the paper for the conference paper discussant, revising the paper based on the discussant's feedback, and sending it to a journal within 1-2 months of returning from the conference. I made a point to do this with every paper that I presented at an academic conference, on the advice of my first department chair at Georgia State University, Wayne Urban. Sometimes it took me a while to get a paper published, even years of revise and resubmits, but I was persistent, and eventually published all of my conference paper presentations, in their original state or heavily revised.

Conferences are also a great time to talk with journal editors and book publishers, who usually participate on panels and spend time in exhibition areas. Take the time to ask journal editors questions, making sure not to be self-deprecating about your work nor to drone on about your topic. Be succinct and ask procedural and topic-related questions. I offer the same advice for talking with book publishers and editors. Ask them about their process and what kinds of books they are looking for. Do not hand them a book proposal, as they are busy talking with many people, and you do not want to overwhelm them. Make sure to do your homework before approaching a publisher; you want to present your best self and convey your intellect and knowledge around your topic during the conversation.

Publishing in Peer-Reviewed Journals and Books

I have talked about publishing quite a bit thus far, but I want to spend some time discussing the specifics, or even the mechanics, of publishing. I begin with peer-reviewed articles, because they are vital across the majority of disciplines. I have spent time discussing how to mine your dissertation and your *next* project. Once you have ideas and have fashioned them into drafts, it is time to begin thinking about where you will publish them. I suggest going back to the list of the journals that are valued in your field that you crafted. Then, spend some time looking at these journals, reading articles that might be similar to yours, and then reading the guidelines for submissions. After doing so, prepare your paper according to the journal's guidelines, which are always posted on the journal's website. Make sure to adhere to the citation style requests and all of the other guidelines, or your article will be returned to you by the editor. You can only send your paper to one journal outlet at a time—it is considered highly unethical to do otherwise.

The peer-review process involves blind review. This means that you must blind your submission, making sure that your name is nowhere in the paper. To do this, you typically replace your name with "author" and delete any citations of your work from the references. If your paper is accepted, it will save you time if you have saved a blinded copy and an original copy in your files. Peer review also means that you will not know who is reviewing your paper. Once you submit your paper, typically through an electronic process, it usually takes 3-6 months for your paper to move through the review process. Once reviewed, you will hear from an editor who will either accept (very rare), ask you to "revise and resubmit" your work, or reject your work. The two most common responses are reject, and revise and resubmit. I have only had one paper accepted with no revisions out of the 100+ peer-reviewed articles that I have had published. We all need the help of our peers to make our work stronger. If you get rejected, review the comments and then strengthen your paper and send it to another journal. Do not dwell on it or let the rejection define you. Just move forward, because you do not have the time to feel sorry for yourself on the tenure track.

If you get a "revise and resubmit," do the work. I often hear faculty complaining about the reviewer comments—rightly so, as some are really quite odd. There is nothing wrong with expressing frustration. However, get over the frustration and then make the revisions. I suggest making a document where you pull out each request for revision, organized by reviewer. Then work your way through them one by one. You do not have to change everything but if you do not address some requests, you need to have a good reason and to communicate that reason to the editor. As you are reading the reviews, you may get angry and defensive about the critique. This is normal. If the comments are really mean—and you will experience this at some point in your career—keep in mind that mean comments are not about you or your work, they are about the reviewer. I once had a reviewer say that my "historical analysis was similar to a Wikipedia article." The article he critiqued went on to be the lead article in the top journal in my field and is my most cited piece of scholarship. Sometimes reviewers are frustrated with their own careers and take it out on others; just let their comments roll off your back.

Once you have revised your paper, you will write a letter to the editor explaining how you revised your paper. Be kind and forthright in the letter, avoiding anger, snide comments, and any sarcasm toward the reviewers. Your paper will then go back out for review, and the reviewers will see your responses; this process may take another 3-6 months. You will then hear whether your paper has been accepted, rejected, or been given another "revise and resubmit." The process is a long one and after your paper is accepted, it will take about six months for the article to be published. Journals with a large backlog of articles can take anywhere from 6-24 months to publish your piece. Luckily, most journals now publish the articles online first so you can note this on your CV.

The book publishing process is similar to the article publishing process, but overall it is quite different. Within the academy, there are two types of book publishers: university presses (e.g., University of Chicago Press, Harvard University Press, Johns Hopkins University Press, University of North Carolina Press) and academic presses (e.g., Palgrave Press,

Routledge Press, Myers Education Press, Jossey-Bass Press). If your discipline requires a published book for tenure, make sure to ask which kind of press is valued or required. Depending on the institution, there will be norms around acceptable publishers. You want to make sure you abide by these norms because they could result in a make or break situation regarding your tenure decision. Keep in mind that if a press does not offer peer-review, it will be very difficult for you to use a book published by it for tenure purposes.

Once you have chosen a press, prepare a book proposal according to the guidelines on the publisher's website. I have always found these guidelines to be very straightforward and easy to follow. Some presses will ask for two sample chapters in addition to your proposal and a CV. Make sure that these chapters represent the best and most polished chapters of your manuscript. Unlike journal article submission, you can send a book proposal to multiple presses as long as you let each of them know in the proposal. However, if you are sending a full manuscript rather than a proposal, you should only send it to one press at a time. Asking people to read a full manuscript is a considerable endeavor and out of respect, I recommend sharing it with only one press at a time.

In most cases, if the editor thinks your work has merit, they will send your book proposal and other materials out for peer-review; this process can take anywhere from one to three months. Publishers are much more efficient than journal editors in their turn-around process—at least from my substantial experience. Once the reviews are in, the editor will let you know if they are interested, and if so, what changes you might want to make as you craft or edit your manuscript. There is usually some back and forth negotiation in this process. Once you have a final draft of the full manuscript, the editor will send it back out for peer-review, usually to the original reviewers. The press will use the reviews to make a case with its editorial board. If the editorial board approves the book, you are on your way to being a published author. I do want to include one caveat here: Some academic presses send work out for peer review and others do not. I suggest that you place your work with presses that use the peer-review process, because it will make your work stronger and shelter you from heavy critique in case of major flaws in or misinterpretations of your work. Peer reviewers are very good at finding the holes in your work.

Once your book is approved, the production process begins. This process includes advising the press on the marketing plan for your book, providing insight on a book cover, either doing the indexing or hiring an indexer for your book, responding to copyeditor queries, and a variety of other small tasks. It is important that you address these matters in a timely matter, to not slow your book down.

After your book is released several important things happen. First, your book may be reviewed by people in your field for various journals. If you are on the tenure track, these reviews are particularly important and you should put them in your tenure dossier. A bad review can be devastating depending on your field. If you receive one, talk to your mentors about how to discuss any negative reviews in your tenure essay, especially if the review is in a very prominent journal. Second, you may want to attend academic conferences in your field and do a book signing or give a book talk. These kinds of events will raise the profile of your book. Third, you can organize a speaking tour around your book that includes stops at local bookstores and libraries as well as talks on college campuses (see Chapter 9 for a discussion on negotiating honorariums and travel fees).

I will also address book royalties. When you first start out, you will not be able to secure a large percentage of the royalties, because you typically do not have the clout or negotiating power. On my first book, I made a 3% royalty. On my last one, I made 15% on hardbacks and 8% on paperbacks, with the percentage moving up for every 5000 books sold; I also received a substantial advance.[3] Royalties are typically on net costs, which means the retail price of your book minus the direct costs pertaining to the book. Often, I hear new academics talk about writing a book and getting rich. Academic books rarely make a lot of money. I have published 27 books and only five of them have made a considerable amount of money. The bulk of the money academic authors make from books is through book talks. Of course, there are exceptions—if you win a Pulitzer Prize or the National Book Award, your books sales and negotiating power will change quickly. At that point, I suggest that you get an agent to assist you with various contracts and negotiations. I do not think a book agent is necessary for most academic authors.

Writing a Third Year Review Narrative and Tenure Essay

Depending on the requirements of your institution, you may have to write an essay when you go through your third-year review (and reappointment), tenure and promotion, and promotion to full professor. This essay is very important—it is a compilation of your work and a chance to talk about your work in an analytical way that demonstrates your knowledge of the field and your place in it. Writing this essay can be a tricky process, because you want to avoid bragging and over-praising yourself and your accomplishments. Christine Tulley, a professor of English at the University of Findlay, has written one of the best guides to writing a tenure review essay that I have come across. She lays out guiding questions across the areas of research/scholarship, teaching, service to your institution, and service to your discipline. Her guiding questions are:

Research/Scholarship

- What concepts or theories do you use in research that you also use in teaching?

- Do you collaborate on research with students as part of course work? When and how?

- Do your scholarly interests align with a service project you are working on for your institution or with your committee work? (For example, if you study writing assessment, are you also on a committee that looks at writing across the curriculum or writing data from the National Survey of Student Engagement?)

- Why are you interested in serving as a reviewer for a particular journal or as a proposal reviewer for a specific conference?

- Where do you share your scholarship expertise outside traditional academic outlets (for example, invited talks to a class at a nearby university or interviews with the local paper)?

Teaching

- What concepts do you teach that also appear (even at a more advanced level) in your white papers, peer-reviewed articles, textbooks, presentations, etc.?

- Where specifically have you changed your classes to reflect new research you are doing? (For example, have you changed an assignment to better reflect changing research practices in your discipline?)

- Are there any areas where you mentor students in scholarship?

- How do you teach your students necessary research skills to complete your courses?

- What faculty development activities do you take part in to enhance your teaching? Are any connected to professional organizations you serve in some capacity?

- Do you have the opportunity to use any of your teaching skills in a service area on your campus (for example, teaching faculty members how to use a new technology tool)?

Service to Your Institution

- When and how do you advise students outside class? Do you write letters of recommendation for graduate school? Do you run additional office hours for tutoring?

- What committees best match your teaching and researching skills? Are you serving on those committees? If not, do you have a plan for getting involved?

- If the committees you serve on do not match your research or teaching, do your skills from either area help strengthen your work on the committee? For example, do you read for details to clarify problems in the course catalog or identify weak arguments in policy writing?

- Do you advise a student club that complements your research area? Do you complete community service activities with students in your major? What disciplinary knowledge do you use in these projects?

Service to the Discipline

- How do you participate in professional organizations and in your larger disciplinary community?

- If you review manuscripts or conference proposals, how do you use this insight in research or teaching? Do you alter classes or design workshops for students after seeing new research or methodologies?

- How does your manuscript review, editing, conference proposal review, etc., benefit the larger university culture? (Tulley, 2018, n.p.)

Answering these questions will ensure that you write a thorough essay. Remember that in order to answer all of these questions, you have to keep a record of everything you do. I beg you not to wait until right before you go up for tenure to gather these materials—collect them along the way and start working on your essay(s) early.

I also suggest that as you move along the tenure-track, you keep a notebook with ideas related to how your work fits together and how it builds upon your previous work. Having this notebook of ideas will make writing these essays easier. According to Manya Whitaker, a professor at Colorado College, your tenure essay as well as your overall tenure dossier must tell a cohesive story of who you are as an academic and intellectual. She notes, "The tenure committee wants to get a holistic sense of who you are professionally" (2019, n.p.). For each of my essays, I told a story that got at the heart of my research. For example, I used the photo below to tell a story about philanthropy, African Americans, leadership, and racism (See Image 2.2)—the major themes of most of my pre-tenure work.

Statement of Academic Research and Publication Plans

Marybeth Gasman
University of Pennsylvania

The story behind this photograph embodies the overarching themes in my research. In 1944, the United Negro College Fund (UNCF) asked John D. Rockefeller Jr., a long-time philanthropist to Black education, to publicly show his support for the fledgling organization. With the passing of the token dollar from little girl to billionaire, the UNCF hoped to demonstrate that African Americans were giving to their own – that they were the agents of change in their own education. The paradox of this scenario, that Blacks should 'give to their own' by turning over their hard-earned cash to a White industrialist begins to make sense when one considers the history of Black colleges and their control by White interests.

What was not intended about this photograph was the positioning of the child on Rockefeller Jr.'s lap. Young Marietta Dockery was frightened by the flash of the cameras and Rockefeller Jr., a grandfather himself, instinctively pulled her up to comfort her. The pictures photographers snapped made the front pages of newspapers throughout the country and spurred an angry backlash from Whites over what appeared to be a breach of racial etiquette. In his response to critics, Rockefeller was careful to indicate that he was in no way advocating for social equality, just showing the importance of thrift and self help. From our perspective, it is ironic that the public's ire was directed against Rockefeller Jr.'s holding of the girl since the dollar was the real culprit. That same dollar would support the Black colleges that educated the leadership of the nascent Civil Rights Movement – forever demolishing the walls of legalized segregation and settling the question about who may sit on whose lap. This photograph marked a watershed moment in the relationships between African Americans and White philanthropy – a moment in which issues of control, philanthropic influence, public perception, and racial equality were being renegotiated. That renegotiation continues in the present day.

Image 2.2 – Lead in to Tenure Essay

I began my essay with the origins of my research and the reasons that led me to my interest. I then moved to an overview of my work for the period being evaluated—how it fit together, built on the knowledge base of the field (contextual and theoretical) and on my past work, and where it was going next (See Appendix D for a copy of my tenure essay). As

I wrote about my own work and contributions, I connected them to the work of scholars that went before me. Writing these promotion-focused essays is vitally important; the essay is the one document that all of your colleagues will read, along with your CV. Not everyone will comb through all of the articles in your tenure dossier (unless they are looking for a reason to deny you tenure), but most people will look at these two documents to judge you. In addition, these documents will be sent to the external reviewers that your institution will procure to offer expert evaluation of your tenure dossier.

Final Thoughts On Your Research Agenda

Overall, your research agenda should be focused and coherent. You should be able to discuss the connections across your research and you should be focused enough to have a deep knowledge of your research area(s). I suggest having a group of colleagues to bounce ideas off of, people you can trust and who want you to succeed. As my mother told me when I was in high school, keep your friend circle small. You need people in your orbit who are going to be honest with you and give you constructive and critical feedback. You do not want people who only tell you how great your work is—that is not helpful. All too often I notice that we academics have lost our ability to be measured in our praise. I have learned to praise only those who actually do good work when they do it, because we often sprinkle praise on people who have done little work, have done mediocre work, and whose work is derivative. I do not want to be praised for this kind of work and I hope you do not either. And when I say good work, I mean work that builds upon the knowledge base in the field, expands it, and challenges it, and work that is well written and argued.

Notes

1 For an outline of a journal matrix, please see Appendix A.
2 Other helpful books include Eleanor Harman's (2003) *The Thesis and the Book: A Guide for First-Time Academic Authors* Toronto, CA: University of Toronto Press and Bill Germano's (2013) *From Dissertation to Book*. Chicago, IL: University of Chicago Press. Please see Appendix B for a list of books pertaining to writing.
3 An advance is a signing bonus that is paid to the author before a book is published. It is paid against future royalty earnings.

References

Sword, H. (2012). *Stylish academic writing*. Harvard University Press.

Tulley, C. (2018). Telling your tenure story. *Inside Higher Education*. https://www.insidehighered.com/advice/2018/04/12/how-develop-cohesive-narrative-your-tenure-and-promotion-dossier-opinion

3

How to Teach at Your Best

If your first tenure-track position is like most, you will probably be teaching courses that you are just slightly qualified to teach (Zimmerman, 2020). When I began as a professor at Georgia State University, I was teaching higher education and the law; a seminar on education, leadership, and policy; a course on college students; and economics of higher education. Did I have enough knowledge to teach these courses? Technically, yes, as I had taken these courses in my PhD program. Should I have been teaching them? Probably not as they were not my areas of expertise. I should have been teaching a history of higher education course, one on philanthropy and fundraising, perhaps a historical methods class, and a seminar on Historically Black Colleges and Universities. However, new professors typically have to contend with faculty who have been at the institution for years already, teaching the courses they might want to teach. Moreover, many times, new assistant professors end up teaching what they are told to teach.

When I moved to the University of Pennsylvania as an assistant professor, I was asked, "What do you want to teach?" and I probably had a look of shock on my face. Immediately, I was able to teach a course on history, one related to philanthropy, and a seminar on Black colleges. While an assistant professor—spanning two institutions—I prepped over 20 new courses. Many of these course preps were by choice, but most of them were requested and assigned by my department chair. Given my experience, I suggest negotiating what you will teach during your hiring process. You may or may not get what you want in terms of classes, but it is worth asking. As I progressed, I learned some valuable lessons; I have included them in this chapter.

As I mentioned in the last chapter, it is important to be realistic about your teaching load and how much time it will allow you to dedicate to research. If you are teaching two courses per semester, you should be able to conduct research and write during the academic year. If you are teaching a heavier load, you may have to do most of your research and writing during the summer. Remember that you are not a superhero, you are human.

Connect What You Teach to Your Research

After several years, I began to realize that the smartest and most efficient way to teach was to try to teach courses that connected to my research, either contextually or methodologically. If you use this approach, you can stay current with the literature in your field, which helps you and your students. I realize you might not always have this option, but if you do, keep it in mind. For me, teaching an historical methods course was easy because I had read widely on this topic, used historical methods daily, and wanted to learn more. I edited a book on historical methods as a result of teaching a course on the topic (Gasman, 2010).

Preparing your Courses

I have some very particular views on preparing courses that others may not agree with, but they work for me, so I am going to share them. I have a secret when it comes to preparing my classes, one that results in me never doing anything last minute and never being overrun with teaching-related work during the academic year. I prepare my courses, including each week's activities, at the end of the academic year. Regardless of my teaching load, I spend two weeks after the semester ends preparing my courses for the next year. I begin by laying out the schedule for the semester, I then assign readings to each day of class. These are readings that I am familiar with and if I want to add something new, I read it to make sure it is appropriate for the class. I then grapple with the organization of the class, making sure it makes sense and moving things around if they seem odd. There are many resources related to creating syllabi and I suggest reviewing them to see what works best for you (Gannon, 2018; Moore, 2019; O'Brien et al., 2008). I have included many of these in the reference list for this book.

Once I lay out the syllabus, collecting articles and noting any books as I go along, I make a separate document focused on class activities. This document includes a play-by-play of what I will do in each class period. I make an outline and design the specific activities for the class. Because I get bored with merely sitting and talking about the readings, I design interactive activities that build upon the readings for each session. I make sure that these activities include opportunities for individual work, group work, public speaking, deep writing, creative writing, research, humor, and data analysis. Once I am done with the syllabus and the activity guides, I prepare my online site for the class (i.e. Canvas, Blackboard, etc.). I do not regularly teach online but I use Canvas to share readings, for grading, and for some course activities.

When the time comes to actually teach the course, I review my syllabus and my course activity guide one week in advance and make sure that I am prepared. I have been using this approach for 20 years; thus, I have many different activities prepared and have quite a bit of flexibility in case I want to switch one activity to another because the class personality is a bit different than I might have assumed or imagined.

When I share my advance prepping strategy with others, they are often resistant because of how much time it takes at the end of the semester. However, believe me, the time is worth it. Unlike my colleagues, I never complain about preparing for class. I always have my syllabus in order, my students know exactly what they will be doing, and I do not have to spend hours preparing for class during the academic year. Of course, I still spend time grading and meeting with students, but my strategy has enabled me to spend time doing research and writing during the academic year.

If you do not use this approach, it will be important for you to prepare your classes prior to the start of the semester. You do not want to be the stereotype of the last-minute faculty member in front of the jammed copy machine, hoping the paper jam goes away so you can get to your class on time. And, you will need to set aside several hours a week to prepare for each of your classes, in addition to the time for grading and meeting with students. I find that many assistant professors who use this approach tend to spend too much time preparing their classes, which results in their not producing scholarship at a level that helps them to secure tenure. My best advice is to prepare well in advance.

Due to COVID-19, many faculty have had to learn—quickly—to teach online. Most people that I know across the nation were teaching online for the first time. If you suddenly have to teach online, I suggest that you seek out mentorship right away as preparing an online course takes considerably more time than an in-person class, because you must manage the technology in addition to the topic. One of my favorite books related to online teaching is Judith Boettcher and Rita-Marie

Conrad's (2016) *The Online Teaching Survival Guide: Simple and Practical Pedagogical Tips* (San Francisco, CA: Jossey-Bass). See Appendix E for my tips for online teaching and virtual community building.

Ensuring That All Voices are Heard in Your Classroom

It is vital, regardless of the topic you teach, to include a variety of voices on your syllabus, in terms of authors, class guest speakers, examples, and assignments. Sometimes I get pushback when making this claim because those in disciplines such a physics, engineering, or math tell me that issues of diversity do not matter in their areas. Having taught a group of 20 biomedical post-docs how to teach for nearly a decade, I know that it matters and that it is possible (Dewsbury, 2017).

As you are crafting your syllabus, include articles written by a variety of people in terms of race, ethnicity, and gender. This takes some work, yes. For my history class, I often go to graduate student conference presentations to see what new research is available, because those doing it are usually more likely to be people of color and women. I definitely use classics in my courses, but I also bring in new ideas, including some I do not necessarily agree with. Because I teach in a highly interactive manner, I also make sure my activities bring in a variety of voices and take place in various contexts.

Most college classrooms are fairly diverse at this point and it is important that all students feel heard, seen, and that their experiences and stories are important and central to learning. In case you are reading along and doubt me when I say "most college classrooms are fairly diverse at this point," here are some statistics on college student diversity in the United States to consider. Between 1975 and 2016, the population of college undergraduates has changed significantly, with increases across most racial and ethnic groups. Hispanic student enrollment has increased from 4% to 18%, Black student enrollment from 10% to 14%, Asian American and Pacific Islander student enrollment from 2% to 7%, and Native American student enrollment from 0.7% to 0.8% (Gasman, forthcoming). And, at some of the nation's most selective institutions, the percentage of undergraduate students of color has increased substantially. For instance, Stanford University, Columbia University, and New York University have a student body that is 66% students of color. Moreover, and commendable, UCLA and UC-Berkeley have an undergraduate population that is 73% students of color. If we move to the middle of the country, both Northwestern University and the University of Chicago have student bodies of nearly 55% students of color.[1] Racial and ethnic diversification has advanced in the undergraduate student population across the nation and even at the nation's most prestigious institutions (Gasman, forthcoming). Unfortunately, the way we teach has not. It is vital to be sensitive to these changes and to be inclusive in your teaching with regard to racial and ethnic diversity. In addition, I strongly suggest that you be as inclusive as possible with regard to LGBTQ+ issues, religious and political beliefs, language, country of origin, and ability.

I work really hard not to center Whiteness in my teaching. For example, most history courses are organized around—thus centering—White men (often heroes) and wars. To be frank, most classes are centered on White men's ideas due to who is writing history and who these authors deem as heroes. As Chinua Achebe said, "Until the lions have their own historians, the history of the hunt will always glorify the hunter." It takes considerable work to decenter Whiteness. It means you have to read extensively and regularly in your field. It means you have to move beyond what your faculty taught you in classes to incorporate new material and voices. However, once you have decentered White men from your curriculum, it becomes easy to bring in the rich contributions of everyone else in addition to talking about the role White men have played in your discipline. I know that this can be challenging for some of you; bringing a diverse group of voices to your classroom may seem unrealistic and unnecessary, depending on what you teach. I beg you to consider the decades of research related to the importance of culturally relevant pedagogy (Hockings et al., 2012; Ladson-Billings, 1995, 2014). We know that when students of all ages see themselves in the curriculum, they are more engaged, perform at a higher level, and have a better learning experience. I believe you want these experiences for your students. Right?

Managing Difficult Conversations in the Classroom

I find that the more diverse your classroom, the more challenge exists among the students. I find respectful disagreement in the classroom to be an important part of learning. However, there are times when students are not respectful and do not realize the difference between ideas that are backed up by research and their personal experiences. I try to give students opportunities to share their personal experiences during course activities and some course assignments. However, it is also important that they understand what the salient research says in their discipline, and that they know how to think critically about it and how to grapple with various ideas. In all of this grappling, there is often frustration, which you need to learn how to manage.

I use a variety of approaches to manage difficult discussions. First, if a student says something offensive in class to another student, I stop the class and work out the situation, taking care of both the person who was offended and the offender. If you do not take care of the offender, they will not learn, and learning is central to your role as a faculty member. In these situations, I try to get the students to understand each other, to listen, and to learn. I also do not tolerate side conversations, and eye rolling, which has become the norm in classes lately, given the popularity of emoji reactions across social media. Second, if I see regular side conversations and mocking of other students, I stop the class immediately and say something. Oftentimes you will have small cliques in class and these students will laugh at and mock other students for not understanding the course material or taking it seriously. I deal with this behavior in real time in class and I also talk to the students after class, following up with an email. Third, I have a section on my syllabus that talks about respect toward others in the classroom and I go over this very clearly on the first day (See Image 3.1). I also make sure that students understand my class participation policy and the percentage of points that I allot to respectful participation.

CLASSROOM DISCUSSION & PARTICIPATION STATEMENT SAMPLE

I have designed the course with the point of view that the classroom must be a place where we all speak freely and share our insights with the other members of the class. I will have my opinions on many matters discussed in class, but this does not mean that you must agree with me. The course will not be truly enjoyable unless we disagree on academic issues and are willing to discuss our opinions. However, at all times, we must be respectful towards each other.

Your class participation will be evaluated at the end of the course. The criteria used to evaluate class participation will be:

(a) attendance as described above, (b) quality of participation (e.g., integration and consideration of course readings), (c) respect for others' views, and (d) consideration of others (i.e., not "hogging" up the conversation, holding side conversations, or talking when others are talking).

Image 3.1 – Classroom Discussion & Participation Statement Sample

It is important to keep in mind that you can prepare for difficult conversations, but in the moment, they typically do not feel good and your heart tends to sink as they happen. I always replay my responses over and over after class because I am very critical of myself while teaching. What is essential is that you address the difficult conversations. The worst reaction you can have is to just move on from the issue, but this is what many faculty do because they do not feel equipped to handle the situation. If you do not feel ready, you need to get ready. Teaching and learning centers on most campuses can help you work through these issues, and I suggest visiting them sooner rather than later. A quick Google search of "how to handle difficult conversations in the college classroom" will result in guidance from most major colleges and universities.[2] My best advice is to prepare yourself and to find a colleague you trust with whom you can discuss these difficult situations and plan your responses. Students are looking to you to step in and provide leadership and guidance. We as professors have an obligation to do so.

Over the years, I have had students say some pretty terrible things in class and I have had to intervene. For example, when I was an assistant professor, I had one student refer to another student as gay in a derogatory manner. The student who was assumed to be gay was not *out* or public to anyone about his sexuality at the time. I could see the look on his face of embarrassment and hurt. I could also see that the student who made the comment immediately realized that what he said was offensive. Likewise, I could see that the class was shocked and they were all looking to me to say something. I asked the class if they could each take a few minutes to collect their thoughts, asked them to write about what just happened in their weekly course journals (that I regularly reviewed), and asked to meet with the two students individually and together after class.[3] After meeting with the students, they decided to talk to the class together the following week. This strategy was productive and cut down on rumors, assumptions, and students' creating their own version of what happened and the outcome. In the end, the two students became friends and remain friends. Both are successful professors now. I was not exactly sure what to do in the moment, but I had spent considerable time reading and preparing in case this kind of situation or something similar happened.

Student Learning

Regardless of the type of class you teach, you want to make sure that your students are learning. There are many ways to do this. First, listen in class and watch who answers your questions regularly. If some students do not engage, I will often ask to meet with them or send them an email to check in on them. Second, I use a variety of small assignments to gauge understanding. You can use anything from clickers in science classrooms, to free writing at the beginning of class in humanities or social science-based courses. You can also develop in-class group activities that require every member of the class to engage the readings and course materials. If students know you are going to ask them to engage regularly, they are more likely to come to class prepared.

I give an assignment that is due the second week of class so that I can gauge student understanding and student writing. There are faculty who believe that writing should not be a part of class evaluation unless the class is focused on writing. However, I wholeheartedly disagree with this approach. It is vital that students learn how to use their voices both in written form and in public speaking. Students work on these skills in all of my classes regardless of what the topic is. I have had students return years later to thank me for helping them find their voice, sharing that very few faculty cared about their ability to write clearly and with argument and perspective. Assigning a short paper, a short data-oriented assignment, or an experiment near the beginning of the semester is also important because it gives students feedback immediately and demonstrates how you grade and assess their learning. All too often, students are waiting until midsemester for any feedback and are wondering and wandering aimlessly.

Another aspect of student learning is variety. I use a variety of assignments for students across my classes (See Figure 3.2). Your students will be unique, possessing skills at different

---

SAMPLE COURSE ACTIVITIES

Historical Document Paper
Obtain a historical document/s related to higher education and write a critical analysis of that document. Please draw on the class exercise in which we examined historical documents. Your critique should include (a) a description or summary of the document; (b) an analysis of the document's meaning that draws upon scholarly work pertaining to the document (outside sources); (c) a description of how the document and your subsequent analysis inform the study of higher education. Questions to think about include: Who wrote the document(s)? What is its purpose? What were the circumstances surrounding its production? What were the agendas of the people involved? Your paper should be 4 pages in length,double-spaced [absolutely no more]. We suggest that you visit one of the many university archives in Philadelphia's colleges and universities or examine some of the many on-line sites for historical documents.

Mini-Documentary
Prepare and record a professional and engaging 3 minute documentary in which you discuss a historical issue related to higher education. We recommend that you use 1-movie. You may also use another movie program if you desire. We expect you to be creative and innovative in your delivery and approach.To procure recording equipment and assistance, please visit media lab at the library. Please make sure to begin working on this project well in advance of the due date.

Persuasive Essay
Write an 800-1000 word opinion essay on a current topic in higher education, rooting it in historical data and literature. The essay should express a firm opinion but that opinion must be based on evidence.

Oral History
Select an individual associated with the history of higher education (you may not interview your boyfriend, girlfriend, partner, significant other, husband, or wife). Craft a list of questions based on your understanding of the historical context. Then, conduct an oral history interview with the individual. When done, write a short essay, including quotes from the interview. Also, please draw from secondary sources to support the individual's perspectives. Your oral history essay should be 5 pages [no more], double-spaced,12 point font. Please hand in a transcript of the interview along with your essay.

Figure 3.2 – Sample Course Activities

levels. Varying assignments allows students to play to their strengths. For example, if I am teaching history, I may begin the class with an assignment in which students write a 3-page history of themselves. This assignment allows me to get to know the student better, allows me to assess their writing and organizational skills, and is low-stakes for the student because they do not have to conduct research and it is usually only worth 5 points. Later in the course, I may ask students to produce a short documentary about a topic of their choice. This assignment is easy for some and really difficult for others depending on their comfort level with technology. I make sure to give them all the tools needed and point them in the direction of tech support. I also give students an assignment that allows them to hone and demonstrate their research skills, such as a research paper that requires an argument backed by data. Sometimes, I provide a menu of 8-10 different assignments and allow students to choose 4-5 for the semester. This strategy allows for agency and students can play to their interests and strengths.

The key to good teaching is to learn what works well for you, what you are comfortable doing, and which approaches ensure that your students learn most effectively. I suggest reading about teaching to increase your knowledge and skills. Some of my favorite books in my library, which are worn due to constant use, are Norman Eng's (2017) *Teaching College*, Chris Palmer's (2019) *College Teaching at Its Best*, Wilbert McKeachie and Marilla Svinick's (2013) *McKeachie's Teaching Tips*, Cyndi Kernahan's (2019) *Teaching about Race and Racism in the College Classroom*, and Ken Bain's (2004) *What the Best College Teachers Do*. These books are all very different and offer many ideas for how to make your classroom a place of learning and inspiration.

Student Teaching Evaluations

Over the years, I have heard faculty complain about student teaching evaluations more than most things in the academy, aside from their pay. Teaching evaluations are tricky. I believe that it is important to have them, to read them, and to see what you can glean from them in terms of ways to improve your teaching. That said, how you are rated on teaching evaluations and the comments on them depend on a variety of factors (Basow, 1998; Centra & Gaubatz, 2000; Chavez & Mitchell, 2020; Downey & Pribesh, 2004; Mengel et al., 2019; Mitchell & Martin, 2018; Reid, 2010). First, if you are teaching a required course, your teaching evaluations will likely be lower. This is not always the case, but it often is, because students often do not want to take the class and are doing so because their program of study requires it. It is important that your evaluations, when reviewed by tenure committees, are viewed within the context of other required courses (Chavez & Mitchell, 2020). Second, if you teach an elective, your teaching evaluations are likely to be stronger because people want to be in your classes. Third, if you are teaching courses within a major, your courses will most likely be rated higher than courses that are part of general requirements (Chavez & Mitchell, 2020). Fourth, if you are a woman, a person of color, a member of the LGBTQ+ community, or have an accent, you may experience racism, discrimination, and lower teaching evaluations from students, and inappropriate comments about your accent, your clothes, your age, your hair, your body, your voice, and other parts of your identity that are not related to your ability to teach (Basow, 1998; Centra & Gaubatz, 2000; Chavez & Mitchell, 2020; Downey & Pribesh, 2004; Mengel et al., 2019; Mitchell & Martin, 2018; Reid, 2010). If this happens to you, you will need to provide research to your department chair and subsequent tenure committee showing that this happens to professors based on identity. When this happened to me, I consulted the research on teaching and demonstrated that I was not the only woman who was regularly disrespected in class and on evaluations. I did notice that this disrespect stopped as I got older and made it clear that I would not tolerate it in the classroom.

When these kinds of situations happened to people of color pursuing tenure, especially during tenure discussions, I made a point to bring in research to tenure committee meetings demonstrating that some faculty are held to a higher standard. It is important that you have colleagues who will have your back and argue on your behalf if you are being discriminated against. For people of color, I suggest having some White allies who will speak up about your teaching strengths. Why? Because all too often White faculty will not believe that bias plays a part unless other White people advocate for you; even though they may not value teaching evaluations, biases and systemic racism makes it all too common that faculty will believe negative characterizations of people of color (Diangelo, 2018; Eberhardt, 2019; Kendi, 2019).

Please keep in mind, however, that although bias can be one factor in negative evaluations, poor teaching, and lack of follow through can also play a part. These issues will be difficult to contextualize even with research to support the impact of bias if they appear in your evaluations. Do your best to put forth your strongest teaching and to mitigate any issues.

Although many factions of the faculty regularly object to student teaching evaluations, they are probably here to stay. From my perspective, they are one tool to judge faculty teaching and student learning. However, it is important that those reviewing teaching evaluations do not fixate on one or two negative comments, ignoring the overall scoring and the majority of student responses (Boysen et al., 2014; Hamilton, 1980; Miles & House, 2015). I find that this fixation happens with faculty in general, no matter what they are reviewing. When I am reviewing student teaching evaluations, I look for patterns of positive comments and negative comments. I look for ways to glean constructive advice. I do not give credence to comments that are mean, spiteful, or insulting (Lindahl & Unger, 2010). As I mentioned, you will not be in the room when your tenure decision is discussed; it is imperative that your mentors and advocates are familiar with the research on teaching evaluations. I suggest you share the research I have cited in this book.

Peer Teaching Evaluations

Some colleges and universities require peer teaching evaluations. Although the thought of a peer watching and evaluating your teaching may make you sick to your stomach—it makes me ill—it is actually very helpful if the peer is in your discipline. Even if your institution does not require such reviews, I think asking a peer—someone you trust—to evaluate you is a smart idea. I would do this early on to ensure that you are in command of the course material, that you are responding to student questions, and that you are clear in your delivery. At some institutions, you can ask the staff in the center for teaching and learning to digitally record your teaching and do a critique with you. Most people do not want to do this because they do not like to see themselves or to hear their voices, but it is an excellent way to see where you need to improve. Whatever you can do to improve your teaching and ability to communicate ideas is valuable.

Final Thoughts

Teaching is an important part of being faculty, and depending on the type of institution where you work, it might play a larger or smaller role. At small, liberal arts colleges and comprehensive universities, teaching is highly valued and is a considerable factor in your tenure package. However, at research universities, especially institutions that fall under the Carnegie Classification of "very high research universities" and/or members of the AAU, research is valued significantly more than teaching. Yes, teaching is important and valued, but great teaching will not lead to tenure if you do not have an equally stellar research record. And faculty who are mediocre teachers are regularly awarded tenure because they are highly productive researchers. I have found that research universities are clear about what they prioritize in terms of research. Finally, if you do not like doing research, do not work at a research university. Far too often, I hear faculty complaining about the research expectations at their institution—a "very high research" institution—and I never understand these complaints. If you take a job at a research-focused institution, research is a way of life. If you do not want to do a lot of research, I suggest working at a comprehensive university or a liberal arts college, where the research expectations are lower and the teaching expectations are higher. I became a full professor in 2011 and I am just as productive, if not more, than I was when I was on the tenure-track and applying for full professor. The expectations at the institutions at which I have worked as a tenured professor are just as high for tenured professors as for those seeking tenure, and they should be. Our role is to produce new knowledge that can advance learning, ideas, society, and beyond and we do this through research as well as teaching.

Notes

1   The majority of the students of color at all of these research universities are from middle and upper income families. Pell Grant eligible student percentages range from 13-21%. 40% of undergraduate students receive Pell Grants overall. For comparison's sake, at Historically Black Colleges and Universities, 71% of students are Pell Grant eligible (Gasman, forthcoming).

2   For example, Vanderbilt University's Center for Teaching and Learning offers "Difficult Dialogues" (https://cft.vanderbilt.edu/guides-sub-pages/difficult-dialogues), Indiana University offers "Managing Difficult Classroom Conversations" (https://citl.indiana.edu/teaching-resources/diversity-inclusion/managing-difficult-classroom-discussions/index.html), the City University of New York provides a handbook for facilitating difficult conversations (https://www.qc.cuny.edu/Academics/Centers/Democratic/Documents/Handbook%20for%20Facilitating%20Difficult%20Conversations2.pdf), and Boston University offers "Challenging Conversations on Campus and in the Classroom" (https://www.bu.edu/ombuds/resources/challenging-classroom-conversations).

3   In classes that are particularly sensitive, I often use journaling as a way for students to express their feelings and to share those feelings with me. I grade students on completing the journal entry and not on what they write, so that the sharing is low stakes for them.

References

Bain, K. (2004). *What the best college teachers do.* Harvard University Press.

Basow, S. A. (1998). Student evaluations: The role of gender bias and teaching styles. In L. H. Collins, J. C. Chrisler, & K. Quina (Eds.), *Career strategies for women in academe: Arming Athena* (pp. 135-156). Sage Publications, Inc.

Boettcher, J. V., & Conrad, R. (2016). *The online teaching survival guide: Simple and practical pedagogical tips.* Jossey-Bass.

Boysen, G., Kelly, T., Raesly,H., & Casner, R. (2014). The (mis) interpretation of teaching evaluations by college faculty and administrators. *Assessment & Evaluation in Higher Education, 39*(6), 641-656.

Centra, J. A., & Gaubatz, N. B. (2000). Is there gender bias in student evaluations of teaching? *The Journal of Higher Education, 71*(1), 17-33.

Chávez, K., & Mitchell, K. M. (2020). Exploring bias in student evaluations: Gender, race, and ethnicity. *PS: Political Science & Politics, 53*(2), 270-274.

Dewsbury, B. (2017). On faculty development of STEM inclusive teaching practices. *FEMS Microbiology Letters, 365*(18), fnx179.

DiAngelo, R.J. (2018). *White fragility: Why it's so hard for White people to talk about racism.* Beacon Press.

Downey, D. B., & Pribesh, S. (2004). When race matters: Teachers' evaluations of students' classroom behavior. *Sociology of Education, 77*(4), 267-282.

Eberhardt, J. (2019). *Biased: Uncovering the hidden prejudice that shapes what we see, think, and do.* Penguin Books.

Eng, N. (2017). *Teaching college: The ultimate guide to lecturing, presenting, and engaging students.* Amazon Services.

Gannon, K. (2018). How to create a syllabus. *Chronicle of Higher Education.* https://www.chronicle.com/article/how-to-create-a-syllabus

Gasman, M. (2010). *The history of higher education: Methods for uncovering the past.* Routledge.

Gasman, M. (forthcoming). *Chasing the thoroughbred: The pervasiveness of systemic racism in faculty hiring.*

Hamilton, L. (1980). Grades, class size, and faculty status predict teaching evaluations. *Teaching Sociology, 8*(1), 47-62.

Hockings, C., Brett, P., & Terentjevs, M. (2012). Making a difference—inclusive learning and teaching in higher education through open educational resources. *Distance Education, 33*(2), 237-252.

Kendi, I. X. (2019). *How to be an antiracist*. Random House.

Kernaham, C. (2019). *Teaching about race and racism in the college classroom. Notes from a White Professor*. University of West Virginia Press.

Ladson-Billings, G. (1995). Toward a theory of culturally relevant pedagogy. *American Educational Research Journal, 32*(3), 465–491.

Ladson-Billings, G. (2014). Culturally relevant pedagogy 2.0: aka the remix. *Harvard Educational Review, 84*(1), 74–84.

Lindahl, M., & Unger, M. (2010). Cruelty in student teaching evaluations. *College Teaching, 58*(3), 71–76.

McKeachie, W., & Svinick, M. (2013). *McKeachie's teaching tips*. Cengage.

Mengel, F., Sauermann, J., & Zölitz, U. (2019). Gender bias in teaching evaluations. *Journal of the European Economic Association, 17*(2), 535–566.

Miles, P., & House, D. (2015). The tail wagging the dog: An overdue examination of student teaching evaluations. *International Journal of Higher Education, 4*(2), 116–126.

Mitchell, K. M., & Martin, J. (2018). Gender bias in student evaluations. *PS: Political Science & Politics, 51*(3), 648–652.

Moore, C. (2019). *Seven ways to make your syllabus more relevant*. Faculty Focus. https://www.facultyfocus.com/articles/course-design-ideas/seven-ways-to-make-your-syllabus-more-relevant

O'Brien, J., Millis, B., & Cohen, M. (2008). *The course syllabus: A learning-centered approach*. Jossey-Bass.

Palmer, C. (2019). *College teaching at its best: Inspiring students to be enthusiastic, lifelong learners*. Rowman & Littlefield.

Reid, L. D. (2010). The role of perceived race and gender in the evaluation of college teaching on RateMyProfessors.com. *Journal of Diversity in higher Education, 3*(3), 137.

Zimmerman, J. (2020). *The amateur hour: A history of college teaching in America*. Johns Hopkins University Press.

How Do I Manage Service?

In this chapter, I will discuss ways for faculty to approach service requirements[1] and how to maximize service work to complement teaching and research. I will also discuss when to say "yes" and "no" to service requests, and how to manage these conversations. The best advice I can give you is to try to do service that complements your research agenda and strengths. This will not always be possible, but attempt to do it. I share some ways, below. There are many kinds of service, at the following levels: departmental, school/college, university, and national. One can also do community service, which may or may not be valued by your institution.

Department-Level Service

Departmental-level service is likely the first service you will be asked to do as an assistant professor. Remember to pace yourself, as new people are usually asked to do things immediately. In addition, students often swarm you because they are excited about the possibility that a faculty member might care about them and be student focused. Typical departmental service includes serving on committees for graduate student admissions, curriculum planning, or tenure and promotion. Your department might have other committees, as well, depending on your institution. Rightfully, tenure-track faculty should be shielded from a high departmental service load, but according to research that is not always the case, especially for White women and people of color (Guarino & Borden, 2017; Harley, 2008; Hirshfield & Joseph, 2012; O'Meara, 2016; O'Meara et al., 2017). I advise only saying "yes" to one committee during your first three years. Saying no to other requests will be hard because you will be in a vulnerable position. If you have a mentor, you may want to ask them for advice and assistance. And, remember that you cannot say "no" to everything, so when someone asks you to be on another committee, say something such as "Thank you. I am already serving on X committee, which takes a considerable amount of my time. It is important to me that I have balance in my career." As my mother always says, "You catch more flies with sugar than you do with vinegar." As you move along the tenure track you will be asked to do more in your department and it is acceptable to do so, but do not take on too much. Ask questions about the workload of the committee and talk to people who have served before. In addition, I recommend discreetly keeping track of who is doing what in your department, to ensure you are being treated in an equitable manner. The best academic department chairs keep track of this information and have it handy whenever they are assigning committee work.

You may also be asked to serve on thesis and dissertation committees—I will discuss chairing dissertations in the next chapter—and I would recommend agreeing to 1-2 initially and more as you move along. I have served on countless thesis and dissertation committees all across the country and do not keep track of them anymore. I like doing it because I love working with students as they grapple with their ideas. However, I do not advise that new faculty take on too much in this area. Again, as you are new, a lot of students will ask to work with you. Saying 'no' will be hard. I found that stating I could only take on so much because I wanted to do my best work with each student was an effective way of explaining my "no."

School/College-Level Service

School or college-wide service is essential to shared governance in higher education. By your second year on the tenure-track, you will usually get tapped by a dean or associate dean, asking if you are willing to be on a school or college-wide committee. I advise serving on one of these committees. These committees include tenure and promotion, scholarships, resources, awards, student grievances, and many more. I even remember a committee on committees at Penn! I bet there are people reading this thinking, "why is she mocking that committee? It makes sense to me." Okay. But for the rest of you, if you want a good laugh, put "Committee on Committees" in Google and see how many universities and organizations have one—it is truly absurd.

I learned early that if you do good work, you will be asked to be on more committees. There are two ways to approach this problem: 1) Continue to do good work and continue to be asked to serve on committees (I take this approach because I grew up Catholic and was taught that follow-through and good work are essential to goodness. Thanks, mom. Thanks, Jesus); 2) Do very little. I have seen quite a few faculty use this approach as the pathway to not being asked to do service. My advice is to do your best work and learn to say no. One school/college-wide committee is enough service each year at that level and there are plenty of faculty across the school who can do service on the rest of the committees.

Throughout my faculty career, I have done a large amount of service. It is easy to me and I can do it quickly. However, I do not like useless meetings. I would prefer to do everything on email. Unfortunately, most faculty prefer to meet and discuss issues until the issues are dead. In order to avoid too much service, you will need to learn how to say a firm but nice no just as noted above. However, when a dean or associate dean asks, it might be harder to say no. I found that having a list of committees on which you are already serving on hand is advantageous. It can also be important to remind the administrator that you are on the tenure track and want to be successful. I will admit that I said yes most of the time when asked by a dean, but I said no once when I realized I was being asked to chair two of the four major committees in the school when there were plenty of other faculty available. After achieving tenure, I did chair both committees, trying to shield tenure-track faculty from doing this work; I still wondered what the other faculty in my school were doing. Here is a secret: I prefer chairing committees rather than being on them, because I can keep the meetings short, do a lot of the work via email, and go in with a strategy for cutting through the minutia of faculty meetings.

University-Level Service

Another type of service within the academy is service at the university or college level. In about your fourth or fifth year, word usually gets out about your talent around campus and you might be asked to serve on university- or college-wide committees. I always said yes to these requests (and still do) because I enjoyed getting to know faculty and staff across campus. These committees are typically not a lot of work, meet infrequently, and they allow you to get acquainted with the inner workings of the university. You do not want to take on too much, but serving on one or two a year can be helpful. I also think it is helpful to get a sense of other departments and schools. All too often, we get stuck in a rut and think that our department's or discipline's way of approaching issues and problems is the only way to do things.

National Service

Many faculty serve on a national scale in addition to their departmental and college/university-wide service. National service can lead to national recognition and provide opportunities for networking. I have served on program committees for national academic organizations, as the website manager for a small history group, as vice president of an organization, on boards of trustees for colleges and nonprofits, and as an advisor to various politicians on higher education policy issues. There are many opportunities for national service and serving in these ways is a choice. You do not have to do it; it is fairly easy to say no because you do not have to face people daily. However, serving on a committee of a national organization or in a leadership role can be rewarding. Not only will you meet new people, establish important relationships, and learn more about your field and discipline, but tenure and promotion committees like to see national service and recognition. I would suggest taking on one service opportunity at a time at the national level. You can do more, but pace yourself and remember that your research and teaching are the most important aspects of your faculty role. As you move along in your career you may be asked to run for elected positions in your discipline's major organization. This type of leadership takes immense time and you have to decide if this is something you want to do and have time for. Do not feel pressured or that it is necessary; it is not. I served as vice president for a large academic association for three years only because a dear mentor asked me to stand for election. I declined to serve in presidential roles because I quickly discovered that individuals in these roles are limited in terms of what they can do or say from the role. Academic organizations are inherently small 'c' conservative and many leaders issue bland statements and talk in mundane policy speak, doing nothing to advance the field in meaningful ways. There are exceptions, but because individuals fear being disliked, they are rare. In my entire career, I have only seen one organizational president make a speech in his role that had a lasting impact on the field—James D. Anderson, the Edward William and Jane Marr Gutgsell Professor of Education at the University of Illinois, in his role as president of the History of Education Society.[2] In 1993, he gave a presidential address entitled "Race, Meritocracy, and the American Academy during the Immediate Post-World War II Era," and subsequently published the speech in the *History of Education Quarterly* (Anderson, 1993). Unlike so many leaders of academic organizations, Anderson's speech tackled a deeply important issue head on and with evidence. He did not stand up and spout platitudes and hopes. He delved deeply into systemic issues of discrimination and institutional racism, and did so with rigor. He demonstrated his craft and pushed the organization to new levels. If you have the ability to do what Anderson did, I beg you to get involved in a national organization as a leader.

You will also have opportunities to serve as a reviewer for journals and perhaps on editorial boards (although this is rare as a tenure-track faculty member unless you have some very well placed articles or the journal is not highly ranked). Depending on how the editor leads the journal, these roles could be manageable or overwhelming. If the work becomes burdensome, you have to speak up and make sure that the editor knows you cannot do any more work. Tenure and promotion committees like to see journal service, especially editorial board service, but reviewing articles takes time and you do not want this work to detract from your productivity. I typically say yes to requests to review articles if they are in my area of expertise because I have learned how to review quickly and it is a good way of staying on top of the new work in the field. I also say yes to editorial board service because I know how to be direct if the workload becomes too large. I am not interested in serving as a journal editor as the workload is immense and I have enough to do with leading a center and institution. Please do not take on an editor or associate editor role pre-tenure. The workload is too demanding and it will take away from your ability to achieve tenure. Moreover, it is unethical to publish in a journal for which you are an editor or associate editor. Doing so appears and is self-serving, regardless of whether or not you see people doing it.

Community Service

You may also choose to be involved in your community, which is always an important thing to do. This type of service will be appreciated more at small liberal arts colleges, Historically Black Colleges and Universities, community colleges, and Hispanic Serving Institutions than at larger research-focused universities, but for the most part, community service will not play a role in your achieving tenure. If you are going to be active in your community, do it for yourself. I have always found it rewarding to be active in the community because it provides a sense of 'realness' that the academy does not.

Keeping Track of Service for Tenure

One of the most important aspects of service is keeping track of it. Remember how I told you to update your CV regularly, with each event that happens in your professional career? You need to update your CV with each act of service you perform, otherwise you will forget (See Appendix F for a guide to outlining your CV). I have sections on my CV titled "departmental service," "school/university service," and "national service." This structure allows you to organize your service and to see if you have balance. You will be asked for all of this information when you produce your tenure dossier so having it on hand is important. Anything that can save you work later is smart to do now. Stay organized and make sure you log the credit for your good service. You will be asked to provide information on all of your service and every other aspect of your career when you go up for tenure so having good records is essential.

Final Thought

Although you will often be told that service does not matter—and, if we are honest, it does not matter as much as research and teaching—it does matter somewhat. Faculty do not like selfish colleagues and I can guarantee you that your internal letters of support from colleagues and students will be much warmer if you are generous with your time (Whitaker, 2019). I want to be sure to note that empirical research shows that White women and people of color are asked to do more service and carry heavier service loads than their White male colleagues (Hanasono et al., 2019; Social Sciences Feminist Network Research Interest Group, 2017). They are seen as the "mothers" and "caretakers" of the academy. As a result, White men are able to have considerably more time to focus on research. It is important that you share this research with your department chair and dean to make sure they realize when asking you to serve on yet another committee, that this action is not equitable and is a form of systemic racism and sexism that derails the careers or people of color and White women.

Notes

1   I do not consider student advising service and as such, advising is discussed in a separate chapter. I realize it is a form of service, but from my perspective it is very different than committee work.
2   I make this statement realizing that I have not heard every academic organization's leader give a speech—but I have heard many—and most say nothing—zip, zero—nothing in the speeches, as they fear offending someone and thus being disliked.

References

Anderson, J. D. (1993). Race, meritocracy, and the American academy during the immediate post-World War II era. *History of Education Quarterly, 33*(2), 151-175.

Guarino, C. M., & Bordon, V. (2017). Faculty service loads and gender: Are women taking care of the academic family? *Research in Higher Education, 58*(6), 672-694.

Hanasono, L. K., Broido, E. M., Yacobucci, M. M., Root, K. V., Peña, S., & O'Neil, D. A. (2019). Secret service: Revealing gender biases in the visibility and value of faculty service. *Journal of Diversity in Higher Education, 12*(1), 85.

Harley, D. A. (2008). Maids of academe: African American women faculty at predominantly White institutions. *Journal of African American Studies, 12*(1), 19-36.

Hirshfield, L. E., & Joseph, T. D. (2012). 'We need a woman, we need a Black woman': Gender, race, and identity taxation in the academy. *Gender and Education, 24*(2), 213-227.

O'Meara, K., Kuvaeva, A., & Nyunt, G. (2017). Constrained choices: A view of campus service inequality from annual faculty reports. *The Journal of Higher Education, 88*(5), 672-700.

O'Meara, K. (2016). Whose problem is it? Gender differences in faculty thinking about campus service. *Teachers College Record, 118*(8), 1-38.

Social Sciences Feminist Network Research Interest Group. (2017). The burden of invisible work in academia: Social inequalities and time use in five university departments. *Humboldt Journal of Social Relations, 39*, 228-245.

Whitaker, M. (2019). *10 things no one told me about applying for tenure*. Chronicle of Higher Education. https://community.chronicle.com/news/2191-10-things-no-one-told-me-about-applying-for-tenure

5

Advising for Success

Aside from writing, advising students is my favorite part of being a professor. I thoroughly enjoy working one-on-one with students or in small groups to help them realize their scholarly dreams. This chapter focuses on advising students, from undergraduates to master's to doctoral students, including how to establish trusting relationships, how to manage student research collaborations, and how to motivate students to excel.

Your Relationship with Students

Your relationship with students often will differ depending on whether they are undergraduate, master's, or doctoral students. In recent years, I think these relationship have become more similar as boundaries have become more fluid. I would advise you to set very clear boundaries with students. Although you may be tempted to share many aspects of your life with students, especially graduate students, I would advise you not to. Far too often personal interactions can be misunderstood, misconstrued, and manipulated by students or colleagues if they do not like you, or do not want you to succeed.

I used to be very open with students, inviting classes to my home, inviting research assistants for dinner to meet my family, and inviting students who did not have anywhere to go for holidays to my home for celebrations. I bought clothes for students who did not have them for upcoming interviews, and purchased plane tickets for students when their parents passed away. I always paid for student meals and coffees, even for large groups of students. I often found myself listening to students pour out their hearts about their relationships, their fears, their pain, and their frustrations with other faculty who did not provide support or acted in racist ways. I do not support students in these ways anymore and I would advise you to be very careful, no matter how big your heart is. My inclination is to always want to help students and listen to them when they need a kind ear, but as faculty we have to remember that no matter how well we think we know students, we do not know them well enough. I would advise you to keep your relationships with students focused on teaching and research and to direct students to use the various mental health and support services on campus for the other aspects of their lives; I would say do the same with your faculty colleagues.

As examples, I have had students come to my office, shut the door immediately, and begin talking about betrayal in their romantic relationships, eating disorders, sexual assault, spousal abuse, bullying by other students, desires to commit suicide, and many other heavy issues. We have to remember that most of us are not equipped to manage these issues; we do not have the training. I used to sit and listen to students and invite them to share. I was a sounding board for them. However, when you are a sounding board, you may be tempted to share your own experiences and stories and here is where you will inevitably run into problems. My best advice is to be very careful about what you share with students, regardless of how close you are with them. I listen to students. I let them know that I am going to open the door to my office, and then I provide guidance on campus resources. In some cases such as suicide threats and issues of sexual assault or harassment, I make a connection to the responsible office on campus. I have a list of contacts and resources in my office so that I am always prepared for these encounters. I realize that my advice may sound cold, and it is difficult to write. However, students who may be suffering from abuse or mental illness may make you the enemy, and you have to protect yourself in these matters. For an informed and research-based discussion of these matters that moves beyond my anecdotes, see Bowman, Hatley, and Bowman's (1995) article "Faculty-student relationships: The dual role controversy."

I am still deeply supportive of students, always a student advocate, and will stand up for justice for students when it is needed, but I no longer go beyond the confines of my faculty role to support students. I would have never imagined ten years ago that I would be advising faculty to focus only on teaching and research in their interactions with students. However, life in the academy has changed, in both good and troubling ways. As a faculty member, you need to protect yourself. Along these lines, I would advise you to always keep your office door open, to document each student interaction using a university provided program (e.g., Advisor in Touch is a good tool) or a personal notebook, and to follow up on each interaction with a summary email. In addition, if you have any issues with students or feel uncomfortable, immediately contact your department chair or dean and ask for their assistance. Yes, faculty have power and, yes, faculty-student relationships are imbalanced, but that power and imbalance can make you vulnerable just as it can make the student vulnerable. For a deeper understanding of why it is important for faculty to protect themselves, and specifically women and people of color, please see Claudia Lampman, Earl Crew, Shea Lowery, and Kelley Tompkins' (2016) important article titled "Women Faculty Distressed: Descriptions and Consequences of Academic Contrapower Harassment," in the *NASPA Journal About Women in Higher Education*. They surveyed 289 professors and found that students were more likely to challenge women professors and their authority. They were also more likely to argue or refuse to follow course policies when women were the professors. And students were more likely to exhibit disrespectful or disruptive behaviors toward women professors than toward men. Lastly, although sexual overtures on the part of students toward faculty are infrequent, women were more likely to report them when they did hap-

pen. I would advise students to take the same precautions, but given that this book is for faculty, that is my emphasis. I would rather not offer this advice, but we live in a society that requires it.

Advising Students

Despite my warnings above, I use an approach to advising that includes warmth and kindness alongside challenge and motivation. I work hard to establish relationships with students, asking for their expectations of the relationship and sharing my own. In recent years, I have asked students I advise to submit these expectations in writing and I do the same. I find this makes the relationship work more effectively.

When working with undergraduate students, I meet on an as-needed basis and let them dictate the schedule unless I do not regularly hear from them. Although I mainly teach and advise graduate students, I have often worked with undergraduates and have found these relationships to be incredibly fulfilling. Undergraduates are rarely jaded and have not been in the academy long enough to pick up the habit of constant critique that many graduate students inherit from faculty. Undergrads are eager and curious and often very driven. I truly enjoy helping them to reach their goals and working with them to shape their aspirations. Because undergraduates—especially those in the 18-25-year-old category, but even those who are older—are often not familiar with the college or university system, it is vital to point them in the right direction and to ensure that they are on the right path to graduation. I regularly review their degree plans to ensure that they are not missing courses and I also encourage them to take full advantage of all that an institution has to offer. In addition, I make introductions for internships and possible mentors in their areas of expertise.

I also advise master's students, as most faculty do. As part of this advising, you may be responsible for advising a master's thesis in addition to the student's program of study, depending on your department and institution. I enjoy working with master's students. I find that they are eager to learn. However, given that I often work with them on writing projects or on a thesis, I would advise that assisting them with analysis and writing can be time consuming. Be prepared. but remember how rewarding it can be. It is also important to get to know the work of your master's students, because they will need a strong letter of recommendation from you if they are pursuing a graduate or professional degree.

When I first began as a professor, I did not understand my responsibilities as an advisor beyond what I experienced throughout school, so I spent time reading about advising and how to motivate and inspire students. There were not very many books to use as resources at the time, but today there are quite a few and I use them when I need support. I recommend the following books for new faculty: *Academic Advising: A*

Comprehensive Handbook (Gordon, 2008), *Academic Advising Approaches: Strategies that Teach Students to Make the Most of College* (Drake, 2013), and *The New Advisor Guidebook: Mastering the Art of Academic Advising* (Folsom, Yoder, & Joslin, 2015). Each of these books offers interesting perspectives on academic advising and is comprehensive in scope. Even if you do not read them from cover to cover, they are good to have for reference.

I am going to dedicate more space to discussing advising PhD students (or other doctoral students), because it is likely that you will do a considerable amount of this type of advising as a faculty member. I have thoroughly enjoyed advising doctoral students and between 2000-2020 have advised 81, mainly students of color. As with any student relationship, I would advise you to begin with a discussion of goals and expectations on your part and theirs. I also suggest putting together a plan for their overall time working with you. Depending on your approach, this plan will vary. I have several goals for those students I work with, including: to graduate with an important research project; to learn research skills; to hone their writing skills; to publish peer-reviewed work; to enhance their teaching skills; to understand the multiple roles of faculty life; and to have a positive doctoral experience. I achieve these goals by making a plan for each year. In year one, I spend time working with students to choose their classes and provide support and feedback when they need it in their classes. I also bring them into a research team that is already in progress so they can learn how to work with others and learn from me and more senior PhD students. This teamwork allows them to work on a publication in a low-stakes and low-stress environment. I do not ask first year PhD students to serve as teaching assistants, because I prefer they take a class with me and experience the way I teach before serving as a TA. Year one is spent getting to know the student, giving them experiences to work with others and me, offering them opportunities to try out various research skills, and delving into their interests and pushing them to think deeply about their potential dissertation topic.

During years three and four, I spend time working closely with students on various research projects, bringing them into the work that I have on my research agenda, but also encouraging them to explore topics they wrote about in classes in more detail. I often have two of my PhD advisees working together on a project, coding and analyzing data, and working with me to develop a literature review and co-author conference presentations and papers. Using this approach helps students secure publications as they move throughout their PhD program and hone the skills needed to become faculty members. It is also beneficial to me, because collaboration has always helped me learn new methodologies, and PhD students challenge me to do better research. In the fourth year (in education, a PhD typically takes 4 years)[1] or if the student needs longer, over the course of their fifth year, I work with them to develop their own, single-authored, peer-reviewed article based on their dissertation work. I want them to graduate with one single-authored, peer-reviewed article as I believe that having this accomplishment gives them an advantage on the job market. In addition, working on peer-reviewed work as a PhD student helps them to understand the publication process from start to finish and gives me an opportunity to help them work through journal revisions or to manage rejections and begin anew. To be successful on the tenure track, students need to understand how these processes work and how to manage rejection and critique. I also make sure that students gain teaching experience as they move throughout the PhD process, asking them to TA or if they want to teach a summer class, helping them to prepare a syllabus. It is vital that PhD students get as much experience that mirrors faculty life as possible during their PhD program, so they know how to manage the work of being a faculty member once they move into that role. For an in-depth guide to advising PhD and other graduate students, I recommend Bruce Shore's (2014) *The Graduate Advisor Handbook: A Student-Centered Approach.*

I realize that my approach is not the norm but I think that it is my job to ensure that PhD students are ready for tenure-track positions, which require a highly productive scholar. Throughout this process, I make sure to give PhD students ample constructive criticism on their writing, their methods, and their abilities to critically analyze data. I also buy them copies of two books that I suggest for anyone pursuing a tenure-track position or currently in one, regardless of academic rank. They are *Stylish Academic Writing* (Sword, 2016) and *Writing your Journal Article in Twelve Weeks: A Guide to Academic Publishing Success* (Belcher, 2019). I read each of these books once a year to motivate myself and ensure that my writing, organizational, analytical skills, and creativity do not slip.

Other aspects of your advising role that are important are providing letters of recommendation, reviewing student CVs and cover letters for faculty jobs, and helping students prepare and practice a job talk. I have seen PhD students stressed out and frustrated from having to beg their advisors to write letters of recommendation. Most of the time, these students have prepared all of the information in advance for the letters and the faculty still have not submitted letters. Do not do this to students. It is incredibly stressful for them and I would argue that it is a form of abuse, whether intentional or not.

My advice is to ask in advance for all the information you need to write the letters. Write a standard template and tweak the letters for each faculty position. It is important to realize that every year you need to make time to write these letters. Please do not hold up your students, as it is not only frustrating to them, but it also is embarrassing when faculty have to make excuses for the lack of follow through on the part of our colleagues. When writing letters, it is important that you write a strong letter and that it include concrete examples and a full understanding of why the student's research is important and rigorous. And, know that you will need to keep writing letters as your students move along the tenure-track and perhaps change institutions. Writing letters of recommendation is a way of life for faculty. If you need help, there are many samples on-line; I have found Andy Tay's (2020) "Writing the Perfect Recommendation Letter" to be a comprehensive source of information on the topic.

I also spend time preparing my students for their job talk and reviewing their CVs and cover letters. I give them considerable feedback because I know that search committees are highly critical during the hiring process. I normally give students an opportunity to formally practice their job talk if they would like, asking other doctoral students to join, if the PhD student is amenable, and providing comprehensive feedback to the student to help them strengthen their talk. Although this can be difficult for the student, I explain that receiving feedback from a group of people who are in your corner is much better than being critiqued by strangers during your job talk. I believe it is my role to support students through the entire job search process and to continue to provide that support as they pursue third-year review, tenure, and even full professor.

Another aspect of advising PhD students that you need to think about is how frequently you meet with them. I do one-on-one sessions with my advisees once per month, giving them time that is just for them to ask questions and to get advice. However, because those students typically also work with me on research projects, I see them almost daily and in research meetings, team meetings, and events. The PhD students I advise have always had my cell phone number and when I had one, my home number. I tell them that they can text me at any time if they need something. I do not have this relationship with all students, but most PhD students can have questions at any given hour and I want to be available to them. I have rarely had a PhD student contact me late at night or abuse the use of my cell phone number.

Advocating for Your Students

One aspect of advising that is vitally important is advocating for your students. There will be times when students need your voice and it is important for you to be there for them. Being there for your students might put you at risk, given that you are on the tenure-track and do not have job security. Ask your department chair or a few senior colleagues about the ramifications of your advocacy for students if the subject matter is controversial. I have found that most of the time when you have to advocate for a student it involves another faculty member, which can cause difficulty. Use your relationships, explore all sides of the situation, and work to ensure that the student is treated well.

Once when I was an assistant professor at Penn we had a situation where African American students were upset about various discriminatory actions by faculty. Because I regularly supported students and my research fell in this area, when random posters appeared across the school detailing examples of racist acts, older White men on the faculty accused me of instigating the poster campaign. I was aware that students were frustrated and I regularly urged students to use their voices both inside and outside of the classroom; however, I did not assist or even know about the poster campaign. I did applaud the thought that went into it and I supported the students in their right to express themselves because they did not feel heard. During this time, I was called out publicly by these older White men on the faculty and felt intimidated and afraid. If you are known for advocating for students, especially if your advocacy pertains to various forms of discrimination, some of your colleagues may not appreciate your stances. Make sure that you have a support system when you speak out around controversial issues.

You may also have to advocate for students as they move through the various systems and bureaucracies of your campus. This type of advocacy is especially important if you are working with first generation students who have little knowledge of how colleges and universities work. As one of these students, I benefited from faculty and staff who were willing to open doors for me and explain how procedures worked on campus. More importantly, these individuals were able to show me how to circumvent policies when these policies blocked my pathway to success. You have to choose your battles, but it is essential that you advocate for your students, sharing with them what you have learned along your pathway.

Student Research Collaborations

While you are on the tenure track and beyond, you may want to work on research projects with students. I have worked with undergraduates, master's, and doctoral students on research projects since my first year of being a professor. In fact, the first book I published, *Supporting Alma Mater: Successful Strategies for Securing Funds from Black College Alumni* (2003), was co-authored with one of my doctoral students, Sibby Anderson-Thompkins, who is still a good friend.

When considering conducting research with your students, it is important to keep in mind a few things. First, you need to find out if research and publishing with students are valued at your institution. I would do it regardless, but you have to be realistic. If it is not valued, keep these kinds of collaborations to a minimum while on the tenure track. If it is valued—and you can tell by looking at what your tenured colleagues published pre-tenure—then consider working with students in this way more often. Second, ask your senior colleagues about the value of single-authored articles. If those who get tenure are more likely to have single-authored articles, it would behoove you to have more of them. Third, be prepared for working with students. It is vital to set ground rules, and I have become better at this over time. Having a verbal agreement with students (or anyone else) is not enough; if you do not listen around this issue, you will end up in a mess.

When working with students—or anyone, I would argue—you need to have an agreement with the student about the work involved; I strongly suggest putting that agreement in writing. Here are some questions to consider: Will the student be working as a research assistant and merely learning new skills by helping you on your projects? Will you be conducting a research project together that you both conceptualize and produce publications from? Will the student be helping on one of your research projects, but also do the level of work that would merit co-authorship? Who will be the lead author and what will that role entail? When I first work with students, I typically serve in the role of lead author and have them work on a literature review, while I take care of everything else, guiding them through the research and writing process. However, sometimes I offer the student the lead role on a project. This offer has resulted in a variety of situations for me. Many times the student does considerable work and I am in the role of co-authoring, editing, tightening, adding, and shepherding the publication through the publishing process. But other times, the student does very little, and I realize right away that I have made a mistake. In this situation, I have always kept the student in the lead role and took the hit, meaning that I ended up doing the work and left the student as lead author. I would never allow myself to be lead on a paper that I did not contribute the most work to; however, students do not always know this or operate in this way, and neither do professional colleagues. You could also have a conversation with the student about contributions and switch the roles. However, it is imperative that you protect yourself in these situations as they can become very dicey. I avoid them.

Engaging in research with students is not always about publishing; it is also about learning to code and analyze data, learning to conduct interviews, or learning how to search for literature. I find it rewarding to involve students in research, but it is also time consuming. It is important to be aware of this time as you move along the tenure track. I recommend working with one or two students and avoiding recent trends of amassing large groups of researchers as part of your "lab" or "group." Scientists may need larger groups in their labs, but most faculty do not, and as a tenure-track faculty member, it is more manageable to stay small. I currently work with many students and a lot of colleagues around the nation. However, when I was working to secure tenure, I only worked with one or two students. I would advise you to do what is manageable for you personally and not to overcommit yourself to keep up with others.[2]

Final Thought

As mentioned at the beginning chapter, I thoroughly enjoy working with and advising students. Hundreds of students have kept up with me for years, even decades. I have watched them get married, have children, and prosper in their careers. It is wonderfully rewarding, and the best part of my role as a professor. I hope you enjoy advising as well.

Notes

1   I took nearly 7 years to finish my PhD because I was trained as a historian; most humanities PhD programs take longer than those in STEM and the social sciences.

2 If you decide to create a research group, I recommend reading "Managing a Research Group," a resource created by Columbia University (https://research.columbia.edu/managing-research-group). It is very helpful and discusses all of the various issues you will need to manage.

References

Belcher, W. L. (2019). *Writing your journal article in twelve weeks: A guide to academic publishing success*. University of Chicago Press.

Bowman, V. E., Hatley, L. D., & Bowman, R. L. (1995). Faculty-student relationships: The dual role controversy. *Counselor Education and Supervision, 34*(3), 232–242.

Drake, J., Jordan, P., & Miller, M. (2013). *Academic advising approaches: Strategies that teach students to make the most of college*. Jossey-Bass.

Folsom, P., Yoder, F., & Joslin, J. (2015). *The new advisor guidebook: Mastering the art of academic advising*. Jossey-Bass.

Gasman, M., & Anderson-Thompkins, S. (2003). *Supporting alma mater: Successful strategies for securing funds from Black college alumni*. Council for the Advancement and Support of Education.

Gordon, V., Habley, W., & Grites, T. (2008). *Academic advising: A comprehensive handbook*. Jossey-Bass.

Lampman, C., Crew, E., Lowery, S., & Tompkins, K. (2016). Women faculty distressed: Descriptions and consequences of academic contrapower harassment. *NASPA Journal About Women in Higher Education, 9*(2), 158–188.

Shore, B. (2014. *The graduate advisor handbook: A student-centered approach*. Chicago, IL: University of Chicago Press.

Sword, H. (2012). *Stylish academic writing*. Harvard University Press.

Tay, A. (2020). *Writing the perfect recommendation letter*. Nature. https://www.nature.com/articles/d41586-020-02186-8.

6

Do I Have to Apply for Grants?

Depending on your discipline, securing grants can either be a requirement or something you rarely do. In the STEM fields, it is often an expectation, with many institutions requiring faculty to fund their salaries with grant support. In other disciplines, for example, philosophy, securing grants is rare and there is much less funding available to support research. In education, discipline-based faculty such as educational historians or anthropologists may have difficulty securing grants whereas those focused on educational policy may find it much easier, given the number of grant opportunities in that area. I often hear faculty complain about the pressure to secure grants. Whereas I do not think that institutions should pressure faculty to apply for grants, I do think applying for grants is an opportunity for freedom as a faculty member—an opportunity to pursue intellectual ideas in full. Although some will disagree with me, that is okay, I also think bringing in grants is a form of service, because the indirect funds in grant budgets help colleagues who might have a difficult time securing grants, and also support students. Some faculty will say that colleges and universities should already provide these kinds of supports and, yes, they need to provide as much support as possible, but I understand how finances work within higher education and believe everyone should contribute.

Why Apply for Grants

Applying for grants can lead to more freedom and the opportunity to scale up your work to have an impact on society in meaningful ways. Having a grant keeps you accountable and can act as a motivating force in your life, because you need to complete the work that you promised to do. Securing a grant also gives you the opportunity to work in partnership with others on projects; these opportunities can help you to grow as an intellectual and hone your skills as a professional (Karsh & Fox, 2019).

In addition, there are very practical reasons to apply for grants. For me, the most advantageous reason has always been to secure summer funding. As mentioned earlier, teaching summer classes detracts from research and requires an incredible amount of work for very little pay. Most funders allow you to include summer pay in grant proposal budgets, and nearly all colleges and universities will allow you to earn up to an extra three months of your academic year salary during the summer. Another practical reason to apply for grants is to financially support students. Working with grant-funded students helps you accomplish your goals and provides students with mentoring opportunities, research skills, and hands-on training. In addition, students can learn how to manage the work of a grant and be ahead in terms of their skill development in this area. Another practical reason for applying for grants is to secure travel support for collecting data or attending conferences. Most colleges and universities offer very little travel support, but funders often ask for a dissemination plan, which can include travel support for presenting the work at academic conferences and for collecting data for you and your research team members.

Defining Your Grant-Funded Project

The most important way to begin applying for grants is to write down 2-3 sentences that succinctly describe your project. Writing clearly is absolutely key for grant proposals (and from my perspective, it is important for every kind of writing). Rather than using academic and disciplinary jargon, you must learn to write for a general audience, since those who will be reading your proposals may not have PhDs, may be from disciplines different than yours, may be non-academics, and may not take the time to look up all of the words that are commonplace in your discipline. Communicating your ideas in clear ways is about 75% of the work of acquiring a grant to support your research (See Figure 6.1 for an example of clear grant proposal writing).

Next, you need to do some homework to see who has produced scholarship in your area of research. How will you build on their work? How will you move the research beyond the existing work? How is your research different from past work? You do not want to produce the same work that someone else has, and you want to be respectful of how you engage others' work, because they may end up reviewing your work if the funder uses outside reviewers. Doing this homework will prepare you to write a literature review, which is a typical requirement of most grant proposals.

I have found that funders love collaboration. They want to stretch their investments and "scale up" ideas and programs. They want to apply research and see it have an impact in real time. Your next step in working toward securing a grant is to think about who you can collaborate with. You may be used to working alone or be hesitant about collaborating, but you will learn a lot from working with others. I have found that my methodological skills and appreciation for diverse ways of understanding issues have increased substantially through working with others on grant funded projects. Ask yourself

The Experiences of STEM Faculty at Minority Serving Institutions (MSIs) in the Midst of COVID-19

Overview

The purpose of this research project is to explore how STEM faculty at Minority Serving Institutions (MSIs) are converting their traditional classes and labs to online courses in the midst of the COVID-19 pandemic. In particular, I am interested in the tools that they are using; the resources that their campuses and the larger scientific community are providing to them to do this work; and their examples of creativity and innovation in teaching. Moreover, given that MSIs are known for being 'high touch,' nurturing environments, I also want to explore how these faculty are providing their undergraduate students with virtual research experiences, supporting student learning in the online context, and advising their students in this new virtual space. In order to carry out the research project, I will conduct open-ended, qualitative interviews with 100 STEM faculty at MSIs across the nation and have an extensive dissemination strategy.

Statement of Intellectual Merit

Researchers have not explored the experiences of STEM faculty at MSIs teaching in online environments with any depth and have not layered on the impact of a pandemic-threatened learning environment. This study, having a rich qualitative sample of 100 STEM faculty, will provide a deep dive into the teaching practices, advising, resourcefulness, innovation, and creativity of these individuals. The voices of STEM faculty at MSIs will be centered in the research, and recommendations will be rooted in the experiences of those who are most fundamental to the success of online learning-faculty. Moreover, this research will explore the perceptions of STEM faculty at MSIs on their students' learning process in online courses that have been, in most cases, haphazardly createdin the midst of a pandemic. Lastly, this research explores the resources available (or not available) to MSI faculty from their institutions and from the large science community, helping us to understand equity issues within the STEM domain.

Statement of Broader Impacts

The proposed project has the potential to advance knowledge across science education and to create new knowledge in an ever changing higher education learning environment. Faculty at both the higher education level (within MSIs and at colleges and universities in general) as well as STEM faculty at the secondary level will benefit from the results of the research project. In addition, these groups can learn best practices, the most appropriate tools for engaged learning, and the types of resources and supports that faculty and students need in order to learn in a virtual STEM environment. Of great importance, this research focuses on highly diverse learning environments and amplifies the voices, ideas, and practices of a highly diverse group of faculty teaching a highly diverse student body. Given the demographic changes in the nation and the importance of having a multitude of perspectives shaping STEM education, this research can have a broad, significant, and relatively immediate impact. As research results and recommendations will be disseminated widely, at no cost, and in practical ways-ways that engage scholarly and general audiences-real time change has the potential to manifest in classrooms across the nation at a time when it is vitally needed. Our national higher education environments are changing rapidly and the impact of the COVID-19 pandemic is unpredictable with potentially long-term results. The findings and recommendations of this study can have an immediate, evolving, and lasting impact on STEM education and especially low-income, first generation, and students of color.

Figure 6.1 – The Experiences of STEM Faculty at Minority Serving Institutions in the Midst of COVID-19

who you might want to work with, what roles you will play, and who will be the lead and co-lead principal investigators. Consider whose institution will sponsor the grant and whose will be the sub-contracted party. If you collaborate, write a memo of understanding around the relationship and have a discussion about your work process and expectations. All too often, collaborations go bad and result in stress, disagreements, and bad behavior. Talking about expectations upfront is key to having open and honest relationships.

The next step is thinking about who might fund your work. Is it only a research project? Does it have both programmatic and research components? Is it theoretical? Scientific? Practical? If you are in the humanities, you may want to engage the Mellon Foundation or the National Endowment for the Humanities. If you are in the STEM fields, you may want to approach the National Science Foundation, the National Institutes of Health, or the Sloan Foundation. If you are more social science-focused, you may want to look into the Russell Sage Foundation, the Spencer Foundation, or the William T. Grant Foundation. And if you are focused on education, and especially educational practice, you would benefit from reaching out to Lumina Foundation, Kresge Foundation, Strata Education Group, or ECMC Foundation (for an extensive list of funding opportunities, please see Appendix G). Regardless of your field and project, you need to do some more homework in this area, reading through foundation websites and taking a look at past and present recipients of funds. I might even suggest reaching out to one of their grantees to ask about their strategies. I provide guidance and introductions for other scholars regularly because I do not see securing grants as something I need to hoard. I think that if you truly care about the work, you should want others to be successful.

Next, think about who you know. Do you know any program officers at foundations or in federal funding agencies? Or, do you know anyone who has received a grant that you could reach out to and ask about their experiences? Knowing someone or having someone make an introduction for you is one way to cut through some of the bureaucracy involved in securing grant funding. It will not get you the grant, but it will get you in the door. Here is something to keep in mind: Funders have to give out money each year—it is required by law and if it is federal money, it is required by Congress. Program officers want to give away money to support important work. If you do know someone, be respectful of their time, have your questions ready, be prepared with a 1-2 page concept paper in case they ask for it, and make sure to treat the relationship with care and respect. I should not have to say this but, I feel I must, as all too often I see faculty talking down to program officers and disrespecting their time and contributions. Program officers have a great sense of the big picture, are constantly learning, and can be very helpful in making connections for you. If you establish relationships, take good care of them.

Although I have talked about some items that you can garner support for through research grants, you will want to think about everything you need to ensure that you can do your work in a timely manner. I suggest including the following in your grant budgets if applicable: Support for course releases, research and conference travel, research assistants, work-study student support, data support, equipment (e.g., computers, printers, lab equipment), transcriptions, and staff support if applicable. It is also important that you inquire about the funder's indirect cost policy. These funds are monies that a funder allots to support the infrastructure for doing the work. Not all foundations provide support for indirect costs, and federal indirect support rates are negotiated by your institution. Although it is wise to become familiar with how to craft a grant budget, you should be able to find support in the sponsored programs office at your university or within your school, depending on the size and resources your institution has.

As you are crafting your grant proposal, you need to consider the timeline. Most funders will provide support for up to three years, but rarely more unless it is a significantly large project. Also be aware that getting a large grant in a short period of time is not advantageous and the monies are difficult to spend quickly. It is best to stretch funds out over a longer period of time. You also want to make sure that your timeline is doable and realistic and appears so to others. Do not take on too much and do not do too little (Karsh & Fox, 2019).

When I am writing a grant proposal, as with nearly everything else, I have others read my drafts before I send it to a funder. It is important that you garner feedback throughout the process and that you find the holes in your proposal before program officers or reviewers do. Although sharing your work can be uncomfortable, it is much better to have mentors and trusted colleagues read your work and find the problems or disconnects than it is to have those making funding decisions find these issues.

One of the parts of a grant proposal that tends to be the most challenging is the evaluation of success that funders ask for. It is essential that you have a plan for how you will learn from both formative and summative evaluation. I often write an external evaluator into the grant proposal because it is helpful to have input from an expert. Other times, I will merely provide an evaluation plan that I will follow. Regardless, you need to be ready to answer this question.

Because funders are investing in your work, they will want to know how you will disseminate your research findings. Depending on the practical focus of the funder, they may require you to disseminate beyond peer-reviewed research articles. I use a variety of dissemination strategies, including policy reports, Twitter chats, infographics, podcasts, webinars, academic conference presentations, invited keynote addresses, and of course, peer-reviewed articles and often a major book. Over the years, most of the major books I have written have been supported by a foundation.

Follow Up and Stewarding Funders

The most frequent mistakes that I see faculty make in terms of grants is that they do not keep the funder informed and do not follow through on their work. Funders understand that life happens and that sometimes a research plan has to change. However, they want to be informed about changes in advance. And, they want to be kept informed about your progress with your research beyond the annual grant report that you are required to submit. It is essential that you learn to *manage up*—or ensure that your program officer is able to speak about your work and the progress you are making to others. Likewise, you want to make sure that all of your narrative reports detailing your progress, and your fiscal reports are in on time. Being late, missing deadlines, and failing to communicate with your program officers are surefire ways to not receive funding in the future (Karsh & Fox, 2019).

Fellowships

In addition to traditional grants, you may want to apply for fellowships while on the tenure track. There are many, including those from the Spencer Foundation, the Ford Foundation, the National Science Foundation, the Fulbright Foundation, and the Library of Congress, and they allow you the opportunity to concentrate on your research and to take time away from your teaching (See Appendix H). If you apply for a fellowship, you will need very strong letters of recommendation from those who know your research beyond that of your dissertation. You will also need to have a concrete and specific project that you want to pursue during your time away from your university. Securing a prestigious fellowship can assist you with securing tenure and can help you hone your research and writing skills.

Final Thoughts

Because I keep my program officers informed, never miss deadlines, and produce the research that I set out to accomplish, I have been able to secure significant grant funding.

However, I do not receive every grant for which I apply. I am rejected regularly and often; I am rejected more than I receive funding. I have grant proposals that took me 5-10 years to get funded. There are instances in which I have done 15 revisions of a grant proposal before getting funded. I have been rejected six times by the same foundation, only to be awarded a much larger grant than I applied for initially. The trick is to be persistent and to not give up on yourself and your ideas. Some of the best ideas that I have launched have been the result of being rejected and having to spend time figuring out why and how to incorporate the feedback.

References

Karsh, E., & Fox, A. (2019). *The only grant-writing book you'll ever need.* Basic Books.

7

Surviving Faculty Politics

In this chapter, I talk about how to manage faculty politics—what to get involved with and what to avoid in terms of politics along the tenure track (Frazee, 2008). I discuss how to manage difficult relationships with colleagues, department chairs, and deans. Because I think it is essential that you truly understand what you are up against in the academy, I am going to be as forthright as I can in this chapter, hoping that my experiences, mistakes, and choices will help you have a better experience than I did.

I want to make it clear that I have loved the majority of my time as a professor. However, I think that the most brutal part of university life is the academic politics. The politics are the reason I have always had a back-up plan, meaning I could pursue another career if needed—as a fundraiser, an interior decorator, a photographer, a nonprofit leader, etc. I am always ready. I would advise you to have a back-up plan, and to save and invest as much as you can as you move along the tenure track. Institutions are not loyal to individuals and it is important for you to realize that although you may give your all to an institution, the institution will not feel an obligation to give its all to you.

Academic politics are vast; you must decide what to get involved with and what to avoid. I made a choice to get involved when issues of equity, opportunity, or racism surfaced, and avoided most other types of political battlefields. I have found that faculty will argue, discuss, disagree, fight, and pout about nearly anything, so you have to choose what you are willing to stand up for and what you will let pass. I hear faculty both inside my institution and across the nation complaining about nearly anything and everything. I ignore 99% of it because it does not matter to my larger life nor to my values. I would advise you to do the same. Decide what you care about, what you value, and what you are willing to speak out about and stick to those values. When issues surface that are not tied to your values, let other people fight those battles.

When I was on the tenure track, I was very open with faculty colleagues about my fears, insecurities, and accomplishments. I would advise you to avoid this type of openness and take a bit of advice from my mother—keep your friend circle small. Unfortunately, the academy is a deeply competitive and hyper-sensitive place that loves gossip (Hollis, 2015; Keashley & Neuman, 2010; Misawa & Rowland, 2015; Taylor, 2012). If you doubt me, visit the #academicchatter or #academictwitter hashtags on Twitter. I honestly have never experienced the kind of gossip that takes place among faculty anywhere else. Some faculty members roam from office to office spreading gossip; some gather gossip as they come to your office asking questions and trying to earn your trust, and then they share your business with others (Hollis, 2015). Be very careful who you share information with.

There are also those faculty who like to have the meeting before the meeting. They caucus before meetings, plotting about how they will influence the outcome of a vote; when you are a tenure-track faculty member one of the most intimidating experiences is having a senior colleague try to force you to vote a specific way on an issue. For example, I had a senior colleague who liked to send me emails asking to meet, but never providing a topic. I fell for this a few times, but eventually realized it was her way of manipulating people into agreeing with her on issues. Eventually, when she sent an email with no topic, I responded with, "Can you please tell me why you would like to meet?" We went back and forth a few times before she told me the reason. I found out later from colleagues that she did not

want any documentation of her manipulation and thus avoided creating a paper trail. I like a paper trail because it keeps you safe in what can otherwise be a cesspool. Experts on the topic of faculty bullying also suggest keeping a paper trail if you are feeling pressured by or uncomfortable with colleagues (Hollis, 2015; Keashley & Neuman, 2010; Misawa & Rowland, 2015; Taylor, 2012)

An aspect of faculty politics that may not seem as obvious pertains to administrative support staff and your relationships with them. I learned early on that it is vital to gain the trust of academic support staff and to treat them well. If you do not, they will not help you, they might disparage you to faculty, and they can make your life miserable—and more than likely, you deserve some of this treatment for mistreating them. I have always had good relationships with the support staff because I value their roles and contribution. My advice is for you to do the same. Never act as if you are better that those who have positions that support your work.

Relationships with Colleagues

It is important that you get to know your faculty colleagues and especially your more senior colleagues who will be voting on your tenure case. I suggest setting up meetings with them over coffee or tea, or perhaps lunch throughout the course of your first year. Ask them for advice and make sure to come prepared to talk about your research and goals in case they ask you these types of questions. I also suggest reading something written by each person in your department so that you have a sense of what they do in terms of research. People like to be known for their work and will expect you to know something about their area of research. I spent some time reviewing my colleagues' CVs, reading one or two articles by each of them, and listening to their perspectives in meetings so that I understood their value systems.

There will be faculty colleagues you do not like and who will not like you. You cannot avoid this situation. Do not beat yourself up over it; work to have cordial relationships with your colleagues, but know you do not have to be friends with them. In fact, after much experience, I would advise you not to be friends with more than a few of them. Having friends outside of the academy is deeply important and something everyone should have. Of course, if you feel close to some of your faculty colleagues, be friends with them. There is nothing wrong with that; however, remember that the academy is competitive and sometimes friendships can go south (Hollis, 2015; Keashley & Neuman, 2010; Misawa & Rowland, 2015; Taylor, 2012). I suggest having one or two people to confide in. Sometimes it is best that these individuals are in another department or across campus.

Early in my career, I had a faculty friend who was at roughly the same level as me; he was one year ahead of me on the tenure track. We talked regularly, shared CVs, read each other's third-year review and tenure statements, and asked each other questions such as, "Is my work crap?" After a while, your work feels old and almost derivative, and you need another person to tell you that it is actually good—if it is. My faculty friend did this for me and vice versa. We trusted each other and shared secrets, including fears and accomplishments. We also strategized about what to get involved in and what to avoid. I would suggest having one person like this in your circle.

Relationships with Department Chairs

When you are on the tenure track, it is essential that you have a positive relationship with your department chair. After achieving tenure, it is desirable but not essential. Something to keep in mind is that department chairs have different degrees of power depending on the institution and the department. For example, when I was a young faculty member at Georgia State University, my department chair had considerable power. He played a part in my reappointment, my raises, and my performance reviews. He also made various decisions that could make my professional life pleasant or not so pleasant, luckily they were pleasant. At Georgia State, a public, regional institution, the departments were large and the department chairs handled any issues or concerns in the department. At the University of Pennsylvania, a private institution, my department chairs had no power, did not levy salaries, and basically served in the role of "person who makes sure we get the paperwork done." Our department, which was really a division, was small and faculty reported directly to the dean. However, as an assistant professor, I needed the support of my department chair as an individual, and thus maintaining a cordial relationship was important. At Rutgers, our departments are midsized and our department chairs have some authority and are involved in annual raises. However, being a union-based, public institution, Rutgers is fiercely egalitarian and faculty have considerable autonomy. It is important to understand the context of your institution and your department, and what role your department chair plays in your professional life. By and large, as an assistant professor, I had very healthy and productive relationships with my department chairs. They were helpful most of the time and one even became a life-long mentor.

As a tenured faculty member, your relationship might change, as some department chairs are power hungry and expect you to acquiesce to their power. You do not have to, and that is something to remember. I once had a former department chair at Penn meet me for coffee to ask why I did not pay them "deference" in our interactions (they were no longer the department chair). Yes, I said "deference." I had to explain to them that when they were the department chair, I respected their role. Now that they are no longer the chair and given that we are both full professors, I was under no obligation to pay them any deference nor would any reasonable person ask someone this question. Often, leadership can overtake individuals, making them believe that they deserve more respect or deference than they do, and that their ideas and perspectives hold more merit than others' (Brown & Moshavi, 2002; Wildavsky, 1992). While on the tenure track, you may have to look the other way as you encounter these individuals, but you do not need to once you earn tenure.

To read more about the various roles of department chairs, I suggest Hyman and Jacobs' (2010) article "What a Department Chair Can—and Can't—Do." Although I have seen department chairs try to assert power over all kinds of things that are not within their domain of authority, this article is a good primer for new faculty curious about whether a department chair can change a grade in a professor's class or intervene if a faculty member is acting inappropriately. The answers are "no" and "yes," respectively. Two additional good reads for understanding the power (or lack thereof) and responsibilities of department chairs are Hecht and associates' (1998) *The Department Chair as Academic Leader* and Chu's (2012) *The Department Chair Primer*, which provide a detailed overview of the role and discuss the chair's relationship to departmental faculty. Understanding what a department chair aims to accomplish is important to your role in the department.

Relationships with Deans

Having a positive relationship with your dean as you move along the tenure track is essential. Depending on the size of your college or university, you may or may not see your dean very often. However, it is important that the dean know who you are. I suggest that you communicate who you are to the dean regularly—not too often, but enough that they know who you are without this knowledge coming only from your department chair or other faculty. I suggest that you ask for a meeting with the dean—request 30 minutes—within your first semester at a new institution. Ask for their advice and guidance for your tenure-track experience. If you are at cocktail parties or events, make small talk with the dean. Deans seem to be the least talked-to individuals at gatherings; people are never sure what non-work subject to engage in with a dean. Go talk to your dean and get to know them a bit. I am not suggesting that you suck up, but merely suggesting that you get to know your dean and make sure they get to know you. Do not email them weekly, do not schedule meetings all the time, do not brag about your work constantly. Just get to know your dean as a person. If you know they have a particular hobby or interest, ask them about it. If they have children or grandchildren, ask them about them. If they like to travel, ask them about it. Get to know them outside of work discussions.

Not having a positive relationship with your dean—depending on your institution—can make your life miserable. I have liked some deans more than others over the years, and respected some more than others as well, but I have never had a destructive relationship with a dean. Work on cultivating these relationships, because they are important and can be beneficial in the long term. To learn more about the role of deans and about their responsibilities, I recommend Buller's (2007) *The Essential Academic Dean*. The book is written for deans but it will give you a deeper understanding of the dean's role and your role in relation to them.

Relationships with Faculty Colleagues in the Field

Given that letters of evaluation and support during your tenure and promotion process will come from people who do research similar to yours, it is essential that you establish positive relationships with academics in your field. You can do this through meeting with them at academic conferences; I will meet with anyone who asks, as long as I have time. Some years I literally had back-to-back meetings at conferences with new scholars on each day of the event. I do not do this as much anymore because I do not like academic conferences, but I talk to new scholars on the phone regularly. Contacting faculty colleagues that you want to meet is a good idea and something I would encourage you to do. However, please keep in mind that some established scholars won't respond to your emails and calls. Please don't internalize their lack of response. It is not about you; it's about them.

You could also ask to collaborate with scholars who are on similar paths as you. However, I would advise you to avoid collaborating with those who could potentially be asked to write tenure letters for you, because they will be disqualified from writing. Anyone with whom you have collaborated is disqualified from writing letters of support; this includes paper co-authors, co-principal investigators on grant proposals, book co-authors, and sometimes even co-presenters, although being on the same panel is not an issue. I personally avoided writing with key people I knew would be asked to evaluate me. You can always collaborate with these individuals after you secure tenure or the rank of full professor. If you want to collaborate with faculty colleagues across the nation, I would suggest writing with people at or around the same place on the tenure track.

Sometimes faculty will create a circle or group of individuals that will meet regularly at conferences, or come together to write in the summers, and support each other. I have seen these types of circles be highly productive and essential, especially for people of color. Others have groups of faculty friends that they get together with—usually around research interests—at conferences. All of these support systems are important. My only word of caution is that you branch out and meet other people as well. Being insular does not take care of all of your needs. In addition, I have seen some of these groups be cliquish and exclusionary. When I was a new scholar, there was a group of White women historians who met regularly for dinner at conferences. They invited me to join them a few times, even though I did not do research related to White women and most of them did. I felt uncomfortable because of the lack of diversity in the group. Later, as I was mingling with some African American women at the same conference, they mentioned that they were never invited to those gatherings— they were left out. I never went to the meetings of the White women historians again. I am not sure if they were intentionally leaving people out, but I do know that as people who say we care about diversity, equity, and inclusion, it is our job to notice exclusion. I also made sure to tell the leader of the White women's historian group that African American women felt excluded. The leader told me they started the women's dinners because they felt left out by the White men historians attending the conference and vowed to do better. We have to be purposeful about being inclusive.

Academic Conferences

I have talked a bit about academic conferences above and in previous chapters, but I would like to add a bit more about the politics of these events. When you are on the tenure track, you feel obligated to attend these conferences. I attended them regularly when I was a tenure-track faculty member. I used them to present work, to have coffee with faculty friends and those I admired, and to attend conferences sessions of interest. Conferences were helpful and because I like to travel, I found it exciting to visit new cities. You may or may not like conferences, but you really need to attend them while on the tenure track.

You do not need to attend them regularly once you earn tenure, unless you want to. Whether or not you attend is a personal choice—you may decide to attend if you have a new book to promote, to connect with colleagues, to introduce your students to colleagues, or to stay visible in the field. You need to do what works for you and what supports balance in your career and mental health. That said, I rarely attend the major academic conferences in my field anymore unless I have a student on the job market, because I find that they are hyper-competitive and filled with gossip. Instead, I attend gatherings of people working on the ground in my field and events that are curated around various issues of interest to me. I especially like to go to events where there will be new people. Why? Because I learn and am challenged. And, most importantly, I am not surrounded by the gossip of my field.[1]

When I venture out of traditional circles in my field, I am reminded of why I became a professor—the search for truth, the hunger for knowledge, and a commitment to helping others and providing opportunities. All fields are different and some have more gossip and back-biting than others. My best advice is to lay low, hunker down, and do your work as you move along the tenure track. Do not get involved in issues that are not related to your area of expertise and remember that if someone is gossiping to you, they are gossiping about you.

As a counterpoint to my dislike of academic conferences, I know many faculty who really like to attend them. They find them motivating and enriching, and they enjoy meeting up with friends to talk about what is happening in their field and to generate new ideas. Whether or not you like academic conferences will depend on your academic discipline and the tenor of the conferences that you attend as well as your personality. I urge you to attend conferences that accept you, where you feel comfortable and included, and that help you accomplish your goals as you move along the tenure track.

Social Media Wars

I will discuss social media in the last chapter, in relation to students. Here, I want to talk about your involvement in arguing on social media as a tenure-track faculty member. If you are active on social media and regularly post or tweet, people will disagree with you and might begin arguments. Or, perhaps you tend to be the one who likes to argue. Regardless, my advice to you is to not argue with people on social media, but to treat the medium as you would an in-person meeting or interaction. Would you argue on and on with someone in person? Perhaps you would, but more than likely you would not. Arguing on social media is troubling because it is on display for everyone to see. Even if you do not start the argument, it often appears that you are in the mud, slinging dirt just like the other person. As Ms. Ruth, a woman I worked with in graduate school, would say, "You can't fly with the eagles if you are running with the turkeys."

Although most social media wars are harmless in the end, some can result in a difficult situation for those involved. Your tweets might appear in a newspaper article, you might be reprimanded by your institution (a bit of a slippery topic), and you might lose your reputation (as well as friendships) among faculty colleagues who see the online arguments. You have every right to argue, to defend yourself, and to engage in online discussions, but be aware of the ramifications of everything you do. For an interesting discussion of academic freedom, free speech, and faculty, see John K. Wilson's (2016) essay "The Changing Media and Academic Freedom." In it, he details how colleges and universities are responding to faculty who are active (and controversial) on social media. In this area, it is better to be prepared than surprised. The American Association of University Professors' *Academe* blog regularly features commentaries related to these types of issues.

Final Thought

Politics are by far the worst aspect of the academy. However, the other areas—being able to pursue your research, living a life of the mind, working with students, and having a positive impact on society—far outweigh the politics of the academy. Try your best to stay focused on the positive and to ignore the negative comments that you hear within the academy.

Notes

1 I am aware that I discuss faculty gossip quite often throughout this book. As I have matured, I have little tolerance for it. I participated in some of it throughout my career, but I made a decision not to at all anymore. Once you make this decision, everything changes and you notice that academic conferences are a hotbed of gossip. Let me provide some food for thought—have you ever given up sugar or salt in your diet? When you go back to eating something sugary or salty, you immediately realize just how much your taste buds have changed and you hesitate returning to your previous diet. I feel the same way about academic conferences because I find that gossip looms around every corner in the form of "catching up," "meals," and "getting a cocktail."

References

Brown, F. W., & Moshavi, D. (2002). Herding academic cats: Faculty reactions to transformational and contingent reward leadership by department chairs. *Journal of leadership studies, 8*(3), 79-93.

Buller, J. (2007). *The essential academic dean: A practical guide to college leadership.* San Francisco, CA: Jossey-Bass.

Chu, D. (2012). *The department chair primer: What chairs need to know and do to make a difference.* Jossey-Bass.

Frazee, J. P.(2008). Why we can't just get along. *The Chronicle of Higher Education.* https://www.chronicle.com/article/Why-We-Cant-Just-Get-Along/45742

Hecht, I., Higgerson, M., Gmelch, W., & Tucker, A. (1998). *The department chair as academic leader.* Oryx Press.

Hollis, L. (2015). Bully university? The cost of workplace bullying and employee disengagement in American higher education. *SAGE Open, 5*(2), https://doi.org/10.1177%2F2158244015589997

Hyman, J., & Jacobs, L. (2010). What a department chair can - and can't - do. *U.S. News and World Report.* https://www.usnews.com/education/blogs/professors-guide/2010/04/07/what-a-department-chair-canand-cantdo

Keashly, L. & Neuman, J. (2010). Faculty experiences with bullying in higher education: Causes, consequences, and management. *Administrative Theory & Praxis, 32*(1), 42-70.

Misawa, M., & Rowland, M. (2015). Academic bullying and incivility in adult, higher, continuing, and professional education. *Adult Learning.* https://doi.org/10.1177%2F1045159514558415

Taylor, S. (2012). Workplace bullying in higher education: Faculty experiences and responses [Doctoral dissertation, University of Minnesota].

Wilson, J.K. (2016). The changing media and academic freedom. *Academe* Blog. https://www.aaup.org/article/changing-media-and-academic-freedom#.X0Uwxi2ZP-Y

8

How Do I Achieve Work/Life Balance?

O ne of the most difficult aspects of being a faculty member is managing one's life alongside one's work. In this chapter, I discuss the importance of work/life balance and how to achieve it. Throughout this book, I have been forthright about my own navigating of the tenure-track life, admitting mistakes and sharing what I have learned from them. In this chapter I reveal that I have not always found a harmonious work/life balance.

As I entered and moved along the tenure track, I was married and had a baby, who eventually became a toddler. This was one of the most difficult times of my life. Like most women, I was constantly torn between paying attention to either my daughter or career. I felt guilty, and sometimes I just put my head down on my desk and prayed that I could manage all of it. During these times, I would think about my mom, who held two jobs—as a housekeeper and a waitress—and took care of ten children over the course of her life, with little help from my dad, few resources, and little education. I had some resources, a husband who helped most of the time, and a good education; in addition, I only had one child. I tried to keep all of this in mind as I struggled, but sometimes I broke down. I remember one particular night, I had a grant proposal due and was working as hard as I could to make it as strong as possible. I was exhausted and really needed sleep. However, life was not offering me sleep or rest. Instead, my daughter woke up screaming; when I went into her room, she was covered in vomit. When I picked her up, she projectile vomited on me. My husband finally woke up and came running into our daughter's room, and she projectile vomited on him. At this point, I knew that it was 3 a.m. and I would need to clean her crib, her clothes, me, and my husband. I stepped into a shower with my daughter and bathed us. My husband took a shower, and I cleaned everything and put the dirty linens and clothes in the washer. Wide awake, I lay in bed knowing I had to be up in three hours. I wanted to scream, and can still remember how frustrated and terrible I felt in this moment. I did not think I would get tenure, nor did I think I was cut out for being a mother or a professor. I did not have balance. Today I do and life is much better. However, there are times in life where balance or harmony are not attainable, and that is okay. When this happens, do the work and get through the stress and then reward yourself in whatever ways make you happy.

During the early years along the tenure track, I kept my work and family separate. Some days I went to the office, some days I wrote, and some days I spent with my daughter and husband. My husband was also a faculty member, so we had to negotiate these days. We were not always successful, which sometimes led to arguments and resentment. It is very difficult when both people are on the tenure track. However, there are times when facing tenure together can be rich and supportive, because you are both driven by intellectual work and a life of the mind, and you understand the demands of academic work.

Setting Boundaries

I am very good at setting boundaries now, but I was not always; I have only in the last three or four years become very good at it. When I was on the tenure track, I often let my work seep over into my non-work hours, driven by fear that I would not secure tenure at Penn—a place that at the time tenured a mere 38% of those who applied. Because I had grown up poor, I lived in fear of not receiving tenure, even though I was overqualified by the time I applied, according to the provost's council that approved my tenure bid. Why? Because I never wanted to be poor again. I knew what it felt like to have neither food nor opportunity, and I never wanted to experience it again.

As I moved toward tenure, I often worked extremely long hours, spending time with my daughter when she was awake and working immediately when she fell asleep. The expectations were high at Penn and I felt the pressure. I often compared pursuing tenure at Penn, and working there in general, to being on a treadmill with no off button. It took me years to realize that work expands and that it is a better idea to confine my work to specific hours and take breaks. Now that I know that taking breaks, exercising, and feeling the joy of family and friends is essential to a healthy lifestyle, this is how I live. I would advise you to learn this lesson early because if you do

not, it can wreak havoc on your life—and create health problems, weight gain, and marriage or relationship issues.[1] I was able to get myself on the right track after noticing where I was going and the toll it was taking on me, but I wish I had noticed earlier. I suggest that you seek harmony, and take care of your body and mind. For inspiration I recommend two books: Michelle Obama's (2018) *Becoming* and Brenè Brown's (2008) *I Thought It Was Just Me (But It Isn't): Making the Journey from "What Will People Think?" to "I am Enough."* Both of these books are written by smart, successful women who have overcome odds, struggled to balance life, and are still struggling. Although these books are written by women and from the perspectives of women, I suggest them for everyone. If that is an issue for you, perhaps it is time for some soul searching and reflection—because women regularly read books by men.

Vacations and Why They are Important

According to research conducted by the U.S. Travel Association (2018), Americans today have taken roughly a week less in vacation than they did in 2000, despite accruing the same amount of vacation days at work. Researchers at the Harvard Business School found that working more does not lead to higher productivity. Instead, it leads to burnout and uneven performance. They found that vacations reinvigorate people and lead to deeper happiness; furthermore, people who actually use their vacation days are more likely to be promoted (Achor, 2015; Achor & Gielan, 2016).

Growing up poor, I never took a vacation until my honeymoon vacation in 1994 to Italy. It was the first time I had left the country and the first time I left the Midwest, outside of one conference in Washington DC when I was a high school senior. My next vacation was a trip to Aruba in 2006, when I realized how exhausted I was from pursuing tenure. I discovered during that trip that I should have taken vacations of any kind between 1994 and 2006. I needed them and so did my family. I urge you to consider planning vacations, even small ones, even inexpensive ones. Get away from the academy and do not work if at all possible while you travel. It may be hard given the low salaries that tenure-track faculty members receive, but try to save for small vacations where you can breathe. And once you can afford to take more extensive vacations, do so several times a year and allow yourself to relax.

I have become fairly savvy about travel and vacations. I recommend staying at the same hotel chain when you travel for both work and pleasure. If you secure a member account that accumulates points for your stays, you will be able to build up enough points to stay for free with the hotel chain you choose. I also suggest getting a credit card that helps you accumulate hotel points, airline miles, or both. I regularly put large purchases on my Marriott Rewards credit card (paying the charges off at the end of the month) and as a result, I stay for free during my vacations. I started doing this as an assistant professor when staying for free was the only way I could travel, but I still enjoy the perks now. In addition to free hotel stays, most rewards programs also waive fees for breakfast and WiFi services and offer early check-in and late checkout services for members. If you do not like hotels, you can also find great deals with sites such as airbnb, VRBO, or similar sites.

I also suggest that you acquire a frequent flyer number with one airline and fly on that airline as much as possible. Not only will you acquire miles to use for vacation travel, you will also move up in status on the airline, which makes flying much easier—you will enjoy priority boarding, waived baggage fees, and a variety of other perks. Once you acquire enough miles to earn free flights, use them for vacations and not for work travel. If your institution does not cover all of your work travel, spend what you need to and deduct the costs from your taxes. Save the perks for yourself and your well-being. You will not always be able to take this approach, depending on your salary, but if you can, take care of yourself first.

Exercise

Another area that is vital to having balance in your life is exercise. Again, I failed in this regard while on the tenure track. For years, I did not exercise regularly, and I paid the price during that time. I now exercise at least five days a week (and usually seven). I have much more energy and am able to accomplish considerably more in terms of my academic work. I am also much healthier. Research shows that exercise not only ensures that you are healthier and that you live longer, but it also leads to greater productivity. According to Robert Pozen (2012) of The Brookings Institute

> Most of your cells contain components called mitochondria, often referred to as the cell's 'power plant.' Mitochondria produce the chemical that your body uses as energy, known as ATP. Physical exercise stimulates the development of new mitochondria within your cells, meaning that your body will be able to produce more ATP over time. That gives you more energy to exert yourself physically, but it also means more energy for your brain, boosting your mental output. (n.p.)

Knowing that exercise helps boost physical and mental energy, I have found ways to fit exercise in throughout the day. For example, I often walk during phone calls. I feel energized after walking through an hour-long call in a way I do not when sitting down. I also sometimes hold meetings across campus so that I have to walk to them, or I ask students or colleagues if they would like to do a walking meeting rather than sitting in my office. I mix this kind of exercise with going to the gym. And, I take the stairs and push myself to be very active when my daughter and I go on vacations. I advise you to do whatever you can to build regular exercise into your day. You will feel better, will thrive immensely from the energy that you gain, and will be happier overall as you navigate both the tenure track and life.

Sleep

I have written many books and published countless articles, but I never work at the expense of sleep. I always get eight hours of sleep. Why? Because getting enough sleep gives you energy, keeps you young, reduces wrinkles, and gives you a better outlook on life in general. According to the Division of Sleep Medicine at the Harvard University Medical School (2020), "sleep plays an important role in memory, both before and after a new task" (n.p.). Lack of adequate sleep can "affect mood, motivation, judgment, and our perception of events" (n.p.). And, a full night of sleep is "optimal for learning" (n.p.). You may want to skip sleep, work at the last minute, or pull all-nighters like you did in college, but these are not good ways to work, and they do not produce your best work.

Mental and Physical Health

Regular mental health check-ups are good for everyone, as are annual physicals with your primary care doctor and check-ups with your optometrist and dentist. In a tenure-track job, you have access to insurance that will cover these appointments and more, and you should take full advantage of this benefit. The more you take care of the various aspect of your person, the longer you will live and the happier you will be overall.

Talking with a mental health specialist on a regular basis can result in: "a reduction in anxiety, improved moods, clearer thinking, a greater sense of calm or inner peace, increased self-esteem, reduced risk of depression, and improvements in relationships" (Miller, 2020, n.p.). If you are in a tenure-track faculty position your health insurance covers your mental health. Yes, there are stigmas about seeking counseling, but who cares. Do it. I went my entire life without seeing a counselor and regret doing so. I began to see a counselor at age 51. After three to four sessions, I realized that talking to a counselor allowed me to breathe and work through a lot of questions. And, because most of my days are spent helping other people and listening to their problems and needs, it is nice to have someone listen to me and provide their perspective and expertise. Instead of waiting until you are in your 50s, consider regularly visiting with a therapist and having some time for just you. I honestly think that if more faculty would see a counselor regularly, the academy would be a nicer and more humane place.

Socializing with People who Aren't Faculty

I have found that many faculty only socialize with other faculty. I fell into this routine for a couple of years while on the tenure track and realized very quickly how essential it is to have other friends outside of academe. These friends will keep you grounded, as the academy is a bubble that is not representative of the rest of the world. Often, when you limit yourself to faculty friends, you begin to talk only about work and happenings within the academy. In addition, you develop a bit of group think, which is not positive for your mental health nor your productivity. I suggest being active in a community-based sports group, joining a book club, taking an art class, or joining a yoga class. Diversifying your friend group and moving away from the academy in your social life will enable you to see the world differently and maintain your stability.

Final Thoughts

The best advice that I can give with regard to work/life balance is to take it seriously. Make time for yourself, including exercise, healthy eating, sleep, vacations, and make time for your family and friends. Remember that being a faculty member is only one aspect of your life. Also remember that institutions and organizations are not loyal to individuals. You need to be loyal to yourself. Aim to have a beautiful life, and the most fulfilling one you can manage.

Notes

1   I divorced my husband in 2011 after 17 years of marriage and 21 years together. Although I do not think the academy was the main cause for our divorce, our experience in it was one factor.

References

Achor, S. (2015). *Are the people who take vacations the ones who get promoted?* Harvard Business Review. https://hbr.org/2015/06/are-the-people-who-take-vacations-the-ones-who-get-promoted

Achor, S. & Gielan, M. (2016). *The data-driven case for vacation.* Harvard Business Review. https://hbr.org/2016/07/the-data-driven-case-for-vacation

Brown, B. (2008). *I thought it was just me (but it isn't): Making the journey from 'what will people think?' to 'I am enough.'* Avery Publishers.

Harvard University Medical School Division of Sleep Medicine (2020). Sleep, Learning, and Memory. http://healthysleep.med.harvard.edu/healthy/matters/benefits-of-sleep/learning-memory

Miller, K. (2020). *The benefits of mental health according to science.* Positive Psychology. https://positivepsychology.com/benefits-of-mental-health

Obama, M. (2018). *Becoming.* Crown Publishing Group.

Pozen, R. (2012). *Exercise increases productivity.* Brookings. https://www.brookings.edu/opinions/exercise-increases-productivity

U.S. Travel Association (2018). *Time off. State of American Travel.* U.S. Travel Association. https://www.ustravel.org/toolkit/time-and-vacation-usage

9

And the Rest of the Job . . .

I have sought in this book to cover the main issues you will face as a tenure-track faculty member, but as I was writing, other small issues and questions popped into my mind. They are questions that people ask me about regularly and as such, I have included discussion of these topics in this chapter. I hope that they are helpful to you as you make progress toward your goal.

Student Relationships on Social Media

When thinking about advising or teaching students, people often ask me if I am friends with students on social media. Here are my thoughts, which have evolved over time. I advise all of my students to have a LinkedIn profile because I believe this is a good idea professionally. LinkedIn started slowly, but has become a powerful engine for meeting people, and I regularly make terrific connections through the platform. I do not add students on LinkedIn, but if they add me, I accept their request. I post my articles, op-eds, and work we do at our center and institute on my LinkedIn page. I rarely post anything personal.

I am also active on Facebook, with about 5000 friends. Facebook is tricky, but the uncertainty can be alleviated. I tell students that if they want to add me as a friend on Facebook, it is their choice. I will not friend them because I do not want to pressure them. Students in my classes will sometimes add me during the class (it is rare) and many will add me at the end of the semester or when they graduate. I used to be sassy on Facebook—giving out advice and sharing do's and don'ts in the academy; I was also very vocal about racial issues and many social justice and equity issues, but in this current climate of nastiness on social media, I am not as fierce. My Facebook page is filled with photos of my daughter, travel adventures, flowers, promotion of our center and institute's work, and news stories that I am quoted in. I do speak out against injustice but I am very purposeful about my voice. Everything we do is scrutinized, analyzed, screenshot, and taken out of context in the current day. Although faculty have academic freedom within the academy and freedom of speech as citizens, it is too risky in the current context to share too much about yourself on Facebook, Twitter, or any social media. Decide carefully who you are willing to friend on social media platforms, and be careful about associating with students.

Anyone can follow you on Twitter. I have no issue with anyone following me unless they harass me or are abusive; I block if needed. I have nearly 10,000 followers so I rarely notice when people follow me—except for Barack Obama, which made my year! Rarely noticing followers means I do not often follow students back. However, if I see a student following me, I typically will follow back. I only use Twitter for professional interactions and political tweets, meaning tweets about national politics. I do not post anything personal on Twitter—nothing about my daughter, where I live, where I travel, etc. Students who follow me will see things I feel passionate about intellectually, news about our center or institute, and articles I write and am quoted in. I never engage in fights with people on Twitter and I only put out positive or motivational messages. If someone tries to draw me into a Twitter fight, I ignore them.

I also have an Instagram account and I use it to post photos—usually flowers, places, food, and people I love. I normally say nothing about the photos. I assume some of my students follow me on Instagram, but I do not pay much attention. My Instagram is public, so anyone can see it. You need to decide if you want your account to be public or private and if you want students to follow your photos. If your account is public, be aware that anyone can use what you post against you.

My rule for social media is that I do not add students unless they request it. And I use the majority of my social media platforms as a way to share goodness and positive messages. I used to be more assertive in my commentary, but I do that almost exclusively on Twitter and I literally think about every word in every Tweet, because I know that words are manipulated, misconstrued, and used against people on the platform. I will speak out vehemently against injustice—that will not stop, but I am precise in how I do it. I understand that many people may not agree with my newly evolved stance. I regularly see faculty (and graduate students) post photos and statements, and retweet highly questionable items on social media. In fact, I usually screen shot these things, because I am fascinated with what faculty will post—I have seen photos of their legs in fishnet stockings with red stiletto heels, photos of themselves in a speedo or barely-there bikini, sexual jokes (e.g., hurricane forecasts that resemble the shape of a phallus), and tweets referring to state governors as Nazis or presidential candidates as "coons." Most faculty consider these posts to be well within their freedom of speech rights and protected by academic freedom in some cases. However, I do not think faculty are protected and in the current climate, I would advise you to be benign with your social media. Anyone at any time can claim to be offended by your posts and tweets, which may possibly matter to your employer. Furthermore, given the "power" that you have as a faculty member, students can claim your tweets/posts intimidate them or scare them, even if those messages do not pertain to them. We live in a world that can be vicious and we cannot be naïve to what people will do with information.

Finally, I often see people subtweeting or subposting about their institution, colleagues, relationships, and student-related issues. I will readily admit that I have subtweeted about items such as poor leadership (I have witnessed a lot in the academy), unnamed people who have missed multiple meetings with me (e.g., "miss one meeting with me and fail to apologize, ok, you are forgiven; miss two, and naw, you'll need to wait for a while for a meeting"), and unnamed colleagues who regularly neglect students or act in racist ways. I regret doing this and do not do it anymore. The best thing to do if you are mad is to call a friend and talk about your frustration, and if you feel comfortable, talk directly to the person who gets under your skin.

If you are on the job market, make sure to review all of your social media and cleanse it of anything that might be considered odd, that represents you in a bad light, or is offensive to others. Search committees regularly review the social media footprint of faculty hires.

Consulting and Keynote Speeches for Hire

As you move along in your career, you are going to be asked to do consulting, especially if your work becomes more well known. I remember the first time I was asked. I had no idea what to say. I am sharing my advice to make things easier for you than they were for me.

The main engagements for which people will offer you pay are consulting, invited talks, commissioned papers and books, and royalties if you are asked to be a series editor for a publisher.[1] I have done many consulting projects, given count-less invited talks, written several books for pay, and written commissioned articles or essays. The pay I received for these tasks differed depending on who was asking and what was involved. Early on, I did not have an organized way of think-ing about work for pay and instead, I would take things as they came along. Now, I am much more thoughtful about what I do and how much I charge.

As a tenure-track faculty member, more than likely, you will not be asked to do a lot of consulting. Most of the offers begin once you are tenured and have established a national reputation. However, you may be asked to give a keynote address, do a workshop, or write a report. As you are thinking about how much to charge for your services, I urge you to think about how long it will take you to complete the project, how much travel time is involved if you are giving a talk, how much prep time is needed for a keynote address, and how much time you will spend preparing supporting materials. All of these items matter in terms of how much you charge. For example, I charge more to give a talk if I need to make an airport connec-tion or if the travel takes a long time. Thus, a talk on the East Coast costs less than one on the West Coast for me because less travel is involved, which means less time away from home and research. If you are working for two straight days and have to travel, you will be tired and intellectually spent—make sure to compensate yourself for this work and time.

How much you charge for talks and consulting is also related to how much experience and knowledge you have. If you are just starting out and building your knowledge base, you cannot charge as much as someone who has a lifetime of knowledge or a major book. What you charge and what you might be offered also have to do with who is asking. I have higher pricing for institutions with larger endowments (but keep in mind that if you do not have a body of expertise, you cannot charge higher rates). I charge institutions that are non-profits and have lower endowments much less, and in most cases offer pro bono work. For example, because most of my research has been focused on HBCUs, I rarely charge HBCUs for talks or consulting unless the project is long-term and grant-funded. I do ask that my travel be reimbursed.

I sometimes do not charge if I see a potential partnership or professional connection resulting due to the collaboration. Some of the very best opportunities in my professional career have resulted from offering my services for free. I regularly tell stories of how good things have come my way because I helped others. For example, I was once asked to attend a dinner in New York City by a foundation program officer and to take notes, summarizing the dinner discussion. At first glance someone might find this insulting. However, the program officer wanted me to provide a thought-provoking overview of the conversation and share it with the dinner invitees. During dinner, I was seated next to a program officer for another major foundation. He and I struck up a great conversation, with lots of laughing. He asked me about my research and requested I follow up with him after the meeting. A year later he encouraged me to apply for a grant from his foundation and two years later I received a multi-million-dollar grant, the largest of my career. If I had refused to take notes at the dinner, I would never have met the program officer and been able to share my good work with him. Stories like this one are important to share, especially lately as I hear many PhD students and tenure-track faculty talking about how much they are worth or, for example, claiming they should be paid for media interviews (that's not a thing unless you have a contract with a media outlet). Feel free to disagree, but I think it is important to give back and I believe that goodness comes back to you many times over when you give back. Most of my major consulting opportunities were the result of volunteering for an organization first.

It can be hard to negotiate hourly rates and honorariums. I suggest you have a standard hourly rate (perhaps $100/hour) and a standard honorarium (perhaps $1200), based on your expertise and the market, and that you move those rates up and down depending on who is asking you to help them. Again, if you are on the tenure-track, you will most likely be paid a standard rate unless you have written a very well-received book, have particular skills, or hold expansive subject-matter expertise. As your expertise and career grow you can ask for a higher hourly rate and honorarium.

To keep track of your consulting and speaking engagements, I advise you to use a spreadsheet and to include the name of the organization, date of the event, contact information, and conditions of pay (See Appendix I). Also include the amount of payment and travel reimbursements expected, and note when the reimbursements and payments arrive. When you first start out, it will be easy to keep track of these consulting opportunities, but once you are further along in your career, there will be many of them and they can get confusing, especially in terms of who has paid you and for what. You will also thank yourself later if you design a standard invoicing form; Google "invoice samples" and you will find many. You may also want to prepare a standard contract. I recommend something basic with your name, address, nature of the services, rate of pay, and a note about recording, live tweeting, and photography. I keep it very simple. Keep in mind that as you move forward with your career, depending on the demand for your work, you may want to hire an agent or speaker's bureau representative. I have personally never wanted to give that many talks, but others do. I have found that my quality of life is more important than flying all over the country non-stop. I have been tempted, but decided it was not for me. You will need to make this decision for yourself. Remember not to let your ego get the best of you.

When giving paid talks and consulting, you should also consider the tax implications, hiring an accountant (I use one), and whether or not you want to establish an LLC (a good idea, but be prepared to pay business taxes). You should also keep track of all of your expenses. I keep every receipt and am organized about the way I manage my financial life. Having an accountant might cost you more initially, but it will save you money in the long run. Accountants can help you deduct a home office and various other utilities if you work from home, they can amortize your library books over time as well as your equipment purchases, and they notice all of the little items that you may not realize are deductible. If you are giving talks around the country or doing consulting in various states, you may owe state taxes in each of those places. An accountant can help you with these issues. One of the most important things you can do for yourself is to be organized and efficient about your financial life, and having an accountant helps immensely with these matters. This type of preparation can begin when you are an assistant professor and will set you up for success throughout your career.

Another issue to think about if you are going to give paid talks and do consulting is your institution's policies about conflicts of interest. Some institutions have very strict rules about the amount of consulting or paid work that you can do per month; others do not. It is important to ask your department chair or dean what the policies are for faculty consulting. I would advise you to take these policies seriously. I always fill out all necessary forms. You may think it is not important; but know that some of your colleagues might report you if you do not do it, because the climate in the academy leads people to do petty things. You can also ask your department chair or dean when and where it is appropriate to use your university affiliation or email. There are times when it will be better to use your private email and other times when using your university email is best. You need to know the difference.

Finally, if you are going to give invited talks regularly and do consulting, make it easier on yourself by having your materials ready to go. Have a professional headshot taken. Your institution will often do this for you, make sure you have the rights to use the photo. When I was a young professor, I found out the hard way that I was not allowed to use my headshot when the school's photographer called me and asked me to pay her $300 per use of the photo. Although other professors were using their photos frequently; I was gaining national recognition and the photographer wanted to collect some money. As the mother of an artist, I think artists should be paid. The problem in this situation is that my school did not buy the rights to the photos for its faculty. Thankfully, the university stepped in, because I was somewhat intimidated by the photographer. I was an assistant professor and unaware of the policies. In addition to a headshot, you should also have both long and short professional biographies, and a document with your social media handles. I would advise you to be proactive in your preparation for invited talks and consulting. Word gets around about the work you do and how prepared you are, and if you want to continue to do this work, you have to do your best work.

Engaging the Media

As your work becomes more well-known or if you do research in an area that becomes a hot media topic, you may be contacted to discuss your research with reporters. My best advice around engaging media is to set up a meeting with the public relations staff in your school or university during your first year as a faculty member. Ask them for their tips on engaging the media, which they will have on hand. Also, do some *mock* media interviews with the public relations staff, both on and off camera. This preparation will be most valuable as you move forward in your career.

There are several pieces of advice that I have around engaging the media. First, you have to remember that no matter what kind of relationship you establish with a reporter, they are nearly always going to place the story above your interests. If a reporter tells you that something is off the record, it is not. Nothing is ever off the record. I have run into reporters who keep their word and whom I trust, but they are rare. I have also run into reporters who are mean, self-serving, and manipulate faculty for their own personal gain. When engaging the media, you need to protect yourself.

If you decide to engage the media, make sure you do so in a timely manner. If a reporter calls, you need to respond right away—not tomorrow, and not in a week. Reporters are operating on short deadlines. If you become known as someone who answers the phone, responds to email, and is respectful of a reporter's time, they will continue to contact you.

When talking to a reporter, you have to speak in clear and precise language devoid of academic jargon; I have told you that many times in this book. Reporters are generalists and do not have the deep knowledge you do. You should also use short phrasing. I once had a faculty colleague tell me she does not talk to reporters because she does not want to *dumb down* her ideas for media sound bites. From my perspective, it takes considerable intellect to take complex ideas and convert them into phrases that are understandable by larger audiences. This is a skill and those who can do it will go far in their academic career and have a much larger impact on society.

You may want to ask the reporter to record you so that you are not misquoted. Reporters will often ask if they can record you and I always say yes, because I prefer exactness in the quotes that are attributed to me. If you are not being recorded, know that there is a chance that you will be misquoted. It has happened to me several times and is not a great situation. However, given the 48-hour news cycle, you will get over it and move on and so will anyone who is offended. If you absolutely want to avoid being misquoted, you can ask that the reporter send you the questions via email and then you can answer them via email, but remember to be succinct and that the reporter will not use everything you send.

In general, a 30-60 minute call with a reporter might result in one quote in a media article or two lines in a National Public Radio interview. Reporters have little control over the final news story—that is under the purview of editors—and as such, even if they want to include four or five quotes from you, an editor is likely to cut them to have more voices in the article. The more voices, the more credible the story, in many people's eyes.

You may wonder if engaging the media is worth the time. I think it is, because it is a way to engage the public with your academic work. You are not paid for your time, but there are often other benefits that result from media coverage. For example, I have secured a book contract as a result of media coverage, garnered consulting contracts, and secured grants due to a program officer or funder reading about my work in the newspaper. In recent years, I have heard new academics talking about demanding pay from reporters or freelance writers for media interviews. Feel free to disagree, but I think demanding pay is unethical and inappropriate, and shows a lack of understanding of how media works. If someone is an official regular contributor on CNN, sure, they will be paid. When I was a regular essay writer for the *Chronicle of Higher Education* for several years, I was paid. However, I have never been paid for being a source because it is not ethical. Freelance writers are paid by the word and very little; they do not have funds to pay you to do interviews. We have to be generous with others and for me, the rewards for media coverage of my work are ample reimbursement.

And the Rest...

There are so many more aspects of being a faculty member that you will eventually learn, more than I can possibly cover in a book. For these matters that are rarely covered in graduate school, make sure to consult your mentors and colleagues and work to make the best choices for your life and career.

Notes

1   Please keep in mind that many of these opportunities do not come about until you are tenured, because you do not yet have the reputation and work available to judge.

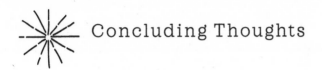

Concluding Thoughts

After reading this book, being a faculty member may seem daunting. I wanted to be honest and forthright with you about many of the issues and situations you might encounter. Yes, some of them are negative, but the majority of what you will experience as a professor will be joyful, exciting, life changing, and will make you proud of the career you have chosen. I wish you the very best in producing knowledge, challenging and even changing minds, and living a beautiful life outside of your faculty role.

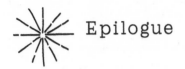 Epilogue

What if I'm a Woman and/or a Person of Color? Three Interviews

The chapters in this book have all been based on my experiences and on findings from literature about navigating the tenure track. And although I am a woman who can write extensively about the sexism I have experienced in the academy, I decided to interview three scholars for the epilogue of this book. These three individuals are people I admire who cut across disciplines and expertise, race, ethnicity, gender, language, and experiences. They are:

Cheron Davis, an African American woman. Cheron is an Associate Professor of Reading Education at Florida A&M University and serves as Co-Research Director for FAMU DRS Freedom Schools (formerly North Florida Freedom Schools), a Children's Defense Fund Freedom Schools® Partner. Cheron's research interests include teacher preparation at Historically Black Colleges and Universities, multicultural reading pedagogy, the promotion of equity and justice through literacy, and early literacy intervention techniques. Cheron serves as a faculty mentor for PURPOSE: Partners United for Research Pathways Oriented to Social Justice in Education. PURPOSE is an Institute of Education

Sciences funded Pathways to the Education Science Training Program intended to increase the diversity of the doctorate in education. Cheron was named the 2016-2017 Florida A&M University Innovative Teaching Award winner and was awarded the 2017 Marguerite Cogorno Radencich Award for Outstanding Teacher Educator in Reading by the Florida Reading Association. She is the 2017-2018 Florida A&M Teacher of the Year. She is an alumna of the 2015 cohort of Center for Minority Serving Institutions' ELEVATE Fellows, the American Association of Blacks in Higher Education (AABHE) Leadership and Mentoring Institute (LMI), and the Asa G. Hilliard III & Barbara A. Sizemore Research Course on African Americans and Education. Cheron has served as a faculty mentor for cohorts of the ELEVATE program at the Rutgers Center for Minority Serving Institutions since 2018. Cheron earned bachelor and master's degrees in elementary education from Auburn University in Auburn, AL. She also holds an education specialist degree in elementary education and a master's certification in school administration from Troy University in Phenix City, AL. Additionally, Cheron holds a PhD in reading education from Auburn University. She is the co-editor of the volume *Underserved Populations at HBCUs: The Pathway to Diversity, Equity, and Inclusion* (Emerald Publishing, 2018) and the forthcoming volume *The Beauty and the Burden of Being a Black Professor* (2021). Among Cheron's greatest accomplishments include managing to marry the smartest and most handsome FAMU alumnus, Terrance O. Davis, and giving birth to two of the brightest and cutest Baby Rattlers known to man, Ava (7) and TJ (4).

Levon T. Esters is an African American man. He is a Professor in the Department of Agricultural Sciences Education and Communication at Purdue University. Levon serves as the Director of the Mentoring@Purdue (M@P) program, which

is designed to increase the number of women and underrep-
resented minorities (URMs) receiving advanced post-sec-
ondary STEM-based agricultural and life sciences degrees
in Purdue University's College of Agriculture. Levon also
serves as a Senior Research Associate at the Rutgers Center
for Minority Serving Institutions. He has established himself
as a scholar within the field of mentoring and is a nationally
recognized scholar on equity and diversity within the STEM-
based agricultural and life sciences disciplines. Levon's
research focuses broadly on issues of educational equity and
access, with a concentration on the mentoring of Black graduate students; STEM career development of racial and ethnic
minorities attending Historically Black Land-Grant Colleges
and Universities; and educational and professional mobility
of Black graduate students and faculty. Levon is among a few
Black scholars in the United States who conduct research
in these areas, and has been able to serve as a national role
model for other Black graduate students who are committed
to broadening participation of URMs in the Ag+STEM disciplines. Levon is a father to three daughters and in his spare
time enjoys watching and attending sporting events, photography, visiting lighthouses, and traveling.

Guillermina 'Gina' G. Núñez-Mchiri is Director of Women and
Gender Studies and an Associate Professor of Anthropology
at the University of Texas at El Paso (UTEP). At the time of this
interview, Gina had become the newly-elected president of
the UTEP Faculty Senate. She received her PhD in Cultural
Anthropology from the University of California Riverside
in 2006, her MA in Latin American Studies in 1998, and her
BA in International Business in 1994 from San Diego State
University. Gina began teaching at UTEP in 2004 and teaches
courses in ethnographic research methods; interdisciplinary
feminist theory and method; anthropology of food, gender,

and culture; and death, dying, and bereavement. Her classes incorporate research and community engagement opportunities through service learning. Gina received the University of Texas Regents Outstanding Teaching Award in 2012. She is an applied anthropologist who promotes service learning and engaged scholarship efforts on the U.S.-Mexico Border. Gina is the academic partner to Wise Latina International, a non-profit organization that empowers Latinas through the arts and entertainment. She is currently co-chair for the L.E.A.D. project, an executive leadership program that prepares women with the skills and tools necessary for them to launch projects and initiatives that support the development of Latinas, their families, and community. She has a 12-year partnership with the City of El Paso's Park and Recreation Department working with older adult athletes who are seeking to challenge the stigmas of aging through active living and competition in physical activities. Most recently, Gina is the co-recipient of an NSF-grant to study, as part of an interdisciplinary research team, older adults and their use of technology to address issues of social connectivity and mobility. Gina specializes in ethnographic research on the U.S.-Mexico border region and has published on a number of topics related to colonias, immigration and human rights, housing and social justice, Latina identity, Latinas in STEM fields, immigrant youth and education, and the applications of ethnography and service learning in higher education. Gina is married and has a teenage son.

I asked each of these scholars questions related to the role their many identities played in navigating the tenure-track. We also discussed their battles with racism and sexism as well as their mentoring experiences. Finally, I asked questions related to parenting while on the tenure track. I hope their voices and experiences will motivate you along your journey.

Cheron Davis

Marybeth: Why did you decide to become a faculty member?

Cheron: I don't know that I ever made that decision. The decision was kind of made for me. The universe brought me to the academy. I was a second grade teacher and had planned on being an elementary teacher forever. At some point I received a fellowship that was intended to recruit and retain minority and women faculty at an institution in Alabama and at that point I decided that it might be a good idea to let them pay for me to go back to school. And so it kind of led me into the idea that they were going to pay for my doctoral degree and then I would come back to the institution to serve in the faculty role. The irony of it all was that as a college student, I didn't like faculty. I didn't like professors. I thought they were all old. I thought they were all mainly White men. I thought they were all conceited and elitist. I did not like that about them. I didn't even like the idea of professorship. And so it's ironic that I actually became one and have had to navigate being one, having the title and still having that very firm, very real connection to K-12 schools and K-12 teachers.

Marybeth: How have your many identities—as a woman, as an African-American, there might be others—had an impact on your experiences as a professor? I also follow you on social media, and see that you take your Christianity fairly seriously as well, right?

Cheron: Yes. My identity as a woman, as this brown-eyed girl, in these spaces and, particularly my Christianity, they've shaped my experiences immensely. Again, like I said before, a lot of the work I do is heart work and unfortunately we don't get paid for heart work. We get paid for hard work. However, everything that I've done has a connection to my passion for mentoring and learning. And I've always wanted to be a life-long learner. I hung a lot of my hat on my smarts as a learner, coming through K-12 schooling. And a lot was expected of me and I wanted to be able to give back a lot. And this is originally why I became a teacher—a K-12 teacher, part of the reason. The other reason was because I don't like adults and they say stu-pid stuff and there's no excuse for that. But the kids were fun. They say silly things, there's an excuse, there's a reason, they're cute. The adults, not so much, but now that I am in this space, I am absolutely confident that everything about who I am plays a part in why I do the things I do, particularly me being a Black woman in my role as a mentor, as a leader to Black and brown women. My Christianity is, it always comes into play. Whether my students recognize that or not, that's questionable. I don't know that they know that, but I do pray for them. I do lift them up. I do spend that time and do the things outside of the box that I do from a place of passion and of wanting to serve my fellow man. I just believe in holistic care for people. I don't know how you can do the job effectively without caring about people, but there are some really cool, really high up folks that don't give two craps about anybody and they've got big titles and a lot of awards, but I just, I don't know how anyone could do it with-out care, I could never do that without care. There are a lot of things that I'm sure are not printed on my CV, but if I didn't do them, I wouldn't be who I am. And I wouldn't want to do what I'm doing, if I could not help others in some way. I know that all of those pieces of me are important to me being in this space.

Marybeth: Because you are at a Historically Black College, do you feel you are able to express your Christianity more readily? At a lot of institutions, especially Predominantly White Institutions, unless they are religiously affiliated, there is pressure to keep religion or spirituality out of your role completely due to the constitutional separation between church and state.

Cheron: The answer is yes and no. An HBCU, much like any other space or institution in America, is very diverse. There's a diversity of people, of cultures, but there's also diversity of religion. There's not a push to remove religion. I don't know that I push so hard to insert that part of me into my teaching. To me, it's like politics. It doesn't matter what I believe, I'm going to do what I would do for all of my students, regardless. However, as a qualitative researcher, I am never far removed from knowing that the lens through which I see the world actually drives how I instruct, how I implement my teaching practices. And so, I don't mind sharing that part, but I'm very, very clear about the fact, about acknowledging that people have different beliefs and religions. I never want it to be uncomfortable. So I never push religion in that space. I'm honest about my position, but I do acknowledge that my position does not matter. It does not matter as to how you're going to perform in this course. Secretly, I'm praying for them and I know they're going to be amazing. So whether they want to or not, they're going to be amazing, because I pray for them.

Marybeth: Thank you. Do you have particular advice to women, mothers, or people of color who are on the tenure-track? What specific advice around issues of race and gender would you give people for pursuing tenure? Where are people trying to trip you up?

Cheron: Oh, Jesus. Everywhere. Mommies, be advocates. I would never tell, particularly, Black women who have families to not acknowledge that part of your life. Of course, it's not celebrated in the same way that we celebrate other parts of higher education and it's not appreciated. However, do recognize that every part of who you become in your career, you owe that to the people who lift you up—friends and family members. And, my little children who give me lots of stories and inspiration for teaching teachers how to teach reading as I go through their youth with them and them growing up. So, you're parenting, you're being a wife, a partner, a mother, that very much is a part of who you are and don't ever let anyone push that down. More advice: publish, publish and publish and publish and just publish and just publish. I don't know how many times I say that and everybody said it to me. I was like, yeah, well, I'll be the best teacher in the world and it'll matter. It matters, but the truth is publishing matters more.

Marybeth: Tell me more about that.

Cheron: Publishing matters, it matters the most. And listen, I've got a whole op-ed in my head about how we need to rethink and re-envision what counts towards tenure and promotion in the academy and why we're still using this patriarchal system that is asinine and archaic. And I don't know when it's going to go away. I would love to say the best way to beat the system is to be the best teacher and win all of the awards for the institution and show them that if you intend for us to be teachers and teach teachers, you want to make sure you have the best teachers. When they get in that room to go over your tenure and promotion packet, if you have not published, it does not matter. It just doesn't. It doesn't weigh as heavily in the decision making process as research. Take it from me, who finally made it through the process: please publish, please, please. And that's not to the detriment of your students, never, ever, I wouldn't say do that. And I've done everything that I hoped I could have done and I wish I could have done more and I don't regret having done the things I did, but I would say to you, don't neglect the publishing piece.

Marybeth: How did you balance your roles of faculty member, wife, and mother while successfully pursuing tenure? What kinds of advice could you offer for women who are in the same situation?

Cheron: It's not easy. I incorporated my family into my work. For example, my daughter and I participated in a series for at-home learning with the Florida Center for Reading Research. This center operates as a gatekeeper for a lot of the research, and dissemination for reading outcomes here in the Southeast. They have done a series where they have parents and students modeling best practices in reading. My daughter and I actively participate. She now calls herself a YouTube star and asks people to subscribe to the channel. To me, that accomplishes so many goals on so many levels, but it also gives me that one-on-one time to spend with my child. I try desperately to incorporate them into every piece of what I'm doing. Yesterday we did a PowerPoint. We were teaching online. We're remote teaching and we were talking about figures of speech. We were going over some pictures and I would show the figure of speech and you'd have to decide whether it was an idiom or a hyperbole and I asked Ava, my daughter, what thoughts she had. We did "a skeleton in the closet" and the students online were chatting and telling me what type of metaphor it was. But we were asking Ava, what she thinks the phrase means. And the picture was of Jada Pinkett Smith[1] [the actress and wife of actor Will Smith], and it said "entanglement" and "the lady has skeletons in her closet." I said what do you think that means? All the students, I could see them chatting. And Ava said well, I think it means when you have skeletons in your closet, that means there aren't a lot of clothes. You don't have a lot of clothes to put on in your closet. And my response was, you are correct, Ava. She probably didn't have a lot of clothes during her entanglement. And they just laughed, they were like, oh my God, I can't even believe you said that. I said but here's the thing. This is relevant to what you're doing, because you'll encounter ELL students, students from different cultures, students who don't get figurative language; and so to practice that and have them see that happening in real time, I thought that was just magical for them anyway, particularly as freshmen students. I try desperately to incorporate my family, my husband. We do sporting events together. We kind of involved ourselves in the community. So immerse yourself in that community in any way that you can. But I have been intentional about the fact that my family members are the most important people on earth to me and they always come first. So if you see them in the classroom with me, or if you see my students tutoring them, it's because I believe in and love both my family and my job.

Marybeth: Often faculty colleagues are not supportive of women who incorporate their family into their professional life. Tell me more about that in your situation.

Cheron: There's a chapter in our newest volume, *The Beauty and the Burden of Being a Black Professor*, in which Alishea Rowley talks about the intersectionality of being a parent, a tenure-track faculty member, and a woman—a Black woman, in particular. She discusses how these roles, how the expectations for us are outside of what we see on the job description. To me, it's all about prioritizing and what is important to you. On top of that, because we're serving a population of students, many of who are first generation or come from vulnerable SES backgrounds, a lot of times we function in parental roles for them. And so we are mothering, even in our careers for students. As we mentor, we are mothering. We did a practice thingy last night when we celebrated my promotion last night at dinner. We were eating outside and I asked these questions, who's the funniest? And they say whether it was mommy or daddy. Who's the sweetest, mommy or daddy? And I ask them who works the hardest? You know what their response was?

Marybeth: Oh God, daddy?

Cheron: Did you hear, she just said it. It was daddy. [Cheron was holding her child during the interview]

Marybeth: Oh my God. Really?

Cheron: Yes. Yes. The perception is that he works harder even though right now, he is sitting right beside me and I've been working all day, they're sitting on the floor, I've been working all day and they've been sitting right here, beside me, doing camps and I'm multitasking. Daddy is the one who works the hardest. And so I'm not naïve to the fact that perception isn't just at home with children. I recognize that that these ideas move right on up into the academy. And so I would say to women, don't ever let anybody tell you you're not working your butt off. Don't ever let anyone diminish what you do as a faculty member and as a parent. And don't neglect your family for this job, because I also have seen folks work to death and then be replaced; the institutions will have an ad in the paper for the faculty job before their obituary is in there. So I have always promised myself, you won't kill me. You will not, you won't kill me. Don't kill yourself. Make sure you prioritize your family, because while this work is important, your family is always going to be there. The work may not. The institution may not.

Marybeth: Right. I always tell people, institutions are not loyal. Are there any special considerations that you had to face as a person of color or as a woman, as you were pursuing tenure?

Cheron: Do your very best work. Work smarter, not harder, work smarter and show up when you need to show up and everything else will fall into place. Those things will happen. It didn't kill me. It was disappointing, but hey, such is life. So don't fall into this race of who's working the hardest, or get in that competitive mindset, because it just becomes that for you. Who are you trying to beat?

Marybeth: I think one of the political things that happens in the academy is there is nonstop competition, with people thinking that your gain is their loss.

Cheron: Yes. Yes. It's unfortunate, but it's just kind of how it works. I remember several years ago I reached out to you for advice about being in the academy, being a faculty member. I told you that I was at the end of my rope; I'm sick of this. Why are they doing this to me? And your advice was pretty much like the reverse psychology of it all. You said, well, maybe you just need to get out. Maybe you're not built for this field. Maybe you just need to get out. And I thought, hold on, hold on. What do you mean? And so that reverse psychology, I have replayed that in my mind over and over again. You're not meant for this. Maybe you should just drop it. And every time I think about you saying that, which is interesting, because I appreciate that. I appreciate now the fact that you said it, because I always say to myself what the hell? I'm not dropping out, I can do this.

Marybeth: I know you can. But I say that to a lot of people—if you do not want to do this, do not do it. Life is short, if you can do what you love, do it.

Cheron: And you were serious. I mean, I had literally mulled over that for years; I still I think about that. When it gets tough, I think about Marybeth saying to me, well, you got to just leave if you don't like it. It was so matter of fact. I was thinking to myself girl, why are you saying that? Like I got a whole job, a whole family to feed and I just get out? No, I can do this. I can do this. Sometimes you need those, you absolutely need those mentors, those people that encourage you and even if that encouragement comes as a push or it comes as pulling you along, you need all of those, to sustain in this environment.

Marybeth: Michael Nettles, one of my mentors, did that to me when I first thought of starting the Center for Minority Serving Institutions. I told him, I cannot do it, because I am afraid I will fail. He just looked at me, he looked right at me and he said, you are acting like a woman. And I thought, what? And he said I am just telling you a man would do it, even if he was afraid to fail. But women, they have to have all their ducks in a row and while you are getting all your ducks in a row, some man is going to go steal your dream. I started planning for the Center for Minority Serving Institutions the next day.

Cheron: Those are facts though. Those are facts, Marybeth.

Marybeth: I am curious, when you have been confronted with racism or sexism, how did you respond as a pre-tenured faculty member? What did you do?

Cheron: How did I respond? I had multiple responses. I can tell you the one thing I did not do, which was what I wanted to do. I never fought. I never fought anybody, but I wanted to lay hands on several individuals, I'm not even kidding, like literally wanted to take it to the streets. I kept it professional. Sometimes I didn't though. In the midst of pregnancy and a day before I was set to be induced to have my second child, one of my colleagues pulled me in her office and yelled at me. And my response to that was tears. You know, some of you know that a lot of times, especially we as women, we will cry—not out of sadness, but rather anger—because there are so many other things that we want to do that we know we cannot do. I knew at the time with an entire baby sitting in my lap, in my belly there was no way I was going to be able to fight her and I needed something to come back to. I needed the insurance. And so my response at that time was to cry. But mostly, the experiences that I've had with racism and even sexism, I have responded to in a professional manner. It's super important not to allow others to create your narrative for you. And so to me, that meant going the route that would be best, that would best situate me as a pre-tenured faculty member. I don't regret having handled the situations the way I did. However, I am more than confident that as a tenured faculty member, I am certain I will feel more empowered to use my voice to speak up, because I don't believe that I spoke up in the ways, or showed up in the ways that I should have, based on my status as a pre-tenured faculty member.

Marybeth: Are there ways that a pre-tenure person can prepare for systemic racism or sexism in the tenure process? Are there things they can do to protect themselves?

Cheron: Yeah, absolutely. I think one of the biggest things for me has been learning the culture. Right? Learning the culture of the institution. Institutions are like people. Everybody has their own little flavor. And so a few years, probably two or three years of really taking a back seat, flying under the radar and listening, figuring out who the players are, figuring out who the gatekeepers are. That was very important for me, because it prepared me, it gave me a peek into how the institution works. Something I actually prescribe for every single individual on earth is that I would encourage them to have a good relationship with whatever God they serve and to also find a good therapist, because there is no way that you can make it and do this without some help. You're not strong enough, like just life in general, like what life is throwing at us right now. You need a therapist to sort through these things, to figure out where you are in this and with the added pressure of academia. Yeah. So a good God and a good therapist.

Marybeth: Did you have any mentors who helped you throughout the tenure process?

Cheron: Some of my mentors were by happenstance. I met them as a junior faculty member at conferences. Adriel Hilton, we won a dissertation award at the American Association of Blacks in Higher Education back in 2009. We both won the award. I think he might've gotten second place and I got third, or the other way around. But anyway, as soon as we got our checks, we went out and cashed them at the bank, literally before the conference was over and went to go party and spend our money. Like it was so much fun, but we always agreed from that point on, we were going to have each other's back. And when you find those people who are mentors and who actually do provide support to you, you have to hang on to those people. Coming to ELEVATE (an early career, faculty workshop) in 2015, I told you one of the reasons why I actually even applied for this was Adriel; he advised me. When I discovered that it was through your Center and I knew of you, I told you even back then and it's the truth: I really needed to sit in this White woman's face and find out who you are, why you're doing this, are you true to this? I needed to have that conversation. It wasn't enough for me that you've done all this work and I knew the name and oh, you were associated with all these rock stars and you are the rock star. I needed to know who is this White woman? I need to have a conversation with her. And to me, that was a goal for getting there. I actually did do that. I've got a picture of me, you, and Chloë at dinner. She told me so much stuff that I'm like, okay, you are true to this, girl. You mean this stuff. But the other part is that I met all these amazing people who ended up being champions for me. They've written book chapters with me. We've done conference presentations together. I've had this amazing network of people who have given me the advice, the support that I needed and not just telling me what I want to hear, because I also had mentors that honestly, probably don't know that they were mentors, in that they pushed me to be great. They didn't just treat me gently because I'm a woman or because I might cry, which I typically do. They see me as a warrior and I'm thankful for that as well, because they didn't take into account my feelings, if you will, but they brought out the best in me and so I'm appreciative of those folks who have supported me in my life. Dr. Henry Frierson, for example. Oh God, the list, I don't want to name them, I'll forget so many people. They have just been amazing.

Marybeth: Often, women and people of color are asked to do a disproportionate amount of service. How would you advise people to manage service?

Cheron: I would be strategic and I have been strategic. If someone who serves on the tenure and promotion committee asks you to be on a committee or do some type of service or speak at an event, then do it. If the people are not anywhere near the tenure and promotion table, if they're not friends with anybody on it, tell them no, because you cannot do everything. And I know there's this common notion that as junior faculty, we can't say no to anything. You've got to do everything. No you don't. I said no several times and I've got more service than I can count on my fingers and toes. You're going to do it, period. But you have to find those places where you can say, you know what? I can't do this. I would encourage junior faculty: You can say no. Make sure you weigh the politics of your no. I weighed the politics. I'm not going to even pretend with you, if a dean asks, of course I'm doing it. Right? You have to know, you have to know the game to be able to play it. So friend of the friend of a person on the committee, would you speak at my event? Of course I would, it would be my honor. And you strap those little kids up and they can get some dinner that night, with the little finger sandwiches and you go and do your speech. But if they are not connected in that way, or if it's something that's going to take away from your productivity, don't say yes.

Marybeth: Have you had to deal with any academic bullying?

Cheron: Hell yes.

Marybeth: Okay, tell me about that. I have had to deal with academic bullying, as you know.

Cheron: Oh, Marybeth, I know. Just bullying period, but yes, Marybeth, they do it, they do it. They use their titles to bully. They use their experience to bully. I've experienced it in faculty meetings where someone will assert their authority. The way that I deal with it most times, in my mind, it functions as either I don't care about what you're saying, or as a challenge to do even better. And so there are a lot of times, especially with junior faculty, that we are made to feel, especially the way we felt as graduate students. Right? We had this impostor syndrome, like do I even belong there? People will capitalize on that. They will move in on that. I think the way to deal with it and with any situation, is in a professional manner. Being very straightforward, always be straightforward, but if they're on the tenure and promotion committee, don't use the bad words. I don't think everybody in higher education has a target on your back. Everybody is not after you, but you have to seek out those people who are genuine and who really want to push you forward.

Marybeth: Any last bit of advice you want to share with readers who are going up for tenure, who might be women or persons of color?

Cheron: Publish. Publish, put your family first, publish again. Take care of home, take care of your partner, take care of your parents and children. Make sure they are first and get a therapist. I am a proponent of mental health. Get a good therapist who can help you to sort through some things and yeah, just make it a thing, incorporate it into your life. I think that has been the thing that has really been helpful for me. I don't ever have these guilty feelings of being away from my kids, because I have incorporated them into what I'm doing, such that I never feel guilty about my role as a wife, as a mom; we're going to do it together. We do it, all of us are going and so I'm thankful for that. I'm thankful for a career that allows me that type of flexibility.

Marybeth: Yes! Thank you for your perspectives.

Levon Esters

Marybeth: I am curious—Why did you decide to become a faculty member?

Levon: That's easy. The driving force for me was my dad. My dad was a psychology professor, so growing up in a household with someone like that had an impact and I remember when I was young I would come home from lunch and even later in the afternoon after school my dad would be home. As I started to formulate ideas of work and what it meant as far as the work he did, I started to see what the life of a professor was like. I thought this is kind of neat that he has a job that allows him to be home at these hours and make lunch for me or do whatever, get off early and do all sorts of things. That was my first interest in a career that allowed that type of flexibility. I grew up in a household where education wasn't stressed, but it was important. I knew it was important because of the way my family carried themselves and approached education. I started to have a fond love of education and learning. Then as I graduated from high school and went to college, I wasn't sure what I wanted to do, like most college freshmen. Then as I matured and graduated, I knew at some point, I started working and then I started teaching for three years after my first job. At that point, I knew I wanted to get a master's degree, so I did that. Then when I got my master's, I started to ask to myself if I could be really good at this. I wanted to try something different. I didn't want to be teaching my whole life. So, that was another motivation for getting a PhD and so I did that. Then as I was in my PhD program, I met a couple of people and had some really good mentors that I still look up to 'til this day; they were the consummate professionals, professors, and faculty members and they were Black men and women. This combined with the fact that again my dad was a professor was what I think collectively made me want to pursue being a faculty member as a career.

Marybeth: How have your multiple identities—as an African American man—shaped your experience as a faculty member, especially pre-tenure?

Levon: Pre-tenure, I was at Iowa State University. That was my first tenure-track position. I was actually lucky being in that department. Of course, I was the only African American faculty member in the department, but to be honest, I was actually in a really good department. I had a department head, a White male, he was really good. I mean, he supported me. He was actually a really good mentor. He helped me. He got me through advising my first master's student. So, he was really good, really supportive, gave me what I needed, helped me through the process of being promoted and tenured. So, I was in a space that I had some supportive colleagues, even though I was in Iowa. But I also realized at the end of the day here I am in agriculture in Iowa. I'm in the college of agriculture and you don't see many Black people, let alone Black men. So, for me, I was well aware of the role of race and how I was going to have to move differently, if you will, to navigate this process. Even though I had supportive people, I realized that my skin color was going to be a factor. I was always aware of the fact that I was Black, not as much about my gender because in agriculture there are a lot more men. Even still for me I think the identity that led the most by far was me being a Black faculty member and just how you kind of feel that pressure and that weight to always have to perform at the next level even when you knew of others who weren't as good as you. I began to realize that there were folks who were average in a lot of ways, but because they were White, they were part of the club already, so they were able to navigate the academy much easier than myself. So, for me, back to your question, by far my race was always front and center with me, no matter the space I was in, whether it was meeting with undergrads that were all White, teaching in front of a class of all White students who were farmers or from farm backgrounds, being in faculty meetings where I was the only Black man, and other service commitments I had. So, again, being Black just permeated everything that I did during those five years that I was at Iowa State. I left Iowa State in August of 2009 to come to Purdue University and I had not earned tenure yet or been promoted. I didn't earn tenure until I came to Purdue three years later.

Marybeth: I have a question for you. I am probably a rarity in that I am a White person who has taught quite a few courses where the students were all Black. However, in society I am still in the majority; you are not. You mentioned being in Iowa, teaching a class of all White students as a Black man. What was that like and what were you thinking as you were on the tenure track? When you were teaching, what was on your mind?

Levon: Good question. So, for me, there are a couple layers to it. The biggest was that not only were these all White students, but they were farm kids. I mean, these were people who lived on their parents' or grandparents'-owned farms of rural Iowa and other parts of the Midwest. So, not only were they White, but they were rural White kids. Here I am a Black guy, not just a Black guy, but I'm a Black guy from the south side of Chicago and I didn't grow up in the rough area of the city, but I had friends who did and my high school was in a pretty bad part of the city. So, for me, I'm like damn, here I am a Black guy from Chicago teaching in Iowa, I mean, you can't get two more polar opposites, the Black guy from the south side of Chicago teaching White farm kids. So, for me, it was I'm here. I'm sitting and standing in front of my class, always trying to figure things out. Of course, there was some level of code switching I had to do, but I mean, I don't use slang and I think I speak well and I guess I know how to be a professional. So, I was always a professional in front of my students, but I also, to some degree back then, I tried to stay true to myself and be myself and not totally just crossover into being someone like Carlton Banks from the Fresh Prince show. I wasn't going to go that route. I was still going to maintain who I was.

Marybeth: Did you say Carlton Banks? You are too funny.

Levon: Right. I was never going to do that. Overall, I had very good relationships with my students. Some are my Facebook friends and we still connect every once and a while. One reached out to me recently. He said he reads what I post on Facebook and I inspire him. So, as you can see, even though my background was different from all of my students, I did connect with some others in various ways. I think what students appreciated about me was my honesty and that I treated them with respect, and also my commitment to doing good work. So, I think that is what enabled me to survive working in that space and achieve some success. But again, back to your question, being in front of that class, it was a bit intimidating because in my classes I averaged about 35 students, so I'm in a class with literally no other Black folks. Although I was the lone Black person in my classes, I'm pretty confident and so I simply focused on doing my job to the best of my ability. When I think about it now and where I am now and the work I do, it's amazing how my career has almost flip-flopped. Even today, I still teach mostly White students, but my faculty appointment is tied entirely to graduate education, whereas when I was at Iowa State my faculty appointment focused on undergraduate education. So, now that my appointment is totally different, the demographic of my students has changed significantly. For example, currently, five of my seven advisees are Black and it's been that way for several years now. It's kind of amazing how the students I work with are polar opposites from those who I worked with at Iowa State.

Marybeth: I just cannot even imagine what that was like. What kind of advice would you give folks as they are pursuing tenure? Any specific advice for African Americans?

Levon: So, I think that the biggest piece of advice I would have and I haven't shared this with many people is that people take their rank seriously as faculty. For example, I have come across people who have been at Purdue 20, 25, 30 years who think that just because of their years of experience, they automatically hold dominion over you in every way possible. What I've learned is that I look at being a faculty member in terms of levels of separation and these levels are what differentiates faculty. For example, when I was an associate professor, there was one clear level of separation between me and the full professors and that was rank. But now having achieved the rank of full professor, this level of separation has been cancelled out. The other level of separation that often comes into play is the amount of institutional knowledge one has as a result of his or her years at the institution. So, what I found helps compensate on this level of separation is to consult mentors, advocates, and allies, many of whom are White men and White women at Purdue who were really good folks like you, and they would give me excellent advice and insight into how things worked and why. Essentially, they would give me the ins and outs of the academy—share with me the "unwritten rules" that would help me navigate various spaces and on campus and situations I would face. They would say "Levon, you have the official policies and procedures of the university and you have the policies and procedures that aren't written—but are allowable." So, there were colleagues who tried to think that they yielded some power over me because they were at Purdue longer. However, I was connected with people who were at Purdue as long as them and so I could get insights on what to do and how to maneuver various situations. Again, the only thing that separated me from my "senior" colleagues when I was an associate professor was the fact that they were full professor and their "years of service", but again, with my promotion and access to information from trusted colleagues from around campus, I was extremely confident in how to navigate within my institution. So, as for advice to other Black and brown faculty, I would say that there are some good White colleagues at all institutions. I've met some and so what needs to happen is that you need to try and identify these individuals and reach out and have them as part of your inner circle or team because they can really help you and give you some damn good advice. So, that's what I've learned.

Marybeth: What would you say to those who might say "I'm not going to have any White mentors" or "I do not trust anybody who is White?"

Levon: I would say that, to be quite blunt, you have to let go of that perspective. I don't separate my mentors by White or Black. I mean, I believe in having good people, quality people in my circle and I'll give you an example. You've heard this story before. When I was on the faculty senate and I was just a member, I was on this committee. There were 15 of us. This is my second year on the committee and then one day a member of the committee who had been at Purdue for nearly 40 years, a White guy I might add, said, "Levon, let's have lunch." I said, "Okay, I'll have lunch. What do you want to talk about?" He says, "Levon, I just want to have lunch with you and tell you that I've been watching you the last couple of years and I think you would be a good candidate to serve as the next chair of our committee." I'm thinking in my head, I am four years into Purdue. You've got people on this committee that have been here for 20, 25 years. What the hell do I know about leading this group of people? He says, "Levon, you can do it. I've been watching you. You have this gravitas about yourself." He said, "I'm sure you can do it." And they voted me in and they voted for me three straight years in a row, reappointed me three straight years. I could have still been doing it, but you have a term limit. So, this is a White colleague that I didn't know until I was on this committee. I trusted him and that was just one example of a White person that was well-meaning and supported me. So, my point is that you have to give people that don't look like you a chance and trust them and in this case I trusted him and that trust and being on the senate has helped me tremendously. I've been able to navigate situations because of the access to information I had, learned a lot about some of the unwritten rules that I never would have learned if I would not have been given an opportunity to be chair of that committee, serve on the provost's search committee and had many other professional opportunities. It was just access I had that I didn't have before. So, my point is you have to learn to trust folks that are non-Black because it can help you tremendously.

Marybeth: I know that you are father to three girls; I am curious about how you balance your various faculty roles along with being a parent.

Levon: People know this about me. You know this, but my colleagues also know. My students know that, of course, your mom is always going to be your mom and you're going to put her needs first, but that aside, everyone knows that when it comes to Purdue work or my daughters, work is always going to come second. I've been blessed to have a job that I can get up and leave when I want and so I've never missed a birthday of any of my daughters' 43 birthdays total, never missed one, well I did miss one this year because of COVID-19, but other than that, never missed a birthday. If it's a major event like a recital or something, a state tournament, I'm there, so my daughters come first and they know that. My students know that. My colleagues know it and I've made it clear with folks. I make it very clear when it comes to family because I don't want people to have any misunderstanding. I also try to make sure that my daughters understand the value of work because work plays a critical role in our lives, not to mention we spend most of our lives working. So, there are times when my daughters will see me working. However, I think I've been pretty good at trying to have some semblance of work-life balance. What I've learned to do is when my daughters are with me and I have work to do; I work in the evening when they're winding down or when they're asleep or early in the morning. I don't want to be the kind of father that they always see working and I don't want to miss out on something, having them grow up and say my dad never checked in on us. They've seen me work. They understand that I have to work, but they are never in a situation where I make it appear that work is more important than them. That's important to me because when they're 30, they're going to remember these times, just like your daughter Chloë is going to remember her time with you.

Marybeth: I do the same thing. When we are on vacation, I do not work at all. I am going to give her as much time as I can. If there is an emergency, I will answer an email or call, but I like the idea of just being present in what you are doing.

Levon: Yeah, because I know people who have missed recitals, they miss their kids growing up, and haven't seen them go to prom. That I'm not doing. That's not an option for me. It just isn't. I've been lucky, but again, being a professor affords me that opportunity. If I was a school teacher or a principal or owned a Starbucks, it would be way more difficult. So, I've actually been blessed to have the job I have as I can just do what I want, leave when I want, come and go when I want. Being a dad is important to me, but at the same time it's important that my daughters grow up to understand that I value work. You have to work hard and if you do those things, then good things come to you. That's kind of how I balance it.

Marybeth: How do you balance teaching, research, and service?

Levon: For me, I've been lucky. So, my research is easy because I have a lot of people on my team. I've had upwards of seven or eight students on my team, so a lot of the work is driven by their theses and dissertations, and I have a couple of pet projects that I have personally—for example, writing a research brief for your Center. Then I also have grant projects that I keep in my back pocket. The research has been easy because I have students that can serve as co-authors and can lead some projects. As far as teaching, my teaching load has been pretty light because I teach nothing but graduate courses, so I don't have a heavy undergrad teaching appointment like I did when I was at Iowa State. Teaching has been easy to navigate; the courses I teach, the load I teach. Then the service, I've always kept that to a minimum. I guess I have been selfish in that way. When it comes to service, I try to make sure that I serve on committees that have high value, high return on my investment like faculty senate, serving on a provost's search committee, or being on a dean's taskforce. Those types of service committees that really have some cachet to them because you meet people. You make connections and I think people look at those types of service activities more highly than being on a departmental social engagement committee. I think my balance has been pretty good because, again, my teaching appointment has been light because of the graduate courses and my department isn't that big, having a research team where I can divvy things out to students who can lead some activities and then, again, the service component, just not being overburdened with service and just learning to say no.

Marybeth: Thank you. I agree. What issues, as an African American man or African American, in general, did you have to especially consider as you pursued tenure? Do you have advice about what people should look out or prepare for?

Levon: I think what I've learned is that, this is from my perspective as a Black man, there aren't a lot of Black men in the academy. So, what I've learned through my observations and interactions is how Black men are treated in society by White people in general outside of the academy, being treated as an enemy or a threat. I've seen that and felt that being in the academy. I mean, I think I'm pretty good at what I do. I think I and my students have done phenomenal work. I have mostly Black students and to be quite honest, they have performed exceptionally well. My college's administration knows this as well. People across the university recognize it. I also think my department knows it, but they seldom acknowledge it. Frankly, I find this extremely interesting, but I'm not surprised. Hell, it happens to a lot of my Black and brown colleagues across the country, especially those who work at PWIs. I'm well aware of the quality of work that I and my graduate lab put out, but I always find it interesting how my colleagues don't like to acknowledge it. Without question I think this stems from: 1) Being Black, and 2) Being a Black man. I guess there's some parallels between how I've been treated and how people try to position me versus how I'm positioned (as a Black man) in the larger society. That's what I've observed. My students observe it as well. My students and I have talked about it because, again, you normally don't see Black people in general rising to the top in the academy and being acknowledged for their work. You just don't see it that often. So, people are surprised when it does occur and then that's when suppression begins. So, it's amazing how, for example, when I see department heads who elevate the work of White faculty and not that of Black and brown faculty or my students for that matter. What I've learned is that you need to figure out ways to bypass folks who do this. For example, develop strategies and approaches to share your accomplishments so that you are helping to build your brand identity. An example could be something as simple as having a relationship with your college's communication department to put out press releases about awards received, national and international accomplishments, grants received, etc. I've also encouraged my students to do the same. In full disclosure, I've learned some of these strategies when I was on sabbatical at your Center. Simply, what I've learned is that, oftentimes Black and brown faculty just have to go around folks and do their own thing because departments won't do the right thing. What I've learned is that if you elevate a Black faculty member such that they are starting to emerge as a leader or star, it upsets the culture of a department.

Marybeth: Can you share some examples of times when you experienced racism as a pre-tenured faculty member and discuss your strategies for confronting it, if you did?

Levon: When I was at Iowa State, I never had and I would remember it, never had an instance where there was anything overtly racist. You always hear it. I was never treated in a way that I felt like the person was being racist. I know race matters in everything we do, so I understand that. But I never felt as though I didn't receive something because I had a lot of access to opportunities. Again, my department head was just a good dude and my colleagues treated me respectfully. So, I felt good about my time at Iowa State. Now, fast forward to Purdue, there was a case where I was being academically bullied. So, once I caught wind of what was occurring and by whom, I started reaching out to my mentors and trusted colleagues across campus to get advice on what to do and how to navigate my situation. My department head at the time was very supportive of me. He knew what was going on and he was on my side the whole time. To make a long story short, what resulted was me getting my faculty appointment changed. One thing I will say is that even though things worked out for me, having to build my case and show what was being done took a lot of energy and involved a lot of labor. Also, one thing I will add, which goes back to your original question was that there is no doubt in my mind that the academic bullying was tied to race— simply, me being Black. So that was by far the biggest instance where I had to confront and address something related to racism and how I addressed it.

Marybeth: Absolutely. Do you currently experience academic bullying, or do you see it happening to others?

Levon: Yeah. I see it happen to other colleagues and they share with me instances. Again, you've got to think about some of these departments like biochemistry and chemistry, huge departments and you may be the only Black person. So, it's a lot tougher to fight. I have a group of Black students and we've won all of these awards. We've done all of this good work. I'm director of the Mentoring@Purdue (M@P) Program. My students go out and do good work and get very good jobs. One thing I've noticed now that I'm a full professor is that the "game" really changes. What I mean by that statement is that I can ignore a lot of stuff and folks just because. For example, I know this White woman faculty member in another department who gives me advice and she's a full professor. She told me one day, "Levon, I'm a full professor. I don't give two fucks about people. I just do my own thing." Again, this is from a White woman. She goes on to say, "you don't have to deal with a lot of dumb shit anymore. Do what you want to do. Pursue that which interests you. Of course be a good citizen and colleague, but being a full professor affords you a lot more privilege than you realize." So, I've definitely taken that approach to things now and it's kind of liberating and empowering, if you will.

Marybeth: I am glad. How can people prepare for walking into what could be potentially a racist environment for their tenure track time and beyond?

Levon: I think some of these spaces are pretty bad. I think the best thing you can do is to have the support of your department head, although many times it doesn't matter. You can say you have the support of the department head, but at the end of the day your faculty can really make your life miserable even if you have that one person. My advice would be to just understand that it's part of the system. Do good work. Don't compromise your integrity. Never do that. That's number one. Do not compromise your integrity, your truth. You cannot do that, number one, but try to do good work because if you do good work by and large good work gets recognized. I think you would tend to agree with that.

Marybeth: Yeah, I do.

Levon: I try to do good work and I try to make sure when I do my research, the mentoring I do with students, the service when I serve on committees that people have nothing but good things to say about me and the work I do. I think if you can do that, that helps out a lot, but understand that if people have an axe to grind, they're going to grind it anyway. So, you have to be prepared for that and have an exit plan, if it happens. You just have to bow out gracefully. Lucky for me, I've had people at Purdue and beyond who support me who have helped me to navigate the system. I think as a faculty member, as a person of color or Black person coming into these academic spaces, you just have to understand that you're probably going to turn over some rocks and you're going to experience some things that aren't going to be very good and that you won't like. And you just have to go in and just try and do the best work you can,

163

try and identify mentors that you can get good advice from and try to make sure you have support from as many people in the department as possible. Also realize that even if you do all of that, at the end of the day if they don't want you around, they will make your life difficult and they will get rid of you. So, you can do what you can, but at the same time, if they want to get rid of you, they will, or they'll force you out. I exerted a lot of energy over that academic bullying issue. It took a lot of labor to do that, but for me, I knew what they were doing was wrong and I wasn't about to put up with it anymore. So, I just went full throttle and addressed it. Lucky for me that my dean and my department head were on my side. I made it very clear that this is what's happening and I researched academic bullying, read a lot of literature on it. One day I'm going to show you my files. I laid everything out to make it so clear that there was no way people could hide from what I was showing them, no way whatsoever. They couldn't do anything but bite their nails, but it took a lot of work. But for me it was worth it because I proved my case and I've been able to thrive ever since.

Marybeth: Thank you. I like your attitude. How did your mentors help you along the tenure track as you were preparing to go up for tenure? How do you use the support of mentors?

Levon: Yeah. I have so many. I have a lot of people I can rely on, but I have a small circle of folks. For me, when it came to the promotion and tenure process, it's learning the nuances of the system and knowing how things should be interpreted. When I was on faculty senate for example, I was just lucky— we revised the P&T guidelines and that came through the faculty affairs committee that I was chairing. So, I knew what was in the document. I knew what our intentions were behind certain things we put in the document. I'd been meeting with the provost and vice provost. So, when it came time to have my annual reviews and my department head would try to say one thing, I was like no, that's not how that should be interpreted. This is how it is. Again, I was lucky to be in that position, but for me, I had several people who were full professors in other spaces on campus, other department heads who I could rely on and get advice from, who told me how to navigate certain situations. There are a lot of vagaries attached to P&T even though you have senior faculty and administrators who say otherwise. As a result, the system allows people to interpret it however they want. So, what I had to do was to make sure that I talked to people who understood what those nuances in the P&T policies and procedures were, and who would say Levon, this is how you need to interpret it because this is how it's viewed at the university level committee.

Marybeth: Did you ever wonder if you should trust people?

Levon: No, because I do my homework on people before I seek out their help. One of my mentors was a dean, an insanely smart person. I trusted him immensely because he had a track record of getting Black folks and brown folks tenured and promoted, so I trusted him. There were also many others who I leaned on for advice who were outside of Purdue. But the people within Purdue I sought advice from were folks I met while serving on faculty affairs and university senate committees. One other thing I discovered was that after a while, I kept hearing the same things over and over. So, that's kind of how I knew that I was getting sound advice.

Marybeth: Do you have any other advice for people of color or for African Americans more specifically, as they're moving along the tenure process? What should they watch out for, or absolutely make sure to do?

Levon: I think this notion of politics is real in the department. Depending on who you align yourself with gives you access or doesn't give you access. So, you need to learn that politics is real. I really didn't align myself with individuals. I had the support of my department head which matters a lot. I think it's important that Black faculty understand that politics is real and how you align yourself and who you align yourself with matters. I think it takes a lot of work, but you have to always keep one eye open all the time. Again, I think it's okay to close one eye but always keep the other eye open knowing that you can't be too trusting of folks because inevitably many folks, not all folks, but many folks aren't on your side or don't want you to succeed. So, until you can grow to trust people, you have to keep one eye open at all times. I think another thing is just knowing that race matters, that it matters in everything that we do. And, the more successful you are, the more successful the students are that you mentor, the more grants you receive, the more awards you receive, this success will rub people the wrong way. So, there's going to be some resentment (e.g., playing games when it comes to promotion and tenure). You have to be mindful of the politics, and the last thing is you have to have outlets to keep your sanity, whether it be a partner, parents, friends, other family members, etc. You have to have an outlet because if you don't, the politics and pettiness will eat at you. Again, have an outlet, multiple outlets if at all possible. You can't be all work and no play. You just can't sustain yourself that way. I know lots of folks in the academy who are always posting to social media about work. I sometimes question if they have lives outside of work, but that's no business of mine so I just keep it moving.

Marybeth: I know. I don't get it.

Levon: It's all the time.

Marybeth: It's the only thing they know.

Levon: For me, I enjoy relaxing on Saturdays and listening to hip-hop music and just watching sports. That's what I like doing. I love sports. I'm a sports junkie. You just have to have outside interests. You can't always be about trying to get in this journal and trying to get in that journal. That stuff is going to come if you stay in this game long enough. So, you have to keep your sanity and have a balance. You've always got to have a balance. You have to. I think that's the advice I would give. Just know that it's tough being a Black faculty member. It is tough. It's a lot of work, but I can say now that I'm a full professor, that now I've achieved the highest rank you can earn within a university and I can do whatever the hell I want to do within reason and no one can say anything to me. So, for me, it was worth it and I'm glad I got to this point. Now, I can pursue all that I want to do, however I want to do it. So, I think it's worth it, but you have to learn how to navigate the system. You just can't think you can be gangster to the system because the system's not going to let you do that. It ain't going to work. It just won't work.

Marybeth: Say a little bit more about that.

Levon: So, what I mean is that I think many folks think you can just push back against the system. The system just won't allow you to do that. They will make an example of you, as you and I have both seen in the media and in print and so you have to learn how to work within the system. Again, don't compromise your integrity, your truth, but you just can't be out here thinking that you can just be like a cowboy in the wild wild west and you can do what you want to do. It doesn't work like that. You have to know how to balance being a good citizen, but at the same time you have to know that you just aren't going to be bullied and pushed around. You can't let that happen either, so you have to find a good balance so that you're respected for your work. At the end of the day if things aren't working for you, then you need to leave, just like you would leave a relationship. If the relationship is not working for you, you need to leave. I would tell my daughter the same thing. If it's not working, you need to leave. It's just that simple. So, that's kind of how I look at it. You have to learn how to navigate. You have to be like whatever they call the person who steers the ship, the captain. You've got to know how to navigate. You have to know. If you don't know, you need to ask people like yourself and others who can help you.

Marybeth: Is there anything else you want to add?

Levon: I just want to say that I appreciate the opportunity and just know that, like I said before, being Black in the academy is tough, just like it is for you being a woman. It's tough, but I think Black people can make it if we surround ourselves with good mentors and we try to do good work. And also keeping an eye out for things that aren't looking and sounding right and figuring out ways that you can call these things out such that you don't compromise your ability to be promoted and tenured. So, that's what I would say. That's what I would end with.

Guillermina 'Gina' Núñez-Mchiri

Marybeth: How did you decide to become a faculty member?

Gina: It was in the early Nineties. I was recruited as a student leader in the state of California. I represented San Diego State University and I was asked to help be a student leader-consultant to a new university, CSU Monterey Bay. They brought students in and I had an eight-hour delay because there was a storm in San Francisco and so by the time I got in, I was really tired. I'm like who brought us here? What am I doing here? And I saw a man with a T-shirt and it was really late at night and I asked, "Who are you?" He said, "I am Steven Arvizu. I'm the provost." I said, "What is that? I don't know what that is." It was just language in higher education that I didn't know and I said who are you? He got his PhD at Stanford and he was an anthropologist. He had worked with homeless populations. He became homeless for six months to do his participant observation and he had a wife and kids, but he knew that he had to live amongst people to understand the challenges of living in the streets. He told me his story, where he came from, that he was from Bakersfield and was raised in a single mom household. I said, "I've never met anyone like you" and I was really flabbergasted. It turns out that for the students that were advising this university, I was the only Chicana. I was the only woman among students that were flown in. It turns out, I'm from a farm working family and I was actually born in that county where the new university was starting up, in Monterey County. All these things coincided. That's how I inherited or got one of my first academic mentors at that level. And then, Dr. Arvizu brought me in and I was 21-years-old. He said, "What do you do at San Diego State?" I said, "Well, I'm doing my master's in Latin American Studies. I am doing a border studies emphasis and I teach Spanish in the Department of Spanish and Portuguese." He said, "Why don't you come do that for us?" He said "I'll double your salary and we'll get you some paid housing on campus and we'll get you some staff and a computer" and then I was all, "Like what?" It was like Fantasy Island, right? But before that he asked me what do you do in the summers? I said "I'm a farm worker." And he said, "no, really? What do you do in the summers?" I said "I'm a farm worker." There was this awkward pause and I said, "My parents are farm workers, so when I'm not at school, I go home and join them in the fields, so I'm a farm worker. I can't just be home when my parents get up at 3:00 and then to the fields at 5:00, 6:00 in the morning, so I get up, I put on my clothes and I go work the fields." He asked, "Do you have siblings?" I said, "Yeah, there's five of us." He said, "I'm sorry, you have to stop." And then I said, Why?" He said "You've got to break the cycle. You're already a grad student and you're still in the fields. Why should your brothers and sisters finish high school? Why should they go on to college and get a degree if you're still in the fields? You're a grad student and you're still a farm worker?" Then he said, "Why don't you come with me in the summer? Come to campus, help me. We're going to file stuff and organize stuff. We're hiring people, we're building a whole university. We'll find something for you to do." That's how I started with him in the summer and then he asked, "What do you do at San Diego State again?" I said, "I'm doing my master's and I teach Spanish. I teach intro classes." He said, "Why don't you come do that here and help us develop the World Languages Center and Culture Center and help me hire the faculty and help me hire administrators? We're starting from scratch." So the school started. My mom was like, "Why are you leaving us? Why are you leaving so far?" She actually thought I was abandoning my family and tried guilt tripping me about this. Higher education is such a mystery for my family. It's always been like, "We don't know what she does." I heard my mom telling her friends, "She's either really smart or really dumb, because she's always in school!" But being there, being so young and then being surrounded by these amazing scholars, at a brand-new university, was a dream come true. It was an opportunity to start something new and people had so many dreams and expectations for this place. To be 21 years old and to see people like Luis Valdez as my colleague, Amalia Mesa-Bains, who is this amazing artist as my colleague. Judy Baca, who's a muralist, as my colleague was truly amazing. When we had our first faculty orientation, I was there. I was the youngest person in the room with some of these people I had written papers about in college as an undergraduate. I said "I've read about you. I've seen your films." I was so star-struck with some of these individuals, pioneers in their fields, all who had been hired to start something new at CSU Monterey Bay.

Marybeth: Wow. Thank you. I did not know all that about you, that was really interesting! I am curious about your journey to tenure. How did your various identities come into play or shape your experience?

Gina: It is tied to this experience I had at CSU Monterey Bay, because I saw all these people were already in their fifties and sixties. Some were a few years from retiring and they thought that they should do something else of importance before they retired, or as a second leg of their journeys. As a new professor, when I decided to become tenure-track, I would take every workshop possible to learn how to do all this. Higher education has always been a mystery for me. I'm usually signing up for this training and that training. Every step of the way, I always ask where should have I learned this? Where should I have learned to write at the master's or PhD level? Where should I have learned to publish as a faculty member? Where should I have learned to pass the GRE with high scores and get my graduate school fully funded? Where should I have learned how to apply to grad school? Because I didn't have those type of mentors growing up. I didn't have people who said, "This is how you do it. I'm going to help you or give me a copy of your work or your application, and I'll take a look at it." I had to figure all that out by myself. My parents could not help me; we didn't have a computer at home. They didn't speak English. I grew up translating for them. So everything I've learned, I've tried to share. That's why I'm like, "I went to this workshop, let me show you what I learned," or, "I'll give you a talk, or I'll give you a workshop," because I am an avid learner and avid reader, because I've made it a personal mission of mine that anything I learn that will help you, I will share with you. If there's a document on how to publish ... I found a book, *They Say, I Say: The Moves that Matter in Academic Writing*. I copied the back part that gives you these sample sentences. I'm like, that's how they write in academia, because that's not how we talk. And so I scanned that one and I share that with graduate students. I'm like here's some writing prompts on how the academics write. They're like, oh, okay. You know, it's all these tools people have to figure this out, it's like a coded language of power that I hope to unlock and understand.

Marybeth: How have you balanced being a mother and being a faculty member? How did you manage that while you were on the tenure-track?

Gina: Well, it was very challenging, because when I was pregnant, I lost my father and everybody tried to protect me. They said, "You need to come home, because I don't think he's going to make it. Dad's really sick." My dad had gone home to Mexico to see his orchards. He had mango trees and he's like, "I'm going to go see my trees. I'm going to go water my trees, I'll be back," and he never made it back to us. One of my older cousins called, and said, "Hey, so I heard your dad's dead." I was eight months pregnant. My cousin was always on something so when he called me, he hadn't understood that people knew I was pregnant and that they didn't know how to tell me my father had died. I just remember I had to leave to be with my family and trying to get a flight to southern Mexico and then getting to Acapulco and then having someone pick me up and drive me two or three hours into our village. My father had died, and they had a bucket of ice under his body, to try to preserve his body until I arrived. In the United States, you have funeral homes and they use chemicals to preserve corpses. In southern Mexico, in the tropics of the Pacific coast of Mexico, they used a large container with ice to keep the body cool. They were just waiting for me to come home so I could say my goodbyes and I was pregnant. Before that, the ultrasound found that my son had a cleft palate and clubbed feet, so I had told my dad my baby was showing up with some problems. The doctor asked me do you want to go forward with the pregnancy, because you have to be ready, to be willing to be okay with imperfection. I said I worked really hard to try to get things right, but you can't control things like that. So not only was I on the tenure-track, I lost my father, and then I had a premature baby with special needs who had to go into the hospital's intensive care unit for four weeks. Since then, he has gone through so many surgeries, Marybeth, so my need to get tenure was based on my need to have health insurance to pay for surgeries for my child and to try to pay for the house. There were many times where I was really in a struggle, wondering am I going to pay for the house or pay for the surgery? I remember thinking, I'm tenure-track, I have insurance, but there's no way I can pay for all those bills. We had this small little house in Santa Teresa, New Mexico right next to El Paso, TX. I just remember, oh my God, being invited to contribute to a book, and someone saying to me if you don't get your chapter in by this time, you're out of the book. Here I was writing, while holding my baby, just trying to figure out how to carry the baby and trying to feed him, he needed special feeding equipment, because I couldn't just latch him on to my breasts to feed him. I had to pump my milk and use special bottles. I had to put him to sleep or just rock him close by me, so I could write. Those were like the darkest times of my life, just trying to write. I needed to get published, because I needed to get tenure and it was brutal. It was 2009, Adam was born in 2007. Around 2008,

2009, the economic recession hit. My husband lost his job. He was on the job market for a year and he applied and applied and applied. He was not an academic, so here I was, basically a single provider of my household with a child with special needs, having a series of surgeries for his cleft lip and cleft palate. From zero to three, he had a team of therapists coming to my house. I taught Tuesdays and Thursdays. So that Mondays, Wednesdays, Fridays, and Saturdays, I would have therapists at my house, helping my son so he could eat, so he could walk, so he could function as a human being and I was on the tenure-track. Right? And so all those things, when you're holding onto a kid with special needs, you're not going to spend a lot of time doing other things, because my major goal was getting him to function and to eat and to be well. Zero to three. At the age of three, no more early child intervention, they cut you off and that's it. There I was with a special needs kid at age three, with no more support until he could go to school, so I would take him to campus daycare. Campus daycare was critical to me, because we had no family in El Paso, so I would drive him to campus daycare. I played Spanish children's music, so he could learn some Spanish on the way to daycare. I'd check in with him during the day, every little break I would get, I'd check in on my kid to see if he was eating. He had a lot of challenges cause of his cleft palette, throwing up, screaming because he had acid reflux and other complications. That's it. I just remember these are my days as a tenure-track professor and a mother with a special needs child and working really hard to publish and to get things in. I just didn't have the luxury to ponder over how to do it. I had to figure things out, figure how to get things published, figure how to turn in my work. I did publish and I think having to tell my story, I remember I did ask for a one-year stop on the tenure clock when he was born, but I don't think I ever stopped working, because I couldn't. I never stopped working because I just couldn't afford it. I just said I might need a little bit more time. I think I might need it just because he's had, I think he had 11 surgeries the first three years of his life, I had to be in intensive care with him and I kept on teaching. I would say to a friend, here, take care of my baby for a little bit. Let me go teach my class, I'll be right back after I teach and have my office hours. I would take him to conferences between birth and age two. I would, at times where daycare wouldn't take him, I said, "You know I have a kid, so either I bring him with me and he sits next to me, or I cancel class." I'll just have him next to me. A lot of times I felt at a crossroad trying to figure what to do if he had thrown up, or if he had a fever, or something like that. I wouldn't expose him or my students if he was sick, I had to always assess what do I do? What do I do? Because my husband is out there looking for a job. I had no one to leave him with. I can't just leave him with a neighbor. It was really hard, because I didn't, we didn't know anyone in this region. Now we've been here for 15 years, but initially, when you have a special needs kid, it's kind of hard for someone to take care of your kid and once daycare says he's sick, we can't take him, you just have to stay home and figure it out. I think that's why I was always thinking figure it out, figure it out, and just keep on going. My kid has gone to conferences with me, gone to class with me, he has spent summers in the office with me. So when I saw you Marybeth, traveling with your daughter, I smiled. People might say why is she traveling with her daughter? We're like, well, because that's our kid and our children are a part of who we are. I can't, like right now I'm in Zoom meetings or Microsoft Teams meetings and there's a kid in the background and they're like your kid does cameos. Well, yeah, he sits behind me. And sometimes I say this is a personal issue I have to address. Can you please wait for me outside and I'll call you back in, but this child, he's 13 years now, he's a teenager and he's always been with me in everything I do. Sometimes I say I have to finish this chapter and he won't sleep. It's okay, I'll be here with you mama, or I can see the light and I can't sleep, you know? So sometimes you have to close the computer and then put your kid to sleep and then get up again. That's how I have done it. I have very thin hair. I think it comes with stress, the weight, and the thinning of your hair. The women in my family have very thin hair. We have curly thin hair, so I know it's not just me. But I know that the stress of the academy of course is going to add the high cortisol levels and into the stress levels of everyday. When I was pregnant, they told me either you lose weight or this baby might not come. I did my Zumba lessons and I would dance. I was the biggest pregnant lady in the class. I'd take some of my dance classes and when I walk in, people call me and say, "You are like a healthy gordita (big girl)." Could I be a healthy big girl? I eat salads every day. I go for walks. I take dance classes, because I need to be well, to be around. I've worked too hard to be here and then to be sick. Diabetes runs in my family and so I was gestational diabetic when I was pregnant and I lost 40 pounds. I had cheese sticks and other protein snacks like peanuts and almonds. I'm like let me know what I need to do to be well and to be alive, because I want to be a mom with a PhD. Because I am a mom, we now have a mama PhD group that another friend and I have kept going. I gather the mama PhDs and say what do you need? What do y'all need? Because I know what it is to be a mom of a child, of an infant and not have any people here to help me. So now, because I've gone through that, I offer to be a point of support or a point of reference to other mothers in the academy.

Marybeth: Do you feel like you have encountered sexism during the tenure-track process?

Gina: Well, I was in a meeting and there was a man, senior professor, who consistently cut off women and a woman senior professor would always fight with him. She would send me a note. Look, every time a woman speaks, he cuts her off. He interrupts me, he interrupted you. But I went through a conflict resolution session. I went a couple of days, they hired Meggin McIntosh to give us a training. She came in and taught us using the book by Susan Scott, *Fierce Conversations*, so this is where I learned about the importance of writing down what is the issue, the causes, the consequences, my contribution to it, and how I wanted to see the issue resolved. So, then I wrote a script and then when I saw him in the mailroom, I knew exactly what I needed to say. I didn't confront him in a meeting. I didn't confront him in front of faculty. I was tenure-track, so when you are on the tenure track you're so afraid of causing conflict or picking sides. People would pick fights in our department and then they would ask me at the copy machine, "Whose side are you on?" I'd respond, "I'm tenure-track. I do not comment. Do not get me involved in your problems, because I need my job. I can't get involved with this stuff. I'm tenure-track." People huffed and puffed, and then they would walk back out without me taking sides. So here I was on the tenure track, taking on the senior professor, who's going to vote on my tenure. I said, "I don't know if you realize this, but every time women speak, you interrupt them and I'm not going to speak for them, but I will speak for myself." I said, "I don't know why you want us to be in meetings, if you don't respect what we have to say. If you think that I'm so stupid and that I have nothing to offer, then why did you hire me?" I used a script and I practiced it. I said, "Next time I'm in a meeting with you and I have something to say, I'd appreciate if you don't cut me off. Let women speak and don't make us feel like we're stupid by interrupting us and completing our sentences. Of course I haven't read all the books you have. I'm just starting. You're already a senior professor. I don't know everything you know." I said, "I don't like it when you make me feel stupid. I don't appreciate it."

Before this, I just didn't have the tools. I would go home or I'd go to the office and cry. I would say to myself, next time I'm going to stand up for myself, next time I am going to defend myself. Next time, I'm not going to stay quiet. I would be angry. I didn't know how to stand up for myself, but I also knew I felt vulnerable. That day, I stood my ground. I used my script and I said, "The next time I speak you don't interrupt me. Good day, sir." You know, that was a watershed moment. I now give that workshop on conflict resolution. I'm really happy. It's based on a book, *Fierce Conversations*, and I give credit to the author Susan Scott for teaching me this. I said I went to this training on how to address conflict and how to defend yourself, just do it on the issue that matters. Don't throw the book at them, because then it overwhelms them and they think you complain about everything. But you know, when you don't have the skill set or you don't feel the entitlement, you just do your job and you end up with shitty jobs, because you have to get paid to pay the bills. Right? And then later on, not that my job, or my institution has been bad, it's just I've done a lot of things now and now I know that I can say yes to this and I can say no to that. Now I'm an administrator/faculty and I'm down to one course for my teaching load, but I'm still doing research. I'm still involved on campus and so it's a very different situation that I'm in, but I've already been through all of those things to know better and to feel stronger.

Marybeth: If you had to give three pieces of advice to a young Latina professor on the tenure track, what would they be? What three pieces of advice would you give?

Gina: I'm an anthropologist, I know how to do ethnography. I know how to do interviews. I can transcribe and code with or without technology and that allows me to create knowledge. A lot of people come out of their graduate programs, some have really good methods and experience in producing knowledge and getting it into publication. Others have not, so I think my advice starts in grad school. Take all the methods classes you can take so that you can have the keys to produce knowledge in the future. Find good mentors, apprentice yourself. Say, "What are you working on? How can I help you?" I remember walking into a professor's office and saying, "What do you need help with?" He laughed, and said, "I actually have two or three hundred dollars left over from a grant. Can you help me organize my office?" I said, "Yes, sir, like, of course." He asked me to separate extra copies of the same books. I kept his signed copies of originals and an extra clean copy. If I found three or four copies of the same book, I put these aside in piles. When I was done cleaning his office, he said to me, "Do you want those books?" I said, "Yes, sir." I walked out with piles of books that this really super-famous professor gave me and people were like how the hell did you do that? I said I came and I said, "Do you need help with anything that I might help you with?" I always needed money in graduate school. I went up to a feminist scholar and I said, "Do you have any clothes that you don't use?" She's like "I have two bags in the trunk that I was going to get rid of." I said, "Because you have suits. I like your style. You dress really nice. I just don't have the clothes that you have to go to classes or to conferences with." She had two bags in her trunk. I go up to people and say, "Do you have any thing that I can learn or that I can help you with?" You can ask people you admire, "What are you working on that I can help you with so I can learn?" So I can gain something and then I'm helping while also benefiting myself from this exchange. So as grad students, a lot of people were like, "Nope, that's not my area. No, it's not my field, so I am not interested in that book you are suggesting I read." I would say, "Stay open, because your area of research and interest might change." Your field is constantly evolving, so stay open to knowledge and then if you come onto a campus that offers you workshops, that offers you faculty development, take them. Take them because your pedagogy has to be strong. Your research has to be strong. Your publication record has to be strong. You can't just say I'm just a researcher. I don't care about my classes, because if you have bad evaluations, why should they keep you? They'll hire someone else that's better. And build relationships with your students and build relationships with senior colleagues. Those people have to vote on your tenure. Right? Learn your field and develop your track record in your field, because you're going to have to send out your whole package to people in your field who can vouch that you're making valuable contributions to your field.

Marybeth: How did you manage service?

Gina: I didn't know, at the time I actually ended up under-reporting a lot of my service, because I was afraid I was going to get dinged for doing a lot of service. Someone pointed this out to me by saying well you're not reporting all of your service. I had not, because I feared that I would be critiqued by the men in my department for doing too much service, so I felt like I had to under-report it and then I had to go back and fill this information in my CV and my tenure package. I know I do a lot. I know I do a lot for my institution and beyond, but everything I did for a reason. I did one of those leadership trainings offered one year and the question that was posed to me is how do you successfully integrate research, teaching, and service? For me, it became like I don't know, I just do. So that question became a challenge for me, so I said okay, I'm gonna figure it out and then I'm going to give you a workshop. So now I have a workshop on how to successfully integrate research, teaching, and service. Every person that faces a challenge has to figure this out. So that is what I do, once I figure it out, I'm going to come and tell you and show how I did it. Then you can ask me to do a workshop for you and then we can figure stuff out. People are like, "How the hell did you do that?" Because I do service learning. I incorporate undergrads, master's and PhD students in my research. We co-author together and those students get back to me and let me know how they have benefitted from these experiences. One student said, "I co-authored with you and that article helped me get into Loyola. I got into a master's. I got into a PhD. I got into law school. I'm a professor." I'm like, you see you learn by doing. So for new faculty, don't be afraid of saying yes to some things. You cannot say yes to everything, but if it's going to add value to your skill set, if it's going to help you produce in your field, if it's going to help you bring someone else under your wing and teach them how, then don't skimp on that. I've invested in so many people over the 15 years I've been at UTEP. If I can help you, I will help you and if I need help, I trust in the Lord that people will respond to my call for help, because they know that it's usually not for me. It's for someone in greater need than us.

Marybeth: Absolutely. I believe that, too. I have always believed that if you help other people, normally you do not have to worry about too much.

Gina: I have done research that integrates my social justice work. I've written about trauma among Central American refugees. Everything that I write about becomes like my life and becomes my research and becomes my pedagogy, it's about integration. So the key nugget here is to integrate your research, teaching, and service to the maximum capacity. If you're going to say yes to something, it's because you're going to be able to document it on your tenure-track file. If not, you're going to probably have to say I can't do this right now, but know, because we're a community, we represent communities of color, the community comes asking for a lot of stuff.

So you might say I can't right now, let me see if my students can help me. So when the community comes knocking, you don't have to be the only one responding. You can say let me see if my students can help, or let me see if my other colleagues can help, because there's no way I could do everything for all immigrants, or for every nonprofit, or for all these causes I care about. I cannot be on every board. I cannot be everywhere, so I have to be very strategic. The word is you have to be very strategic with your time and your energy, or you will collapse and it's not worth it. It's not worth having a heart attack before you get tenure. I find a lot of people, once they get tenure, they're angry. There's all these hoops we have to go through. We have to go out there to prove ourselves worthy of being in the academy and I don't want us to lose our health or our soul in that process.

Marybeth: Are there any other things that you want to share? Any advice?

Gina: Well, I think it's important to have boundaries. When are you going to write? Have appointments with yourself. Sometimes we put other people ahead of our needs, so just find out what I need to teach my classes. I need to have time to prepare. I also need time to have a family, I need time to rest. That's the hardest thing, you're on survival mode for five years, you have to show everything. Everything you do, you have to document, have a digital copy and a hard copy. The hardest thing is keeping track of everything. I know I do so much and the hardest thing at the end of the year is trying to count everything I've done, because I forget. I'm like, oh yeah, I did that. Oh yeah, I did that. Oh yeah, I've done that. But if I don't keep a good accounting system, I will likely under-report it. And I know I under-report, people don't understand how I get things done. They're like you're one person. How can you possibly do all this? Well, I do. I do. I've done monologues, performances, and community theater. Last year, we did public presentations on how to do theater to address gender-based violence and my husband said to me really, you have nothing else to do? Now you're doing theater? I'm like, yeah. We find out that if you talk to people in community settings, you can get through to them. And if they invite you, they want to hear what you have to say and I don't have to do it alone. So bring in some fun, bring in the arts, bring in some joy, do things together with your friends and your students. Dance, I do Zumba. I love to dance. I have a happy hour group. I have a happy hour group I started a long time ago and there were people outside of my field. It's so cool to have friends outside of your own profession, your own field, to have friends that are non-academics. I have mom friends too. Develop different support groups that you need to survive, whether it's your faith community, your religious, your cultural community or people with affinities, people who also have small kids or kids in the age range similar to yours that you could do play dates with. And then, I knew that for me, going home was part of my survival. My family is in California, so in the summers, winters, and spring I go home. My degree, my title, everything kind of gets hung up at the door and they're like, okay, she's home. She's going to take care of meals now. She's gonna help us take care of mom. Now, I get to switch roles and say I'm a daughter, I'm a sibling. I'm an aunt. I'm a mom, I'm a wife. These other roles matter. Sometimes we put the academy before our family. I've seen colleagues who never found time to find a partner or have children and time has gone by. You know, we live once, so we have to think about what's important to us and there's never a perfect time to have a child. If you want to be a mother, then be a mom and know we will figure it out. We will figure it out. We're not the first and the last ones to have children in the academy. Kids need to be held. They get sick. They throw up on you. I walked into my class with boogers on my lapel. My students pointed this out, I had something on my clothes. Oh, yes, I'm like they are probably my child's boogers, I was carrying my baby into daycare before coming to class.

Marybeth: Boogers are a good look.

Gina: That's real. But being a mom has helped me be more empathetic to working moms with children and working class students with kids. They'll say my kid got sick. I've got to go. All right, we'll catch up later. I'll send you an email. I have this tool called Personal Interest and Commitment Form. I ask my students to give me their emails and their phone number if I need to get ahold of them. I ask, "What are your career goals and interests? What's your schedule like? How many jobs do you have?" That is like the first thing, that's the first assignment every single one of my students turns in to me, because it allows me to get to know them as human beings, as complex human beings. And then I incorporate that in how I'm going to deal with assignments or schedules. That student is working long hours so I extend my deadline times to 11:59 pm instead of 5 pm. Right after the El Paso shooting of August 3rd, I had a student who was working as a security officer at Walmart. Her hours went up. She said to me, "I'm a security officer, they're calling me in." I said "all right, you go take care of security, come back and then we'll figure things out." Or someone will say, "Dr. Nunez, my kid got sick." And I say, "You go take care of your kid, come back, and then we'll just figure this out." That's what matters more. Not whether you took the test on time, or submitted the paper by 5:00 PM. I don't even have 5:00 PM deadlines any more. My deadlines are 11:59. Just get it done. My students, many work 9:00 to 5:00 and they just need a couple more hours to come home, feed their kids, get something to eat themselves, and then turn in their work. So I think being human and seeing others with humanity comes first, and then everything else will follow. You can tell when we have graduate seminars or workshops and students worry about how to prove themselves in the academy. I have found that students want to know that you care about them, that you are invested in their success as human beings, not just on their grades. Now, out of the blue, I get unexpected emails. Out of the blue, like I was recently in an episode of Taste of the Nation [a Hulu food show hosted by Padma Laskshmi], and I found my last roommate. Her name is very common, Maria Garcia. I'm like, "How will I ever find a Maria Garcia in California?" I said, "I Googled you. I've looked for you Maria 'Sisi' Garcia and could not find you for the life of me," she laughed and laughed. She contacted me. She says "I saw you on TV and I realized you were my roommate and I needed to connect with you again because I have missed you." I have had so many friends and former students email me saying you saved me a plate, you were kind to me, and this kept me in school when I thought I could not do this anymore.

[During our interview, Gina's son came in with a new song he had composed on her cell phone with the use of an app. He interrupted her to share his song with her.]

Gina: You made this up? (Asking her son.)

Gina's Son Adam: Yeah, I made a song.

Gina: You made a song? That's beautiful. Can you give me five minutes and then I'll hear it? Wait for me.

Gina: It wasn't until I was tenured that I said, can I teach a class I want to teach now? And I taught the Anthropology of Food and Culture because I love food and my research was with farm working communities in the Hatch Valley of

185

southern New Mexico where the famous green and red chile comes from. I never thought that as a big girl I could seriously study food. I do ethnography and I study political ecology, housing, immigration, social justice, but once I got tenure, I'm like I want to teach my own class now. In a regular semester, this class doubles in size, because my students like to bring a guest to the class. I asked, "How come there's so many people in the class?" Well, "I brought my co-worker. I brought my husband. I brought my kid. I brought my friend." They want to be in the class because they're learning about food, culture, gender, and society. Everybody eats so this brings us togethers. I also have food demos and I invite food scholar friends that come and do demos and we will do food tastings. We meet at restaurants and take cooking lessons there. We have potlucks at the end of the semester and if someone is pregnant, then for sure we're going to do a baby shower for her, because that is what I love to do and that is what we do in my culture. I bring in my love for my students, my love for community and love of food and culture into my classes and so no class is ever the same. No class is ever boring and at the end of the day, there are memories, students who remember you and will say, "You did a baby shower for me. I lost my baby later on and that was the kindest thing someone ever did for me." And I'm like, "Oh, I'm glad you remembered and I am glad that was meaningful." You don't know how you're going to touch people's lives. They often don't remember the books they read. They don't remember the tests they took. They remember that I taught them how to interview their grandma and that they kept a recording of their grandmother and they'll always be able to hear her voice. That's what I do. I teach them how to do ethnography and how to be the storytellers of our community. Once I teach them skills to create new knowledge and to document their people's stories, nobody can unteach them that. Once I teach them how to become social scientists, how to be critical thinkers, critical writers, how to care for their communities, and how to give back, there is no going back. I integrate community engagement in every single one of my classes. My students have done something of value for their community and I trust that once they graduate, they will be people of value and people of action. I teach them that education is not just learning how to pass an exam or write a paper, but it's to care for others, to make their skills come to life by being of service to the communities we're a part of. I've been doing that for 15 years, that's thousands of students, that's thousands of community hours. There's a ripple effect of impact there, that I hope people will remember.

Marybeth: Absolutely. Thank you so much. I really, really appreciate your spending an hour with me.

Notes

1   Jada Pinkett Smith used the word "entanglement" to describe an affair she had while married to Will Smith.

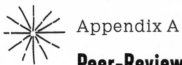

Appendix A

Peer-Reviewed Journal Matrix

	Top Tier	General Discipline-Based Journals
	Top Tier	Sub-Discipline-Based Journals
	Second Tier	General Discipline-Based Journals
	Second Tier	Sub-Discipline-Based Journals
	Third Tier	General Discipline-Based Journals
	Third Tier	Sub-Discipline-Based Journals

Note: Ask your department chair or dean, which journals in your field fit into each of these categories and what the tenure expectations are across the categories. Also, encourage your colleagues to fill in the matrix above together so that you have an idea of what they value in the area of research. Remember, they will be voting on your tenure.

Appendix B
Books on Writing

Clark, R. (2008). *Writing tools: 55 essential strategies for every writer*. Little Brown Spark.

Germano, B. (2013). *From dissertation to book*. University of Chicago Press.

Goldberg, N., & Cameron, J. (2016). *Writing down the bones: Freeing the writer within*. Shambhala.

Goodson, P. (2016). *Becoming an academic writer: 50 exercises for paced, productive, and powerful writing*. Sage Publications.

Hanika, T. (2017). *Writer's workbook: A personal planner with tips, checklists, and guidelines*. CreateSpace Independent Publishing platform.

Harman, E. (2003). *The thesis and the book: A Guide for first-time academic authors*. University of Toronto Press.

Janzer, A. (2016). *The writer's process: Getting your brain in gear*. Cuesta Park Consulting.

King, S. (2020). *On writing: A memoir of the craft*. Simon & Schuster.

Koppelman, H. (2020). *The gifts of writing: Exploring the mystery, magic, and wonder of the creative process*. Hope Koppelman.

Lamott, A. (1995). *Bird by bird: Some instructions on writing and life*. Anchor.

Sheldon, S. (2019). *Academic writing genres: Essays, reports, & others genres*. Evident Press.

Soles, D. (2009). *The essentials of academic writing*. Wadsworth Publishing.

Sword, H. (2012). *Stylish academic writing*. Harvard University Press.

Syme, B. (2019). *Dear writer, you need to quit*. Hummingbird Books.

Zinsser, W. (2006). *On writing well: The classic guide to writing non-fiction*. Harper Perennial.

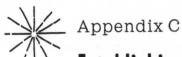

Appendix C

Establishing a Center or Institute

In 2014, long after achieving tenure, I established a national center. I am often asked how to do this by scholars across all ranks. The first thing I caution is, "be careful what you wish for." Having a center or institute may sound prestigious, but it is an incredible amount of work, especially if it is more than a website and a bookshelf in your faculty office. Having a center or institute changes the nature of your work and your relationship with your institution. I cannot stress this enough. It can also create jealousies and issues with your colleagues who are not successful in creating their own centers. If faced with the decision again, despite the significant success and impact of the center I established (and the subsequent institute), I would probably choose not to do it—although I am not 100% sure about that. Let me explain.

I began planning the center in 2012, a full two years prior to opening it. My first step was to create a vision to share with trusted colleagues, who provided me with feedback that helped shape the work agenda and facilitated a better understanding of similar centers. I also shared it with my dean Andy Porter, who was very supportive, but encouraged me to think through my plans for eventually closing or leaving the center. Given that I had not yet opened a center, I definitely had not thought about when I would close it. I thought his comment was odd; however, since then, I have realized it was an important point. I will elaborate as I continue. Next, I secured a mentor who had successfully launched a center, a faculty member in the Wharton School at Penn. He was kind and gracious about sharing his journey as well as the challenges he had faced. I began reaching out to funders who had supported me and my work in the past to ask if they would support the center I envisioned. I was able to get a planning grant from a foundation to think through the idea. I spent this time assembling an advisory group of scholars and practitioners; began writing grant proposals for signature center projects; and started thinking about staffing and support needs. During this thinking time, I was also able to prepare for the launch of the center. My strategy was to apply for several large grants and use these funds to support a small staff. Based on hard work and past relationships with funders, I was able to secure the necessary funding to open the center and to demonstrate that I was serious.

In 2014, in the middle of one of the worst snow storms in Philadelphia, the Penn Center for Minority Serving Institutions hosted its grand opening. When we started, I imagined the center as a research center only and had not considered the impact we could have programmatically. After its first year, I was ready to hire more staff, including a program coordinator. By 2015, I had four staff members in place—an operations coordinator, a program coordinator, a part-time communication coordinator, and an administrative assistant. I also had several PhD students working <u>with</u> me. Today, in 2021, after six years and having moved from Penn to Rutgers, the center has a Director for Operations and Strategy, a Director for Programs and Communication, an Associate Director for Assessment and Research, a program coordinator, an assistant director for operations, a finance coordinator, and a communications coordinator. We also have PhD students, post-docs, visiting scholars, and interns. This growth may sound exciting, but it is also a constant sources of stress because I have to raise money to support all of these individuals and the work we do together. If this is not the kind of stress you want in your life, I beg you to stick to your traditional faculty role. I am still a faculty member, but I have a reduced course load, supported by grants, in order to lead a center and institute. In addition, if you are not good at motivating and managing people, please do not open a center, and honestly, if you are me-focused—as many faculty are—you cannot open a center. A center or institute is about *team* work—if you cannot come to terms with this fact, move on to something else. If you can embrace team work and use the word "we" instead of "I," you will be fine.

One of the secrets of the academy is that most "centers" and "institutes" exist without physical space. They are online through a website or someone's faculty office. Why? Because space is coveted and expensive on college and university campuses and people rarely give it to faculty to open a center. At Penn, I had an agreement that if my indirect costs were equal to at least one-half of the rental costs, the school of education would pay the balance. I was able to honor this agreement during my time at the institution. This agreement was not public, because Penn is a private university with behind-closed-doors, negotiated deals based on retention offers, etc. However, I was comfortable talking about the agreement I had with the dean. Rent was expensive and all of my indirect cost monies went to cover it; if they had not, I would not have had the space. I received about 1.5% of my indirect cost monies back each year in a small fund. If your institution is willing to let you keep the indirect costs monies in your grants, you will have an easier time finding and paying for space. Please note that space is always at a premium and if you are renting space, other people will regularly want that space and may try to move you out of it. This happened to me on several occasions. If you do not want to get involved in space issues, I suggest sticking to a website or your faculty office. Just make sure you are upfront with people about what your "center" or "institute" really is.

Depending on the size of your center and workload, you may or may not have a staff. If you do, you need to get supervisory training immediately, because your role as a faculty member will immediately change from one of advising students and working with a shared administrative assistant, to one in which you are responsible for human resources policies and their implementation. If you are not interested in this role, do not start a center. As a center director, you will have to manage personalities, staff members who dislike each other, and the day-to-day work of all staff members. Eventually, you will master this, but it takes time, and most faculty have little experience in this area. My best advice is to become familiar with human resources policies and to get a friend in the department. When I started the center at Penn, no one advised me on this matter, and human resources and faculty rarely interacted. Things have changed in recent years but you have to prepare yourself for any situation. As a faculty member, there is a power differential between you and staff members and students. Be careful with that power. Be cognizant of how it is viewed and be aware that you are in a vulnerable position when you supervise people.

If your center or institute focuses on research, you need a research team. You cannot produce all the research by yourself. While there are many professors who run centers alone from their office, that is not what I am talking about here. To produce good work regularly, you need a team. My team was and is made up of three groups of people—PhD students, postdocs, and visiting scholars. Occasionally, I include master's students, but they must have the maturity level and commitment required to do the highest quality work. If you create a research team, you must lead them. Your research productivity will increase, but so will the time that will devote to mentoring. Moreover, you must constantly consider equity issues among the team and decide how to leverage the strengths of the various team members. Most importantly, you must spread the opportunities around. One of the most disheartening and disturbing trends I see in the academy is the faculty member, who leads a center, taking all of the credit for the work. You cannot be first author all the time, you have to learn to say "we" and ensure that everyone on your team has a chance to shine.

Another aspect of having a center that is not obvious at first is that you need superb communications and technology support. When we first opened, I did all of the communications—for exactly six months. After that, I could not keep up and hired a part-time communications specialist. Six years later, we have a Director for Programs and Communications, a communications assistant, and two interns working on communications. We have grown from a few social media posts, a website, a blog, and one or two reports a year to having a full-scale communications arm—with podcasts, Twitter chats, four social media channels that are updated throughout the day, videos, op-eds, research briefs, reports, infographics, an 8000-person distribution list, webinars, and much more (and that is just our center, I am also now leading an institute). If you want to communicate on a large scale, you must invest in staff and the various technologies to support it. When we started, I had no idea that I would be buying tech programs including Zencaster for podcasts, SoundCloud for audio, and In Design for graphic design. I assumed I would be purchasing software for qualitative and quantitative research—which I do—but in order to communicate on a large scale, you have to expand and learn new things constantly.

The biggest change for me since opening a center—and I am still not sure I like it—is how my work changed drastically. When I was only a faculty member, I taught, attended meetings, and conducted research. I spent days behind closed doors in my office or at home, in yoga pants and a tank top, writing. I still do that twice a week. However, the other three days are filled with meetings, phone calls, team brainstorming sessions, and fundraising to support the staff and our work. I love what I do but my life as a faculty member is not the norm in any way. If you are not prepared for this change, do not do it. You will fail, and you will hate it. If you are disorganized, selfish, or lack patience, please do not open a center. You will hate it. To lead a center, you must be able to balance large amounts of work, be comfortable with public speaking, be willing to be very active on social media, be willing to speak regularly to the media, be comfortable with the constant stress of raising money, and be comfortable with people talking about you in the public domain. You are no longer just you doing your professor role; you are taking on a much larger enterprise. Each day I ask myself if starting our center was worth it. Yes, we have done some incredible work and have had an impact on so many, but if I want to stop it and shut it down, how does that work?

Appendix D

Sample Tenure Essay

Statement of Academic Research and Publication Plans

Marybeth Gasman
University of Pennsylvania

The story behind this photograph captures the overarching themes in my research. In 1944, the United Negro College Fund (UNCF) asked John D. Rockefeller Jr., a long-time philanthropist to Black education, to publicly show his support for the fledging organization. With the passing of the token dollar from little girl to billionaire, the UNCF hoped to demonstrate that African Americans were giving to their own—that they were the agents of change in their own education. The paradox of this scenario, that Black people should "give to their own" by turning over their hard-earned cash to a White industrialist, begins to make sense when one considers the history of Black colleges and their control by White interests.

What was not intended in this photograph was the positioning of the child on Rockefeller Jr.'s lap. Young Marietta Dockery was frightened by the flash of the cameras and

Rockefeller Jr., a grandfather himself, instinctively pulled her up to comfort her. The photos that were captured made the front pages of newspapers throughout the country and spurred an angry backlash from Whites over what appeared to be a breach of racial etiquette. In his response to critics, Rockefeller Jr. was careful to indicate that he was in no way advocating for social equality, just showing the importance of thrift and self-help. From our perspective, it is ironic that the public's ire was directed against Rockefeller Jr.'s holding of the girl, since the dollar was the real culprit. The same dollar would support the Black colleges that educated the leadership of the nascent Civil Rights Movement, forever demolishing the walls of legalized segregation and settling the question about who may sit on whose lap. This photograph marked a watershed moment in the relationships between African Americans and White philanthropy—a moment in which issues of control, philanthropic influence, public perception, and racial equality were being renegotiated. That renegotiation continues in the present day.

My interest is in the study of higher education from a broad perspective, with special attention to African Americans, philanthropy, and issues of access and equity. By examining historical and current manifestations, my research brings the evolving picture of race, philanthropy, and education to the fore. I have concentrated my research in three areas: the history of Black colleges, current issues facing African American higher education, and philanthropy. By and large, when I conduct research, I use historical methods to examine archival papers, new and existing oral history interviews, photographs, advertisements, newspapers, etc.[1] To explore contemporary research questions, I use various qualitative methods, including individual interviews, document analysis, open-ended surveys, and media analysis. This essay will describe my completed projects and my future research trajectory.

Philanthropy and African American higher education are two distinct subjects, yet they overlap in very specific ways. From its beginning, philanthropy has been a driving force behind American higher education.[2] For African Americans, however, the dilemmas surrounding the funding of Black colleges have been particularly acute. The leaders of Black colleges grappled with whether they should cooperate with or shun White involvement in and financial support of their institutions.[3] Rather than acquiescing to the will of White philanthropists, some Black college leaders chose to cultivate giving among their own people, often paying a heavy price for their independence. Although this freedom came at a cost, it also spawned a legacy of African American philanthropy.[4]

The majority of my research pertains to historically Black colleges and universities. These institutions, which were primarily established after the Civil War, have been and continue to be a driving force in the lives of African Americans. Prior to *Brown v. Board of Education* (1954), they were, apart from the rare exception, the only educational option for Black people. Yet, more than 50 years after *Brown*, Black colleges still enroll 16 percent and graduate 20 percent of all African American undergraduates. Moreover, the majority of African Americans who go on to attend graduate and professional schools receive their undergraduate degrees at Black colleges.[5] For example, Xavier University of Louisiana sends more Black students to medical school than any other institution in the country, including Harvard.[6] Likewise, Bennett and Spelman colleges, both small African American women's institutions, educate over 50 percent of the Black women who enter doctoral programs in the sciences.[7] Because Black colleges are vital to African American access to higher education and because they have enriched the nation's intellectual life and society at large, it is important that we know their history.

Beyond the details of their founding and operation, I am interested in Black colleges because they are rich examples of African American agency and the ability of Black people to develop, in the midst of a racially divided society, their own approach to undergraduate and graduate education. Much of my work is focused on the post-World War II era, with Cold War and civil rights struggles serving as an historical backdrop. As the nation freed itself from the shackles of legalized segregation, Black college campuses changed, sometimes becoming havens for progressive ideas and Black-focused curricula. At the same time, in an era when Black people were *legally* able to attend historically White institutions, critics began to question the need for Black colleges. To this day, the same issues are raised in relation to these historic institutions: the desire for a more Black-focused, supportive curricula and environment on the one hand, and the disdain for a group of institutions that are seen as the poor stepchildren of segregation on the other.

Research on the History of Black Colleges

The first strand of my research examines the history of Black colleges. I am interested in the social dynamics and power struggles in philanthropic relationships within these institutions. My initial inquiries into this topic focused on the life of sociologist and Fisk University president Charles Spurgeon Johnson (covered in *Charles S. Johnson. Leadership beyond the Veil in the Age of Jim Crow*, co-authored with Patrick J. Gilpin).[8] Examining Johnson enabled me to address my research interests using his life as a lens. In this book, I explored the efforts of an African American intellectual to broker race relations during an era of Jim Crow, cultivate cultural and artistic talent during the Harlem Renaissance, and most importantly, counter the racist mythology of intellectual inferiority by creating an authentic African American center for research and scholarship at Fisk University (an historically Black institution). In order to accomplish his goals, Johnson had to navigate the often treacherous waters of a White-dominated philanthropic world. This book received favorable reviews in both the *Journal of American History* and the *Journal of Southern History*. I also published several articles related to Johnson that explored issues and questions not covered in the book, including Black colleges and international relations, African American intellectual rivalry, and the use of modern art in campus curricula.[9] Each of these articles provides an understanding of the various strategies Johnson employed while president of Fisk University to chip away at American racism.

Recently, my areas of interest, including Black colleges, fundraising, and philanthropy, intersected in a book entitled *Envisioning Black Colleges: A History of the United Negro College Fund* (UNCF).[10] This book builds upon my previous one in that it broadens the exploration of the social dynamics of philanthropy and fundraising. Etched into the American consciousness by the phrase "A Mind is a Terrible Thing to Waste," the UNCF's fundraising effort on behalf of Black colleges is perhaps the quintessential expression of African Americans helping their own. Yet the reality is much more complicated. My research interrogates the notion of the UNCF as a Black-controlled organization working for Black higher education. Through historical analysis, including review of archival documents and images as well as the use of oral history, I paint a picture of an evolving institution—one that started in the 1940s as an auxiliary of White industrial philanthropy but, through the crucible of the Cold War and Civil Rights-era turmoil, became more Black-centered during the 1960s and 70s. In its comprehensive treatment of the organization's publicity materials, considering text and image as a unit, this book is a unique contribution to historical research. Published in 2007 by Johns Hopkins University Press, the book uses publicity images and fundraising messages to demonstrate the changing mindset within the UNCF. Prior to writing this book, I published several articles using data collected in the UNCF archives. These articles focused on outsider influence on Black colleges, early appeals used to raise money for Black colleges, and early images used to represent Black colleges.[11]

Continuing an interest in Black education and the use of images, I recently finished a co-edited manuscript with Michael Bieze entitled *Booker T. Washington: A Non-Traditional Reader*.[12] Booker T. Washington attained national fame within a decade after his 1881 founding of the Tuskegee Normal Institute in rural Alabama. Tuskegee developed as a largely industrial school serving economically struggling southern Black men and women. Washington steadfastly believed that education was the answer to race problems during the aftermath of Reconstruction and the rise of Jim Crow. The tactics he employed in his attempt to achieve this vision made him both one of the most beloved and hated figures of the Progressive Era. Although much has been written about Booker T. Washington, what makes this book unique is that, like my work on the United Negro College Fund, it treats each of Washington's publications as a comprehensive package, with text and visuals working collectively to convey a message. The book explores the life and work of Washington through the use of his speeches, writings, photographs, and never before published documents detailing the man behind the legendary persona. It argues for an expanded definition of "primary sources" that includes not just the words of a document but the actual object: the juxtaposition of text and image, the type style, and even the type of paper used. The book shows that Washington carefully manipulated these elements to craft his message along race and class lines for the diverse audiences he sought to persuade.

It was not until a colleague asked me to contribute to a book on gender and education that I realized I had approached my work without much thought to the issue of gender or the role of Black women. My first book on Charles S. Johnson focused on Johnson's relationships with White male philanthropists and Black male intellectuals and did not consciously consider gender. My recent book on the United Negro College Fund spends considerable time looking at the roles of Black and White men and their relationships with the White women in the organization; however, I included only a few examples of the roles that Black women played in this story. To rectify my oversight, I undertook a historiography of gender and Black colleges, which uncovered the omission of women and gender relations throughout the historical literature on these institutions. In doing so, I used an integrative framework, conceptualized by Evelyn Nakano Glenn, which considers race and gender to be mutually interconnected, revealing a different picture than might be seen by considering these issues independently.[13] The resulting article will be published in the *American Educational Research Journal* this fall 2007.[14] During the review process the article was well received, with one of the seven reviewers commenting, "I have to commend this author because the work is path breaking. Few dare provide a gender critique to Black educational history. . . It will become a classic and an important article in the canon on Black and women's educational history."

Research on Current Issues Pertaining to African American Higher Education

While conducting research at many Black college archives for the Charles S. Johnson biography, I noticed that the campuses were in dire need of financial support. Buildings were physically deteriorating; the homes of African American luminaries who had lived on the campuses were boarded up; archival papers were crumbling in my hands as I read them. Through my research and that of others, I knew how Black colleges were funded historically, but I wondered where the funding was coming from in the current day. After much thought and exploration, I decided to pursue a line of inquiry into Black college alumni giving, examining contemporary fundraising strategies and donor motivation. My research on Black college fundraising resulted in a book entitled *Fund Raising from Black College Alumni: Successful Strategies for Supporting Alma Mater* (with Sibby Anderson-Thompkins).[15] This study collected the wisdom and experiences of Black college fundraisers, alumni directors, and alumni in order to understand fundraising language and strategies. It explores fundraising approaches that are tied to African American traditions and culture. The book is a scholarly study that addresses an enormous gap in the fundraising literature, but it was written first and foremost for practitioners. In 2004, the book received the H. S. Warwick Award for Outstanding Research on Philanthropy from the Council for the Advancement and Support of Education. It also received favorable reviews in both the *International Journal of Educational Advancement* and *Chronicle of Philanthropy*. My research for this fundraising book led to three additional articles, which focused on the role of faculty in Black college fundraising, Black college presidents and their impact on fundraising success, and fundraising strategies to be learned from the Black church.[16]

In an attempt to examine other salient questions pertaining to Black colleges and gain a deeper understanding of how these institutions operate in the twenty-first century, I also conducted research projects related to student experiences, graduate and professional education, the impact of Hurricane Katrina on Black colleges in New Orleans, and the influence of media coverage on the reputations and public images of Black colleges. Each of these research projects resulted in published articles.[17] Moreover, I served as the guest editor (with Michael Jennings) for a special issue on Black colleges for the *Journal of Educational Foundations*, authored two review essays exploring the state of research on Black colleges (published in *Educational Researcher* and *Teachers College Record*) and wrote a policy report on the future of Black colleges for the American Association of University Professors' *Academe*.[18]

Historically Black colleges are one type of institution that serves minority students in the United States. Hispanic Serving Institutions (HSIs) and Tribal Colleges and Universities (TCUs) are two others. Collectively, these colleges and universities are referred to as Minority Serving Institutions (MSIs), and as my work overlaps in several ways with scholarship on HSIs and TCUs, it is a logical step to collaborate with scholars who study them. Toward that end, I recently co-edited a book on MSIs with higher education scholars Ben Baez and Caroline Sotello Turner. This book offers a comprehensive treatment of these institutions using various disciplinary and interdisciplinary perspectives. At present there is only one small monograph on the subject of MSIs.[19] With a growing number of students of color attending these institutions it is crucial that we understand the needs of MSIs. Little has been done, however, to systematically study them, particularly in a way that highlights the relationships *among* MSIs of the same type and *between* MSIs of different types.[20]

My experience advising African American graduate students within historically White institutions has led to a scholarly interest in the subject. Accordingly, I have co-authored three papers with my students. For example, "Corridors and Coffee Shops: Teaching about Race and Research Outside the Classroom," written with Sibby Anderson-Thompkins and Nia Haydel, explores the teaching that takes place in advising sessions and informal discussions about research.[21] Another project examines the ways in which faculty and students can converse across status, race, and gender in an effort to enhance the learning experience in a doctoral program. This article, "Developing Trust, Negotiating Power: Transgressing Race and Status in the Academy," was published in *Teachers College Record*.[22] Most recently, I began working with my students on research related to African American graduate student experiences at historically White institutions. The resulting article, "'Difficult, Yet Rewarding': The Experiences of African American Graduate Students in Education at an Ivy League Institution," is currently under review with the *Journal of College Student Development*.

Research on Philanthropy

Within both my historical and contemporary work on Black colleges, I have maintained an interest in philanthropy and fundraising, especially, but not limited to the African American context. With regard to Black philanthropy specifically, I found that this area of research had received very little attention by scholars. I realized that by studying Black philanthropists, I could address many of my overarching research questions about Black agency. My research in this third area focuses on the role of individual and organizational philanthropy within the Black community, incorporating education as a central theme. For example, in a book chapter entitled, "Sisters in Service: African American Sororities and the Philanthropic Support of Education," I explore the philanthropic endeavors of African American sororities and examine charges of elitism often lodged against these women's groups.[23] I expand upon this research in a forthcoming book chapter entitled, "Giving and Getting: A History of Philanthropic Activity among African American Fraternities and Sororities," written with Patricia Louison and Mark Barnes.[24]

Further exploration of Black philanthropy led to my editing a book with Katherine Sedgwick entitled *Uplifting a People: African American Philanthropy and Education*.[25] This book was awarded the Association for Fundraising Professionals'

Skytone Ryan Prize for Research on Fundraising and Philanthropy and received favorable reviews in *Educational Review*,
the *International Journal of Educational Advancement*, and
the *Chronicle of Philanthropy*. Although significant to society
at large, African American philanthropic contributions are
often ignored by the academic community and the general
public because they fall outside the standard view of philanthropy (monetary donations given by wealthy Whites). This
book traces African American philanthropy from its begin-
nings among the freedmen to the efforts of individual Black
donors and philanthropic organizations in the current day. It
also encourages scholars in philanthropic studies, sociology,
and history to broaden their understandings of philanthropy.

My explorations of philanthropy have extended to gender
as well, with an edited volume of new and classic works on
the subject (co-edited with Alice Ginsberg). This book, entitled *Gender and Educational Philanthropy: New Perspectives
on Funding, Collaboration, and Assessment*, explores the complex questions funding agencies and foundations face as they
struggle to understand and define gender equity in education. As a collection of writings, some authored by critics of
philanthropy and others by the foundations themselves, the
book engages readers in different approaches funders use to
define gender equity, target limited resources, and create collaborative relationships that seek to make schools more equitable and engaging for boys and girls of a variety of cultural
backgrounds.[26]

In a similar vein, yet broader in scope, I edited an anthology
entitled *Philanthropy, Volunteerism, and Fundraising in Higher
Education* with Andrea Walton.[27] The anthology contains classic works in addition to new essays written by Walton, myself,
and our associate editors that seek to contextualize the study
and practice of philanthropy. With this book, we aim to more
centrally locate the study of philanthropy within the field of

higher education, so that scholars and students will grasp its significance.

Future Plans for Research

The projects I have planned for the next five years complement my current research agenda and expand the extant knowledge base. These projects are at various stages and reflect each of the research strands discussed in this essay.

Uncle Tom? Accommodationist? Authoritarian? The Representation of Black College Presidents in Scholarship, Fiction, and the Media.

Scholarly and popular accounts often paint Black college presidents with a broad brush. Negative characterizations embodied by the words "Uncle Tom," "Accommodationist," and "Authoritarian" have existed for more than 100 years, appearing in the works of Black authors Langston Hughes and Ralph Ellison; the studies of White scholars Christopher Jencks and David Riesman; the writings of Black conservative thinker Thomas Sowell and the recent pages of the *Atlanta Journal Constitution*.[28] But how did these characterizations come to be? On which incidents and actions are they based? How are they perpetuated? Conversely, how do the individual presidents see themselves and their actions? Building on my past research related to Black college leadership, I plan to complete a historiography of the Black college president. I will also review fictitious accounts of Black college presidents such as Dr. Bledsoe in Ralph Ellison's *Invisible Man*, as these accounts tend to be composites of real events and have a lasting impact. Likewise, because media depictions hold enormous sway, I will look at the media's treatment of Black colleges and their presidents throughout these institutions' existence. Based on this research, I will use prosopography (collective biography) to examine the lives and actions of Black college presidents from the post-Civil War period through the current day.[29] I will juxtapose the characterization of these individuals in scholarly literature, fiction, and media with their self-assessments. These assessments will be gleaned from autobiographies, personal papers, presidential papers, and oral histories. My examination will take into account significant periods and movements throughout the history of Black colleges. I am just beginning this project and foresee working on it over the next five or six years. I will apply for external funding from the Spencer Foundation and National Endowment for the Humanities to support this research.

New Essays on Black Colleges: Triumphs, Troubles, and Taboos

This project took root last year in my *Historically Black Colleges and Universities* seminar and includes a group of essays on Black colleges that explore new territory and previously taboo subjects such as sexuality, colorism (i.e., discrimination based on complexion), and gender issues. Half of the chapters were written by students who took the seminar, while others were written by my doctoral advisees and colleagues throughout the country. I am working with the individual students to revise their chapters, teaching them about the publishing process along the way. I am also mentoring Chris Tudico, my PhD advisee and co-editor, on the editing process, proposal writing, and other tasks related to publishing a book. This project has afforded me an opportunity to push the research on Black colleges ahead and in new directions.[30] We will complete this project in the spring of 2008.

A Growing Tradition? Examining the African American Family Foundation

Building upon my work related to African American philanthropy, I am doing research that explores the recent growth of African American family foundations.[31] Family foundations are of particular interest to African Americans, who prefer to put their trust in organizations that are close to them and that aid the surrounding African American community.[32] To date, there is limited scholarly research on family foundations in general, and *none* related to African American family foundations.[33] Little is known about the motivations of the founders of these organizations, their make-up, or their operations. Using qualitative methods such as interviews, open-ended surveys and document analysis, I will attempt to understand where African American family foundations operate, how they are developed, and to what kinds of causes they allocate their monies. Upon completion, this research will help scholars and practitioners to further understand African American philanthropic behavior, assist more African American families who want to establish foundations, and provide a comprehensive overview of the growth and development of African American family foundations. Funded by the Aspen Institute, this project will take place over the next three years. I plan to publish the results in several peer-reviewed journal articles. I will also write articles and op-ed pieces for more general audiences.

Summary of Research:

With higher education access currently in flux, and in particular, with affirmative action in an uncertain state, it is critical that we look at the history of African American education, and specifically Black colleges, for clues about how to attain educational equity. My research explores new ground in the area of African American higher education and philanthropy, examining data that have often been ignored. It has yielded a wealth of information about the story of Black colleges, complicating our picture of African American higher education and compelling us to recognize African American agency.

Notes

1 For an in-depth explanation of historical methods, see Martha Howell and Walter Prevenier, *From Reliable Sources: An Introduction to Historical Methods* (Ithaca, NY: Cornell University Press, 2001); Gilbert J. Garraghan, *A Guide to Historical Method* (New York: Fordham University Press, 1946); Louis Gottschalk, *Understanding History: A Primer of Historical Method* (New York: Alfred A. Knopf, 1950).

2 Merle Curti and Roderick Nash, *Philanthropy in the Shaping of American Higher Education* (New Brunswick: Rutgers University Press, 1965); John R. Thelin, *A History of American Higher Education* (Baltimore: Johns Hopkins University Press, 2004).

3 James D. Anderson, *The Education of Blacks in the South, 1860–1935* (Chapel Hill: University of North Carolina Press, 1988); Eric Anderson and Alfred Moss, *Dangerous Donations: Northern Philanthropy and Southern Black Education, 1902-1930* (Columbia, MO: University of Missouri Press, 1999); William Watkins, *The White Architects of Black Education: Ideology and Power in America, 1865-1954* (New York: Teachers College Press, 2001).

4 Emmett D. Carson, *Black Philanthropy and Self-Help in America* (New York: University Press of America, 1993); Marybeth Gasman and Katherine V. Sedgwick (Eds.). *Uplifting a People: African American Philanthropy and Education* (New York: Peter Lang, 2005).

5 National Center for Educational Statistics, 2004.

6 American Medical Association, 2006.

7 Frederick D. Patterson Research Institute, 2004; National Center for Educational Statistics, 2006.

8 Patrick J. Gilpin and Marybeth Gasman, *Charles S. Johnson: Leadership behind the Veil in the Age of Jim Crow.* (New York: State University of New York Press, 2003). Foreword by Pulitzer Prize winning author David Levering Lewis.

9   Marybeth Gasman, "Scylla and Charybdis: Navigating the Waters of Academic Freedom at Fisk University during Charles S. Johnson's Administration (1946-1956)," *American Educational Research Journal*, vol. 36, no. 4, Winter, (1999), 739-758.

Marybeth Gasman, "Passport to the Front of the Bus: the Impact of Fisk University's International Program on Race Relations in Nashville, Tennessee," *The Interdisciplinary Journal of North American Studies*, no. 7, (2001), 10 pp.

Marybeth Gasman, "The President as Ethical Role Model: Instilling an Ethic of Leadership at Fisk University during the 1950s," *Journal of College and Character*, vol. 2, (2001), 12 pp.

Marybeth Gasman and Edward Epstein, "Modern Art in the Old South: The Role of the Arts in Fisk University's Campus Curriculum," *Educational Researcher*, vol. 31, no. 2, (March 2002), 13-20.

Marybeth Gasman, "W. E. B. Du Bois and Charles S. Johnson: Opposing Views on Philanthropic Support for Black Higher Education," *History of Education Quarterly*, vol. 42, no. 4, (Winter 2002), 493-516.

10   Marybeth Gasman, *Envisioning Black Colleges: A History of the United Negro College Fund* (Baltimore: Johns Hopkins University Press, 2007). Foreword by John Thelin, author of *A History of American Higher Education*. 290 pp.

11   Marybeth Gasman, "A Word for Every Occasion: Appeals by John D. Rockefeller, Jr. to White Donors on Behalf of the United Negro College Fund," *History of Higher Education Annual*, (2002), 67-90.

Marybeth Gasman, "Rhetoric vs. Reality: The Fundraising Messages of the United Negro College Fund in the Immediate Aftermath of the *Brown* Decision," *History of Education Quarterly*, vol. 44, no. 1, (Winter 2004), 70-94.

Marybeth Gasman and Edward Epstein, "Creating an Image for Black Colleges: A Visual Examination of the United Negro College

Fund's Publicity, 1944-1960," *Educational Foundations*, vol. 18, no. 2, (Fall 2004), 41-61.

Gasman, Marybeth, "Salvaging 'Academic Disaster Areas': The Black College Response to Christopher Jencks' and David Riesman's 1967 *Harvard Educational Review* Article," *Journal of Higher Education*, vol. 77, no. 2 (2006), 317-352.

12 Michael Bieze and Marybeth Gasman, *Booker T. Washington: A Non-Traditional Reader*. Under review with Oxford University Press, passed external review process and now negotiating revisions. 612 pages.

13 Evelyn Nakano Glenn, The Social Construction and Institutionalization of Gender and Race: An Integrative Framework in Myra M. Ferree, Judith Lorber, and Beth Hess (Eds.). *The Gender Lens: Revisioning Gender* (Thousand Oaks, CA: Sage Publications, 1998).

14 Marybeth Gasman, "Swept Under the Rug: A Historiography on Gender and Black Colleges." *American Educational Research Journal*, vol. 44, no. 3 (Winter 2007), 73 pp.

15 Marybeth Gasman and Sibby Anderson-Thompkins, *Fund-Raising from Black College Alumni: Successful Strategies for Supporting Alma Mater*. (Washington, D.C.: CASE Publications, 2003), 119 pp.

16 Marybeth Gasman, "The Role of Faculty in Fundraising at Black Colleges: What is It and What Can It Become?" *International Journal of Educational Advancement*, vol. 5, no. 2, (2005), 171-179.

Marybeth Gasman, "Charles S. Johnson and Johnnetta Cole: Successful Role Models for Fundraising at Historically Black Colleges and Universities," *The CASE International Journal of Educational Advancement*, vol. 1, no. 3, (2001), 237-252.

Daryl Holloman, Marybeth Gasman, and Sibby Anderson-Thompkins, "Motivations for Philanthropic Giving in the African American Church: Implications for Black College Fundraising," *Journal of Research on Christian Education*, vol. 12, no. 2, (Fall 2003), 137-169.

17   Robert Palmer and Marybeth Gasman, "'It Takes a Village': Social Capital and Academic Success at Historically Black Colleges and Universities," *Journal of College Student Development*, (forthcoming Jan/Feb, 2008), 40 pp.

Meredith Curtin and Marybeth Gasman, "Historically Black College MBA Programs: Prestige, Rankings, and the Meaning of Success," *Journal of Education for Business*, vol. 79, no.2, (Winter 2004), 79–84.

Gasman, Marybeth and Noah D. Drezner, "A Rising Tide: New Orleans' Black Colleges and Their Efforts to Rebuild After Hurricane Katrina," *Multicultural Review*, vol. 15, no. 4 (2007), 34–39.

Marybeth Gasman, "Truth, Generalizations, and Stigmas: An Analysis of the Media's Coverage of Morris Brown College and Black Colleges Overall," *Review of Black Political Economy*, vol. 34, no.2 (2007), 111–135.

18   Marybeth Gasman and Michael E. Jennings, Guest Editors, "Historically Black Colleges and Universities," *Educational Foundations*, Special Double Issue (Winter/Spring 2007), vol. 20, no. 1–2.

Marybeth Gasman, "Coffee Table to Classroom: A Review of Recent Scholarship on Historically Black Colleges and Universities," *Educational Researcher*, vol. 34, no. 7 (2005), 32–39.

Marybeth Gasman, "Education in Black and White: New Perspectives on the History of Historically Black Colleges and Universities," *Teachers College Record* (www.tcrecord.org, January 25, 2006); in print (2007), 24 pp.

Marybeth Gasman, Benjamin Baez, Noah D. Drezner, Katherine V. Sedgwick, and Christopher Tudico, "Historically Black Colleges and Universities: Recent Trends," *Academe* (Jan-Feb, 2007), 69–77.

19   Jamie P. Merisotis and C. O'Brien, *Minority Serving Institutions: Distinct Purposes, Common Goals, New Directions for Higher Education*, No. 102, (San Francisco: Jossey-Bass, 1998).

20 Marybeth Gasman, Benjamin Baez, and Caroline Turner (Eds.), *Understanding Minority Serving Institutions* (Albany, New York: State University of New York Press, 2008), 400 pp.

21 Marybeth Gasman, Sibby Anderson-Thompkins, and Nia Haydel, "Corridors and Coffee Shops: Teaching about Race and Research Outside the Classroom," *Journal of College and University Teaching*, vol. 17, no. 1/2 (2006), 79–95.

22 Marybeth Gasman, Cynthia Gerstl-Pepin, Sibby Anderson-Thompkins, Lisa Rasheed, and Karry Hathaway, "Developing Trust, Negotiating Power: Transgressing Race and Status in the Academy," *Teachers College Record*, vol. 106, no. 4 (2004), 689–715.

23 Marybeth Gasman, "Sisters in Service: African American Sororities and the Philanthropic Support of Education," in Andrea Walton (Ed.). *Women, Philanthropy, and Education.* (Bloomington, Indiana: Indiana University Press, 2005), 194–214.

Marybeth Gasman and Lucretia Payton Stewart, "Twice Removed: A White Scholar Studies Black Sororities and a Black Scholar Responds," *International Journal of Research and Method in Education*, vol. 29, no. 2 (2006), 129–149.

24 Marybeth Gasman, Patricia Louison, and Mark Barnes, "Giving and Getting: A History of Philanthropic Activity among African American Fraternities and Sororities," Tamara Brown, Gregory Parks, and Clarenda Phillips, *African American Fraternities and Sororities: The Legacy and Vision*, Vol. II (Louisville: University of Kentucky, 2008).

25 Gasman, Marybeth and Kate Sedgwick (Eds.), *Uplifting a People. Essays on African American Philanthropy and Education* (New York: Peter Lang, 2005), 204 pp. *Winner of Association of Fundraising Professionals' Skytone Ryan Prize for Research on Fundraising and Philanthropy.*

26 Ginsberg, Alice E. and Marybeth Gasman (Eds.), *Gender and Philanthropy: New Perspectives on Funding, Collaboration, and Assessment* (New York: Palgrave, 2007). Foreword by Andrea Walton, editor of *Women, Philanthropy, and Education.*

27 Walton, Andrea and Marybeth Gasman (Eds.), *Philanthropy, Fundraising, and Volunteerism in Higher Education.* (Upper Saddle River, New Jersey: Pearson Publishing, 2007). Foreword by Ellen Condliffe Lagemann, author of *The Politics of Knowledge: The Carnegie Corporation, Philanthropy, and Public Policy.*

28 Langston Hughes, "Cowards from the Colleges," *Crisis* (August 1934), 226–228; Ralph Ellison, *Invisible Man* (New York: Random House, 1952); Christopher Jencks and David Riesman, "The American Negro College," *Harvard Educational Review*, vol. 37, no. 2, (1967), 3–60; Thomas Sowell, *Black Education: Myths and Tragedies* (New York: David McKay Company, 1972); Cynthia Tucker, "Morris Brown College: Ailing Institution Must Face Awful Truth: It's Time to Close," *Atlanta Journal Constitution* (October 23, 2002), 17A.

29 According to Lawrence Stone, "Prosopography is the investigation of the common background characteristics of a group of actors in history by means of a collective study of their lives." See Lawrence Stone, "Prosopography," *Daedalus* 100.1 (1971), 46–71. This article is considered the germinal work on the method.

30 Marybeth Gasman and Christopher Tudico (Eds.), *New Essays on Black Colleges: Triumphs, Troubles, and Taboos* (New York: Palgrave, forthcoming 2008), 300 pp.

31 Charles S. Weiss, "Family Foundations: A Case Study Approach," *New Directions for Philanthropic Fundraising*, no. 28 (Summer 2000).

32 Council on Foundations, *Cultures of Caring: Philanthropy in Diverse American Communities* (Washington, D.C.: Council on Foundations, 1999); Marybeth Gasman and Sibby Anderson-Thompkins, *Fund Raising from Black College Alumni: Successful Strategies for Supporting Alma Mater* (Washington, D.C.: CASE Books, 2003).

33 The last scholarly article written on Black foundations specifically was Robert S. Browne, "Developing Black Foundations: An Economic Response to Black Community Needs," *Black*

Scholar, vol. 9, no. 4 (1977), 25-28. There is one published family foundation reflection. It is a chapter in the edited volume, *Faith and Family Philanthropy: Grace, Gratitude, and Generosity* (Washington, D.C.: National Center for Family Philanthropy, 2002) entitled "An African-American Family's Experience." The chapter focuses on Betty and Jean Fairfax and the establishment of their family foundation.

Appendix E

Tips for Online Teaching

Preparation

1. Be organized and plan in advance as much as possible. If you are teaching asynchronously, prepare the syllabus, readings, assignments, videos, exercises and more, in advance.

2. Make sure you are completely familiar with your virtual platform.

3. If you regularly lecture, record the lectures instead of doing them live, and make the lectures short. If you do not lecture, have live interactive conversations with students.

Teaching

4. Create a warm greeting and an online icebreaker to encourage interaction on the first day. I also advise a very short interaction at the start of each class.

5. If you use online discussions, monitor them for full participation as well as respect issues.

6. Use videos (TED Talks, YouTube), real-time polls, and breakout rooms to provide interaction in the classroom. Practice using these strategies before going live.

7. Invite guest speakers for variety, and moderate a Q&A.

8. Encourage student sharing and prepare questions to engage students about the course material.

9. Encourage students to take the lead during portions of the course so that you are not doing all the talking; let them know in advance and make it part of the course assignments.

Organization and Communication

10. Post all announcements and changes to the course on your virtual platform to avoid rumor and confusion.

11. Communicate clear expectations and add these to your platform to eliminate confusion. Be clear about camera use in synchronized courses, attendance, and due dates.

12. Keep track of who submits and misses assignments and make sure to reiterate deadlines. Not being in a physical class may make it difficult for students to remember and prioritize course assignments.

13. Because of students' various levels of comfort with the virtual platform, use multiple forms of assessment. I do this with all of my classes, but it is especially important in virtual environments because many students who can typically focus and shine will be lost in this new environment.

14. Regularly check in to see if students are logging in and keeping up with coursework. These are stressful times and students will need encouragement.

15. Respond to all student inquiries within 24 hours. As a teacher, you have an obligation to respond to students. This is not an option; saying you are too busy is not student centered.

16. Provide timely feedback on assignments to keep students on task and motivated.

17. Regularly communicate with the entire class; try writing an email to the entire class on a set schedule once a week.

18. If you have a TA, make sure you and they are on the same page regarding expectations; communicate those expectations to students, as well.

19. Make virtual office hours available twice a week for students to check in with you.

20. Conduct regular, informal evaluations with students to make sure they are learning and getting the most out of the course.

Overall Success

21. Do not try to do too much. Be simple. Less is always best.

22. Be flexible and nimble, because the world is changing quickly.

Appendix F

Suggested Outline for CV

Name
Contact info
- personal
- professional
- Twitter handle

Education
- PhD degree
- Master's degree
- Bachelor's degree
- do not include prep schools

Research Related Positions/Faculty Positions

Books
- authored
- edited

Peer-reviewed articles
- highlight your name in the list of authors

Book chapters

Essays
- scholarly and opinion

Reports/White Papers/Working Papers

Book Reviews

Works in Progress
- only serious items, be ready to explain these works in progress
- do not include too much

Presentations
- peer-reviewed presentations
- invited presentations

Awards
- avoid high school and undergraduate awards unless highly prestigious

Grants
- awarded
- those applied for but not awarded should go in annual performance reviews, not on your CV

Service
- professional organizational membership
- service to journals
- departmental/college/university service
- national service
- consultancies
- media engagement

Other Relevant Professional Positions

Appendix G

Select Funders for Academic Research

Name of Funder	Interests	Website
Fulbright Program	Travel, teaching, research	https://us.fulbrightonline.org/about/types-of-awards/study-research
National Endowment for the Arts	Visual, performance, written arts	https://www.arts.gov
Spencer Foundation	Education research	https://www.spencer.org/grant_types/small-research-grant
William T. Grant Foundation	Research to improve the lives of young people	http://wtgrantfoundation.org
Russell Sage Foundation	Improvement of social and living conditions	https://www.russellsage.org
The Pew Charitable Trust	Environmental, economic, and health issues	https://www.pewtrusts.org/en
Social Science Research Council	Social science research	https://www.ssrc.org/fellowships/
Harry Frank Guggenheim Foundation	Natural and social sciences, humanities	https://www.hfg.org/rg/guidelines.htm
National Endowment for the Humanities	Humanities research	https://www.neh.gov/grants/research/collaborative-research-grants
National Science Foundation	Basic science research and science education	https://www.nsf.gov/funding/
Alfred P. Sloan Foundation	Science, engineering, education, economics	https://sloan.org/grants/apply/
National Institutes of Health	Science and medicine, science education	https://grants.nih.gov/grants/oer.htm

Name of Funder	Interests	Website
Lumina Foundation	Education, student success, educational policy	https://www.luminafoundation.org
Strada Education Network	Education, student success, educational policy	https://www.stradaeducation.org
ECMC Foundation	Education, student success, workforce, educational policy	https://ecmcfoundation.org
Kresge Foundation	Cities, environment, arts & culture, education, health, social investment	https://kresge.org
Mellon Foundation	Arts and humanities	https://mellon.org
Kellogg Foundation	Education and social justice	https://www.wkkf.org
John Templeton Foundation	Religion, free speech, discovery	https://www.templeton.org
Bill & Melinda Gates Foundation	Education, science, global issues	https://www.gatesfoundation.org
David & Lucile Packard Foundation	Lives of children, families, and communities, environment	https://www.packard.org
Ford Foundation	Civil engagement and government, free expression, equitable development, gender, racial, and ethnic justice, youth opportunities	https://www.fordfoundation.org
Henry Luce Foundation	American art, East Asia, theology, religion, public policy, environment	https://www.hluce.org
Robert Wood Johnson Foundation	Improvement in health and health care	https://www.rwjf.org

Appendix H

Select List of Fellowships

Name of Fellowship	Sponsoring Organization	Topics of Interest	Website
Jameson Fellowship	American Historical Association	history	http://www.historians.org/awards-and-grants/grants-and-fellowships
Gilder Lehrman Fellowships	Gilder Lehrman Institute of American History	history	http://www.gilderlehrman.org/programs-exhibitions/fellowships
National Endowment for the Humanities Fellowship	National Endowment for the Humanities	arts and humanities	http://www.neh.gov/grants/research/fellowships
Strategy and Policy Fellowship	Smith Richardson Foundation	political science, public policy, policy analysis, history	http://www.srf.org/grants/international_strategy and_policy_fellows.php
Hunt Postdoctoral Fellowship	Wenner-Gren Foundation	anthropological theory	http://www.wennergren.org/programs/hunt-postdoctoral-fellowships
Postdoctoral Research Leave Fellowship	American Association of University Women	research related to women	https://www.aauw.org
ACLS Fellowship	American Council of Learned Societies	classical studies, English and American literature, American history	https://www.acls.org
Postdoctoral Research Awards	Canada-U.S. Fulbright Program	environmental studies, community development, economic development	https://www.fulbright.ca/programs/american-scholars/primary-awards/post-doctorate.html

Name of Fellowship	Sponsoring Organization	Topics of Interest	Website
Guggenheim Foundation Fellowship	The John Simon Guggenheim Memorial Foundation	open to any field	https://www.gf.org/about/fellowship/
Huntington Library Fellowship	The Huntington Library	history, literature, art, and history of science	https://www.huntington.org/fellowships/
Kluge Center Fellowships	Library of Congress	research related to the Library of Congress collections	https://www.loc.gov/programs/john-w-kluge-center/chairs-fellowships/fellowships/kluge-fellowships/
Translations Fellowship	National Endowment for the Arts	translation of prose, poetry, or drama language to English	https://www.arts.gov/grants-individuals/translation-projects
Cullman Center Fellowships	New York Public Library	journalism, creative writing, visual artists	https://www.nypl.org/help/about-nypl/fellowships-institutes/center-for-scholars-and-writers/fellowships-at-the-cullman-center
Scholars in Residence Program	New York Public Library	history, politics, literature and culture of Africa and diaspora	https://www.nypl.org/help/about-nypl/fellowships-institutes/schomburg-center-scholars-in-residency/application
Lapidus Center Fellowships	New York Public Library	research related to transatlantic slave trade	https://www.lapiduscenter.org/category/fellowships/

Name of Fellowship	Sponsoring Organization	Topics of Interest	Website	
Mellon Emerging Faculty Leaders Award	Woodrow Wilson National Fellowship Foundation	humanities and social sciences	https://woodrow.org/fellowships/facultyleaders/	
Ford Foundation Fellowship	The National Academies of Sciences, Engineering, and Medicine	racial and ethnic diversity	https://sites.nationalacademies.org/PGA/FordFellowships/index.htm	
NAEd/Spencer Postdoctoral Fellowship	Spencer Foundation	education	https://spencer.org	

Consulting and Public Speaking Log

Name of Engagement	Date of Engagement	Amount of Pay	Travel Expenses	Expected Pay Date	Reimbursement Received Date

Consulting and Public Speaking

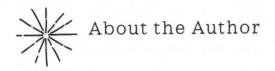

Marybeth Gasman is the Samuel DeWitt Proctor Endowed Chair in Education and a Distinguished Professor at Rutgers University. She serves as the Executive Director of the Samuel DeWitt Proctor Institute for Leadership, Equity & Justice and the Executive Director of the Rutgers Center for Minority Serving Institutions. Prior to joining the faculty at Rutgers, Marybeth was the Judy & Howard Berkowitz Endowed Professor in the Graduate School of Education at the University of Pennsylvania. While at Penn, Marybeth also served as the founding director of the Penn Center for Minority Serving Institutions (MSIs). Her areas of expertise include the history of American higher education, Minority Serving Institutions (with an emphasis on Historically Black Colleges and Universities), racism and diversity, fundraising and philanthropy, and higher education leadership. She is the author or editor of 26 books, including *Educating a Diverse Nation* (Harvard University Press, 2015 with Clif Conrad), *Envisioning Black Colleges* (Johns Hopkins University Press, 2007), and her newest book *Making Black Scientists* (Harvard University Press, 2019 with Thai-Huy Nguyen). Marybeth has written over 250 peer-reviewed articles, scholarly essays, and book chapters. She has penned over 450 opinion articles for the nation's newspapers and magazines and has been ranked by *Education Week* as one the most influential education scholars in the nation. Marybeth has raised over $23 million in grant funding to support her research and that of her students, mentees, and MSI partners. Marybeth has served on the board of trustees of The College Board as well as Paul Quinn College, Morris Brown

College, and St. Augustine's College. She considers her proudest accomplishment to be receiving the University of Pennsylvania's Provost Award for Distinguished PhD Teaching and Mentoring, serving as the dissertation chair for over 80 doctoral students since 2000. She has one daughter and enjoys photography, jewelry making, and international travel in her free time.

About the Illustrator

Chloë Sarah Epstein is an illustrator, comic book and graphic novel artist, and writer. She attended Bryn Mawr College with a major in fine arts (with a printmaking specialty) and minors in creative writing and art history. Chloë has illustrated poems for major publication outlets and poets. She has also shown her work in solo art shows at both the University of Pennsylvania and Haverford College. Chloë has curated an award winning collection of graphic novels and comic books. She lives in Philadelphia and enjoys fencing and traveling extensively in her free time.

Index

#academicchatter, 96
#academictwitter, 96

A

Academe, 106
*Academic Advising: A
    Comprehensive Handbook*, 75
*Academic Advising Approaches:
    Strategies that Teach Students to
    Make the Most of College*, 76
Academic Job Search Handbook, The,
    xxxii, 7
accountants, importance of having,
    126
Achebe, C., 48
Achor, S., 112
administrative support staffs, 97
advising, 71
    advocating for students, 80–81
    job talks and, 79
    letters of recommendation and,
        78–79
    master's students, 75
    PhD students, 76–80
    relationship with students, 71–74
    research teams and, 76–77, 81–83
    undergraduates, 74–75
    Also see teaching
Advisor in Touch, 73
agents, 125
Aguilar, S., 7
American Association of University
    Professors, xvii, 106
Anderson, C., 5
Anderson, J.D., xx, xxi, 66
Anderson-Thompkins, S., 81
Arvizu, S., 169
Asian American and Pacific
    Islander student enrollment, 48
Atlanta University Center, 22

B

Baca, J., 170
Bain, K., 54
Basow, S.A., 54
*Beauty and Burden of Being a Black
    Professor, The*, 134
Becoming, 112
Belcher, W.L., 78
*Black Academic's Guide to Winning
    Tenure, The*, xxxii
Black student enrollment, 47–48
Blackboard, 45
Blake, D., 12
Blake-Beard, S., 2
Boettcher, J., 46
book publishing. *See* writing/
    publishing
Borden, V., 62
boundaries, setting, 110–12
Bowman, R.L., 73
Bowman, V.E., 73
Boysen, G., 56
Brookings Institute, 114
Brown, B., 112
Brown, F.W., 100
Buller, J., 102
bullying, xxvii, xxviii, 72, 97,

C

Canvas, 45
Carnegie Classification, 57
Centra, J.A., 54
*Changing Media and Adademic
    Freedom, The*, 106
Chavez, K., 54
Chronicle of Higher Education, The,
    7, 129
Chu, D., 101
class activities, 45, 53

classroom discussion and
    participation statement, 50
*Coach's Guide for Women
    Professors, The*, xxxii
College Teaching at Its Best, 54
Colorado College, 38
Columbia University, xxvii, 22, 48
Committee on Committees, 63
conferences, academic, 29-30, 102,
    104-5
conflict resolution, 177, 178
Conrad, R.-M., 46
consulting and keynote speeches for
    hire, 122-27
COVID-19, 46
Crew, E., 73
CSU Monterey Bay, 168, 171
culturally relevant pedagogy, 49
curriculum, Whiteness and, 48-49
CV, 67

D
Davis, C., 133
    advice about service, 148-49
    advice for people of color,
        139-40
    advice on pursuing tenure,
        143-45
    balancing role as woman, 141-42
    being mentored, 147-48
    bullying and, 149-50
    Christianity and teaching,
        138-39
    family and professional life,
        142-43
    her background, 133-34, 137
    identity impacting role as
        professor, 137-38
    publishing advice, 140, 150
    response to racism and sexism,
        145-47
deep knowledge, 21
Delpit, L., xxv

*Department Chair as Academic
    Leader, The*, 101
Department Chair Primer, The, 101
Diangelo, R.J., 56
dissertation
    importance of, 1-2
    mining for journal articles, 14, 20
    turning into book, 14, 20
Donovan, J., 5
Downey, D.B., 54
Drake, J., 76

E
Eberhardt, J., 56
ECMC Foundation, 89
Economist, The, 14
editorial boards, 66
Education of Blacks in the South, The,
    xx
email, 126, 127
Eng, N., 54
entanglement, 141
Epstein, C.S., xxiv
Essential Academic Dean, The, 102
Esters, L.T., 134, 150
    advice for people of color, 165-66
    advice on pursuing tenure,
        154-56
    balancing teaching, research,
        and service, 158-59
    bullying and, 161-62, 164, 167-68
    his background, 134-35, 151-52
    his decision to become
        professor, 150-51
    family and professional life,
        157-58
    mentors and, 164-65
    response to racism, 161-62,
        163-64
    teaching White students, 153-54
    trusting people, 165
    White mentors and, 156-57
exercising, 111, 114

INDEX

F

Facebook, 119-20
faculty politics, 95-97
    academic conferences and,
        104-5
    relationships with colleagues,
        98-99
    relationships with deans, 101-2
    relationships with department
        chairs, 99-101
    relationships with colleagues in
        field, 102-3
    social media and, 105-6
faculty positions. *See* jobs/faculty
    positions
Faculty-student relationships: The
    dual role controversy, 73
fellowships, 92
Fierce Conversations, 177, 178
Fisk University, 22
Florida A&M, 133, 134
Folsom, P., 76
Ford Foundation, 92
Fox, A., 86, 91, 92
Frazee, J.P., 95
frequent flyer accounts, 113
Frierson, H., 148
Fuhrman, S., xxvi-xxviii
Fulbright Foundation, 92

G

Gadsden, V., xxviii
Gallo, C., 5
Gannon, K., 45
Garcia, M., 185
Gasman, Marybeth (author), xxiii, 48
    background of, xix-xx
    bullying and, xxvii, xxviii,
    decision to become professor, xx
    management of CV, xxvii
    mentoring of, xxi, xxvii
    promotion of African American
        women, xxvii-xxviii

TEDtalks and, 5
tenure process at Penn,
    xxviii-xxix
Gaubatz, N.B., 54
Georgia State University, xxi, xxiv,
    xxv, xxvi, 13, 17, 22, 30, 99
Gielan, M., 112
Gordon, V., 76
gossip, 24, 96, 104, 106
*Graduate Advisor Handbook: A
    Student-Centered Approach, The*,
    78
grants, 85-86
    defining a project, 87-91
    fellowships and, 92
    follow up and stewarding
        funders, 91-92
    reason for applying for, 86
Guarino, C.M., 62

H

Hamilton, L., 56
Hanasono, L.K., 68
Harley, D.A., 62
Harvard Business School, 112
Harvard University Medical School,
    115
Hatley, L.D., 73
Hecht, I., 101
Heestra, J., 1
Hilliard, A., xxi, xxii-xxiv, xxx
Hilton, A., 147
Hirshfield, L.E., 62
Hispanic student enrollment, 47
Historically Black Colleges and
    Universities, 21, 22, 43, 67, 133
History of Education Quarterly, 66
History of Education Society, 66
Hollis, L., 96, 97, 98
hotel stays, 113
House, D., 56
Hudson, T.D., 4
Hyman, J., 100

I

I Thought It Was Just Me (But It Wasn't), 112
identities, 136, 137-38
Indiana University, xxi
indirect cost policies, 90
injustice, speaking out against, 121
Instagram, 121
Iowa State, 152, 161

J

Jacobs, L., 100
jealousy, academic, xxiv-xxvi
job/faculty positions, 1
    establishing work patterns, 13-15
    job searches with a partner, 11-12
    letters of recommendation and, 2-3
    mentors and, 2
    negotiating offers, 7-13
    negotiating salary offers, 7-8
    post-doctoral positions and, 3-4
    PowerPoint presentations and, 5
    preparing to apply for, 1-7
    reduced course loads and, 10
    research assistants and, 9
    sabbaticals and, 10-11
    social media and, 122
    start-up packages and, 10
    summer salary support, 8
    travel funds and, 9
job talk, 4-7, 79
Johns Hopkins University Press, 23, 32
Johnson, C.S., 22
Joseph, T.D., 62
Joslin, J., 76
Jossey-Bass Press, 33
Journal About Women in Higher Education, 74
journals
    publishing in top-tier, 18-19
    service and, 66
    Also see writing/publishing

K

Karsh, E., 86, 91, 92
Keashley, L., 96, 97, 98
Kelsky, K., xxxii
Kendi, I.X., 56
Kernahan, C., 54
Klimek, P., 14
Kresge Foundation, 89

L

Ladson-Billings, G., 49
Lampman, C., 73
Laskshmi, P., 185
Laszloffy, T., xxxii
Leeming, J., 10
letters of recommendation, 2-3, 78-79
Library of Congress, 92
Lindahl, M., 56
LinkedIn, 119
Lowery, S., 73
Lumina Foundation, 89

M

MacArthur Genius Award, xxv
manage up, 92
Martin, J., 54
McIntosh, M., 177
McKeachie, W., 54
McKeachie's Teaching Tips, 54
media, engaging with, 127-30
Mellon Foundation, 89
Mengel, F., 54
mental and physical health, 115-16
mentors, xx, xxi, 2, 133, 135, 147, 152, 155, 164-65, 169, 171
    grants and, 86
    service and, 62
Mesa-Bains, A., 170
Miles, P., 56
Miller, K., 115
Misawa, M., 96, 97, 98
Mitchell, K.M., 54
mitochondria, 114

Moore, C., 45
Moshavi, D., 100
Myers Education Press, 33

N
NASPA, 74
National Endowment for the
    Humanities, 89
National Institutes of Health, 89
National Science Foundation, 89, 92
National Survey of Student
    Engagement, 36
Native American student
    enrollment, 48
Nature, 10
Nettles, M., 145
Neuman, J., 96, 97, 98
*New Advisor Guidebook: Mastering the
    Art of Academic Advising, The*, 76
New York University, 48
Nikolioudakis, N, xviii
Northwest University, 48
Núñez-Mchiri, G.G., 135
    advice on pursuing tenure,
        178-80
    balancing family and profes-
        sional life, 172-76, 183-84
    caring for her students, 184-85
    experiencing sexism, 176-78
    her background, 135-36
    her decision to become a profes-
        sor, 168-71
    importance of boundaries,
        182-84
    mentors and, 169, 171
    pursuit of tenure, 171-72, 181-82
    service and, 180-81
    teaching about food, 185-87

O
Obama, B., 120
Obama, M., 112
O'Brien, J., 45
Olena, A., 1

O'Meara, K., 62
online discussions, 106
online teaching, 46-47
Online Teaching Survival Guide, The,
    47
Other People's Children, xxv

P
Palgrave Press, 32
Palmer, C., 54
paper trails, 97
Parkinson, C., 14
Parkinson's Law, 14
partners, job seeking with, 11
Payton-Stewart, L., xxiii
peacocking, 6
peer review, 11, 30-35
    PhD students and, 77
    revise and resubmit, 31-32
peer teaching evaluations, 56-57
perfectionism, xxii
post-doctoral positions, 3-4
PowerPoint, 5
Pozen, R., 114
Pribesh, S., 54
private email, 126
pro bono work, 124
professional biographies, 127
Professor is In, The, xxxii
Purdue University, 152, 154, 156, 161,
    162
publishing. *See* writing/publishing

R
racism, xxviii, 19, 38, 55, 56, 66, 68, 96,
    136, 145-47, 161-62, 163-64
reduced coarse loads, 10
Reid, L.D., 54
research agendas, 17-19
    department expectations, 19
    improvement of writing and,
        23-29
    presenting work at conferences,
        29-30

reading regularly and, 23
second-year goals, 22–23
setting annual goals, 21–22
research assistants, 9
Rockquemore, K.A., xxxii
Rosenbluth, F., xxxii
Routledge Press, 33
Rowland, M., 96, 97, 98
Russell Sage Foundation, 89
Rutgers University, 14, 99–100

S
sabbaticals, 10–11
Seltzer, R., xxxii
San Diego State University, 168, 169, 170
Scott, S., 177, 178
service, 24, 61, 68, 148–49
    community, 67
    department-level, 61–63
    to discipline, 38
    editorial boards and, 66
    to institutions, 37
    journals and, 66–67
    mentors and, 62
    national, 65–66
    school/college-level, 63–64
    thesis and dissertation committees, 62–63
    tracking for tenure, 67–68
    university-level, 64
service learning, 181
sexism, xxvi, xxvii, xxviii, 68, 133, 145–47, 176–78
Shore, B., 78
sleep, 115
Sloan Foundation, 89
Smith, C., 1
Smith, J.P., 141
social media, 105–6
    student relationships on, 119–22
Social Sciences Feminist Network Research Interest Group, 68
socializing, 116

speaker's bureaus, 125
Spencer, M.B., xxviii
Spencer Foundation, 23, 89, 92
Stanford University, 48, 169
start-up packages, 10
Statement of Principles on Academic Freedom and Tenure, xvii
STEM, 3, 4
Strata Education Group, 89
student learning, 52–54
student teaching evaluations, 54–56
Stylish Academic Writing, 24, 78
summer classes, teaching, 86
summer salary support, 8
Supporting Alma Mater, 81
Svinick, M., 54
Sword, H., 24
syllabi, 45

T
Taste of the Nation, 185
Tay, A., 79
Taylor, S., 96, 97, 98
Teachers College, xxvii
teaching, 36–37, 43–44, 57–58
    class activities and, 45
    connecting research to, 44
    creating syllabi and, 45
    diversity of voices in the classroom, 47–49
    establishing work patterns in new positions, 13–15
    managing difficult classroom conversations, 49–51
    online, 46–47
    peer teaching evaluations, 56–57
    preparing for new classes, 13–14, 44–47
    student evaluations and, 54–56
    student learning and, 52–54
    summer classes, 86
Teaching about Race and Racism in the College Classroom, 54
Teaching College, 54

INDEX

TEDtalks, 5

tenure, xvii
    benefits of, xvii
    conflict in writing of recommendation letters, 102-3
    consulting and, 123
    faculty politics and, 96
    identities and, 136
    institutional expectations for, 19
    mental health and, 115
    objection to, xvii-xviii
    research collaboration and, 81-82
    review essay, 35-40
    service and, 62-63, 67-68
    setting work boundaries, 110-12
    sexism and, 133
    social media and, 105-6
    types of colleges and universities granting, 57-58
    writing and, 25

Thelin, J., xxi

They Say, I Say: The Moves That Matter in Academic Writing, 172

third-year review narrative, 35-40

To Postdoc or Not to Postdoc?, 4

Tompkins, K., 73

Top 10 Tips on Negotiating Start-Up Packages, 10

travel funds, 9

Tulley, C., 35, 38

Twitter, 96, 120-21

U

Underserved Populations at HBCUs, 134

Unger, M., 56

United Negro College Fund (UNCF), 22

university email, 127

University of California Berkeley, 3, 48

University of California Los Angeles, 48

University of Chicago, 48

University of Chicago Press, 32

University of Findlay, 35

University of Illinois, xxi, 66

University of North Carolina Press, 32

University of Pennsylvania, xxvi, 4, 12, 13, 18, 43, 63, 99

Urban, W., xxi, 30

U.S. Travel Association, 112

V

vacations, importance of, 112-13

Valdez, L., 170

Vick, J., xxxii

W

What a Department Chair Can—and Can't—Do, 100

What the Best College Teachers Do, 54

Whitaker, M., 38, 68

Whiteness, 48

William T. Grant Foundation, 89

Wilson, J.K., 106

Women Faculty Distressed, 73

work/life balance, 109-10, 116
    exercising and, 111, 114
    mental and physical health, 115-16
    setting boundaries, 110-12
    sleep and, 115
    socializing and, 116
    vacations and, 112-13

writing/publishing, 140, 150
    applying for jobs and, 3
    author-supported promotional activities, 34
    blocking time for, 25-26, 28-29
    book publishers and, 11
    book royalties, 34
    improving, 23-29
    lead roles in, 82-83
    PhD students and, 77
    planning writing time, 14-15

publishing articles and books,
32–35
revise and resubmit, 31–32
taking breaks and, 26
two types of book publishers,
32–33
writing day schedule, 26–27
Writing the Perfect Recommendation Letter, 79
*Writing Your Journal Article in
Twelve Weeks*, 78

Y
Yoder, F., 76